Valid?
The Resignation of Benedict XVI

The Case against the Benepapists

By

Steven O'Reilly

Valid?
The Resignation of Benedict XVI

The Case against the Benepapists

By

Steven O'Reilly

Hartwell Publishing Company

Atlanta / Woodstock, GA

The prayer beginning "O Ineffable Creator" and found near the front of this work is excerpted from a *Prayer Before Writing or Preaching* by St. Thomas Aquinas. It may be found in *An Aquinas Reader* edited by Mary T. Clark (published by Fordham University Press: New York, 2000), p. 438.

Cover design by Rafael Andres

Copyright © 2022 by Steven O'Reilly.
All rights reserved. No part of this publication may be reproduced, stored in a retrieval system, or transmitted in any form or by any means, electronic, mechanical, photocopying, recording, scanning, or otherwise, without the prior written permission of the publisher and author. Requests to the author for permission should be addressed to StevenOReilly@aol.com.

Library of Congress Control Number: 2022918080

ISBN 978-1-7341260-4-4 (Paperback)
ISBN 978-1-7341260-5-1 (e-book)

Published by Hartwell Publishing Company
P.O. Box 2163
Lawrenceville, Georgia 30046

Ad Maiorem Dei Gloriam
Beataeque Mariae Virginis in Honorem

To my wife Margaret

"O Ineffable Creator...inspire my beginning, direct my progress, bring all to an end, you who art true God and man, who livest and reignest one God, world without end. Amen."

—St. Thomas Aquinas

Contents

About the Author i
Foreword ii
Preface v
Introduction 1
   The Origins of Benepapism 2
   The Rise of the Benepapists 5
   Whither Benepapism? 8
   The Case against the Benepapists 11
Chapter 1: The *Declaratio* 13
   Objections, and Replies to Those Objections 16
   Objection 1.1: Resignation was not freely made 16
   Objection 1.2: BXVI did not renounce the "munus" 17
   Objection 1.3: An appropriate synonym for *munus* was not used . 19
   Objection 1.4: BXVI withdrew only from his function as pope. ... 25
   Objection 1.5: "Substantial error" re "partial" resignation 27
   Additional Thoughts on Canon 188 31
   Objection 1.6: BXVI believed in a "sacramental papacy" 32
   Objection 1.7: Deficient consent due to "substantial error" 39
   Another Argument against the Objection 41
   Reductio ad Absurdum 42
   Objection 1.8: BXVI intentionally "sabotaged" his resignation 42
   Objection 1.9: The *Declaratio* contained errors in the Latin 47
   Objection 1.10: Effective date of resignation was deferred 48
Chapter 2: *Normas Nonnullas* 50
   Objections, and Replies to Those Objections 54
   Objection 2.1: *Normas Nonnullas* is irrelevant 54
Chapter 3: Benedict's Last Audience 57
   What Did Pope Benedict XVI Mean by the "Always"? 58
   What Did Pope Benedict XVI Mean by the "Forever"? 61

Objections, and Replies to Those Objections 67

Objection 3.1: BXVI said the "always is also a forever" 67

Objection 3.2: BXVI said the resignation "does not revoke" his office 70

Objection 3.3: The "forever" suggests BXVI kept the *munus* 72

Objection 3.4: Admits to resigning only the "active" ministry 75

Objection 3.5: BXVI bifurcates the papacy into "active or passive" parts 78

Chapter 4: Pilgrims from Albano 81

Objections, and Replies to Those Objections 84

Objection 4.1: Irrelevant due to "substantial error" 84

Objection 4.2: BXVI is speaking in a "Ratzinger Code" 85

Chapter 5: Gänswein's Speech 92

Objections, and Replies to Those Objections 104

Objection 5.1: BXVI wears white; still called Your Holiness 104

Objection 5.2: BXVI created the "pope emeritus" 106

Objection 5.3: BXVI still gives "apostolic blessings" 108

Objection 5.4: Gänswein spoke of an expanded Petrine ministry 110

Objection 5.5: BXVI "has not abandoned the Office of Peter" 116

Objection 5.6: Violation of law of non-contradiction 119

Objection 5.7: Plain meaning of the words proves Benepapism .. 123

Objection 5.8: BXVI edited and approved Gänswein's speech ... 126

Chapter 6: Summation 128

"The 'Always' Is Also a 'Forever'" 128

Benedict XVI: Theological Fool or Strategic Genius? 130

A "Pope Emeritus" Wearing White? 136

If the Roman Pontiff Renounces His Office (*Munus*)............. 137

That the Renunciation Be Freely Made… 141

That the Renunciation Be Duly Manifested… 142

Not That It Be Accepted by Anyone 143

Concluding Remarks 143
Bibliography and Works Referenced 147
End Notes 163

About the Author

Steven O'Reilly writes on Catholic and general Christian apologetics topics. He has written articles for *This Rock* and currently writes for his own Internet blog, *Roma Locuta Est*.

He is currently writing a historical-fiction trilogy entitled, PIA FIDELIS, which is set during the time of the Arian Crisis of the fourth century A.D., and the rise of Julian the Apostate. Book I of this trilogy, *PIA FIDELIS: The Two Kingdoms,* is now available.

He graduated from the University of Dallas with a Bachelor of Arts in Economics. He also received a Master of Science in Management from the Georgia Institute of Technology.

He served in the Central Intelligence Agency and currently works in private industry. He and his wife, Margaret, have four sons (Patrick, Peter, Brian, and Kevin). The author and his wife live in the Atlanta area. He can be contacted at:

StevenOReilly@AOL.com.

Foreword

The safest guiding principle in the crucial question for the life of the Church regarding the validity of the papacy of Pope Francis should be the prevailing practice in the history of the Church, which includes resolved cases of presumably invalid papal renunciations or elections. In this prevailing practice was shown the *sensus perennis ecclesiae* (the perennial meaning of the Church).

The principle of legality applied *ad litteram* (to the letter) or that of juridical positivism was not considered in the great practice of the Church an absolute principle, since the legislation of the papal election is only a human (positive) law, and not a Divine (revealed) law. The human law that regulates the assumption of the papal office or the dismissal from the papal office must be subordinated to the greater good of the whole Church, which in this case is the real existence of the visible head of the Church and the certainty of this existence for all the body of the Church, clergy and faithful. This visible existence of the head and the certainty about it are required by the very nature of the Church. The universal Church cannot exist for a considerable time without a visible Supreme Shepherd, without the successor of Peter, since the vital activity of the universal Church depends on its visible head, such as e.g., the appointment of diocesan bishops and cardinals, appointments that require the existence of a valid pope. In turn, the spiritual good of the faithful depends on a valid appointment of a bishop, since in the case of an invalid episcopal appointment (due to a presumably invalid pope), priests would lack pastoral jurisdiction (confession, marriage). From this also depends those dispensations that only the Roman Pontiff can grant, and also indulgences, all this for the spiritual good and eternal salvation of souls.

Guided by this truly pastoral principle, the instinct of the Church has also applied the *supplet ecclesia* or the *sanatio in*

FOREWARD

radice (the healing in the root) in the case of doubts about a renunciation or a pontifical election. Concretely, the *sanatio in radice* of an invalid pontifical election was expressed in the peaceful and morally universal acceptance of the new Pontiff by the episcopate and the Catholic people, for the same fact that this elected (presumably invalid) Pontiff was nominated in the Canon of the Mass practically by the entire Catholic clergy.

The hypothesis of Benedict XVI's invalid renunciation, and therefore of the invalidity of the papacy of Francis, properly presents itself as a dead end, a cul-de-sac. For nine years the Apostolic See would have been de facto vacant, since Benedict XVI did not make any act of government, no episcopal or cardinal appointment, no act of dispensation, of indulgences, etc. For this reason, the universal Church would be paralyzed in its visible aspect. Such an assumption would amount in practice to the attitude of sedevacantism. In the past nine years all the appointments of Apostolic Nuncios, diocesan bishops and cardinals, all the Pontifical dispensations, the indulgences granted and used by the faithful would be null and void, with all the harmful consequences for the spiritual good of souls (illegitimate bishops, invalid episcopal jurisdictions, etc.). All the cardinals nominated by Pope Francis would be invalid, that is, there are non-cardinals, and this would apply to the overwhelm-ing number of the current cardinals.

The hypothesis that Benedict XVI is still the only valid pope, and therefore Pope Francis is an invalid pope, contradicts not only the proven and reasonable practice of the great tradition of the Church, but also simply common sense. Furthermore, in this case one absolutizes the aspect of legality, that is, in our case of the human norms of renunciation and pontifical election, to the detriment of the good of souls, since there is created the uncertainty of the validity of acts of government of the Church and this undermines the visible nature of the Church, and thus one approaches the mentality of sedevacantism. The surer way (*via tutior*) and the example of the constant practice of the great tradition of the Church must be followed also in our present case.

The rudder of the boat of the Church holds Our Lord Jesus Christ in his hands even in situations of heaviest storms, such as exists in a time of a doctrinally ambiguous pope. Such storms are relatively short compared to other great crises during the two-thousand-year existence of the militant Church. The extremely rare case of a heretical, or of a semi-heretical pope, must ultimately be endured and suffered in the light of the faith in the Divine character and in the indestructibility of the Church and of the Petrine office. Pope Saint Leo the Great formulated this truth, saying that the dignity of Saint Peter is not abated in his successors, however unworthy they may be: *"Cuius dignitas etiam in indigno haerede non deficit"* (Serm. 3, 4).

One has to welcome the initiative of Steven O'Reilly with his convincing analysis of the question of the validity of the papacy of Pope Francis in the present book. May this book bring clarity in the midst of the confusion among Catholics and convince them to assume a more supernatural view of the current crisis of the papacy in firmly believing that even in our day the Church is in the almighty hands of God.

June 2, 2022

+ Athanasius Schneider, Auxiliary Bishop of the Archdiocese of Saint Mary in Astana

Preface

In February 2013, Pope Benedict XVI renounced the papacy of the Roman Catholic Church. However, around 2016 voices began to arise claiming that Benedict's renunciation was invalid. Various writers both then, and since, have put forth theories attempting to justify this claim. If any of these theories were in fact true, it would necessarily follow that the election of Pope Francis was invalid.

There are various factors which contribute to the belief of some that *Benedict is (still) pope*; a belief or theory which is called *Benepapism* in this book. Ultimately, this belief is rooted in the confusion and concerns of many Catholics with the election of Pope Francis, and with his words and deeds over the course of his pontificate.

There are suspicions of a group of progressive, modernist cardinals, who called themselves the St. Gallen Mafia. Meeting in secret for years, this group attempted to prevent the election of Cardinal Ratzinger as pope in 2005. Then in 2013, its members played a questionable and murky role in the conclave to elect their candidate, Cardinal Jorge Bergoglio, SJ, to forward their agenda to change the Church.

In 2016, the Apostolic Exhortation *Amoris Laetitia* was promulgated, which allowed Catholics living in public, adulterous relationships to receive Holy Communion in "certain cases." This exhortation, certainly on its face, contradicted the perennial teaching of the Catholic Church on this question. Various documents have been penned by Catholic scholars and theologians raising the alarm over *Amoris Laetitia*. Several cardinals addressed a number of so-called *Dubia*, or questions, to Pope Francis in hopes of receiving clarification. Unfortunately, to date, Pope Francis has neither answered the *Dubia*, nor responded to the various filial appeals addressed to him.

Other concerns involve the Scalfari interviews in which Pope Francis is quoted to have said heretical things, and which have not been directly denied. There was the incident over the Pachamama idol during the Amazon Synod, and the wording and meaning in the Abu Dhabi document on Human Fraternity.

The confusion caused by such doings has led many otherwise faithful Catholics to ask, *how could a pope do such things?* Unfortunately, some have definitively answered this question for themselves, essentially declaring, *Benedict is still pope, and therefore Francis cannot be.* This belief has been defended by variety of erroneous and fallacious arguments.

Given the above, it is understandable that questions have arisen in the minds of the faithful over the last nine years of this current pontificate. The author shares the concerns of many Catholics with regard to these events, as well as with the confusion caused by a seemingly endless stream of negative developments and news from Rome. He is not dismissive of such concerns.

However, even if one might speculatively entertain some hypothesis hoping to understand or explain the current crisis in the Church, one should not definitively settle upon a seeming solution apart from, or in opposition to the Church; and nor should one anticipate the judgment of the Church on the matter. As Catholics, we must have faith these controversies will one day be resolved, either by those with the appropriate authority within the Church, or by the Lord himself.

Some Benepapists have taken it upon themselves to issue a Declaration and Petition in which they affirm they remain faithful to Benedict XVI as the still reigning true pope. Furthermore, they have issued a set of conditions necessary for them to accept the result of any future conclave. This is an ominous development. The potential for schism is very real.

Regrettably, many Benepapists do not even exhibit the slightest hesitancy in their views, or any sign they admit the possibility that it is they who might be in error. There is no indication in this Declaration and Petition that they obediently await and submit to the Church's judgment on the question.

Over the last few years, the Benepapists have assiduously advanced their beliefs through various media and platforms, including blogs, videos, several books, and podcasts. Where they

PREFACE

have appeared on popular podcasts, their theories have rarely been critically challenged by hosts.

However, seeing the effort put forth in propagating Benepapism, particularly the several books published in favor of it thus far, I thought a book that provided the case against the Benepapists might be of some use. Having already written much on the topic in article form, I had long toyed with the idea of this project. When I was in doubt as to whether to proceed, I received encouragement from an unexpected and unlikely corner, for which I am grateful.

This book is for those who have been confronted with Benepapist arguments, and for those who have accepted them. Again, I certainly share concerns over the crisis through which we are living. However, we must remember in searching for a solution, a bad theory is *never* a substitute for a good one; and Benepapism is a demonstrably bad one. Therefore, it cannot be the solution to this crisis, particularly when the logic of Benepapism counsels schism.

The resolution of the current crisis is beyond our vision in this moment. What *the* solution ultimately is may yet be in doubt, but that it will unfailingly come is not. The Lord will provide it in His time—not ours. Therefore, until then, let prayer, prudence, and patience be the order of the day.

I pray the Lord will be pleased with this effort.

Steven O'Reilly

On the feast of Saints Peter and Paul, 2022

VALID? THE RESIGNATION OF POPE BENEDICT XVI

Introduction

As I am writing this in June of 2022, Pope Francis and the Pope Emeritus, Benedict, are still with us. While this may seem an odd way to introduce a book, a controversy involving the papacy and these two men has been festering over the last few years. Following the death of Benedict or Francis, a group of Catholics will likely be led into a schism from the Church. The great majority of the faithful are unaware of both the controversy and this possibility of schism.

This papal controversy involves a group of Catholics who have come to reject the validity of the resignation of Pope Benedict XVI on February 28, 2013. It will seem odd to most that any confusion may have arisen over the resignation of Benedict. After all, the resignation document, the *Declaratio*, is quite straightforward. In it, Benedict said that his *"strengths, due to an advanced age, are no longer suited"*[1] to exercise the Petrine ministry. Benedict would then go on to declare:

> For this reason, and well aware of the seriousness of this act, with full freedom I declare that I renounce the ministry of Bishop of Rome, Successor of Saint Peter, entrusted to me by the Cardinals on 19 April 2005, in such a way, that as from 28 February 2013, at 20:00 hours, the See of Rome, the See of Saint Peter, will be vacant and a Conclave to elect the new Supreme Pontiff will have to be convoked by those whose competence it is.[2]

Benedict's intent and meaning are quite apparent. He has renounced the "ministry of the Bishop of Rome, Successor of Peter" in "such a way" that as of February 28, 2013 (at 8 p.m.) the "See of Rome, the See of Saint Peter, will be vacant" and a conclave will need to be convoked to elect "the new Supreme Pontiff." Nothing could be clearer.

Yet, despite the clear wording and manifest meaning of the *Declaratio*, there are those who have come to reject the validity of the resignation. For such Catholics as these, "Benedict is (still) pope." This theory or belief is sometimes called BiP.[3] However, in this work, we will refer broadly to the BiP theory under its various forms as *Benepapism* and those who lead this movement as *Benepapists*.[4]

The Origins of Benepapism

The theory that "Benedict is (still) pope" finds its origin in the concerns which many Catholics share, Benepapists or not, with regard to the pontificate of Pope Francis. These concerns became evident in 2016 with the publication of Pope Francis' Apostolic Exhortation, *Amoris Laetitia*, following the 2015 Synod on the Family. Many lay and religious Catholics around the world, including members of the hierarchy, bishops and cardinals, were shocked and confused by *Amoris Laetitia* and remain so. This Exhortation, on its face at least, and certainly in the view of its public apologists, allows those living in public, adulterous relationships to receive Holy Communion in "certain cases."[5]

Such a teaching certainly appears to contradict the perennial teaching of the Catholic Church against giving Communion to those who live in objective situations of adultery. John Paul II reaffirmed this perennial teaching in his own Apostolic Exhortation, *Familiaris Consortio*,[6] and *Reconciliatio et Paenitentia*,[7] etc. The Congregation of the Doctrine of the Faith, in a document approved by John Paul II, said no exceptions to this rule were possible.[8] Furthermore, Pope Benedict XVI reaffirmed the teaching in *Sacramentum Caritatis*.[9]

Within a few months of the publication of *Amoris Laetitia*, a group of Catholic scholars published their grave concerns about various aspects of it.[10] In the fall of 2016, in a separate initiative, several cardinals,[11] following a longstanding practice, submitted five *dubia* or questions to Pope Francis.[12] The cardinals hoped to receive clarification as to how *Amoris Laetitia* should be

INTRODUCTION

interpreted and reconciled with prior Church teaching. Surprisingly, even up to now, six years after the *Dubia* were submitted to Pope Francis, he has yet to provide an answer to any of them.

Aside from these attempts to engage Pope Francis with regard to the confusion over *Amoris Laetitia*, there were others. In July 2017, a group of Catholic scholars and theologians addressed a *Filial Correction*[13] to Pope Francis. In Easter week of 2019, a group of 19 scholars and academics published an *Open letter to the Catholic Church* accusing Pope Francis of the canonical delict of heresy.[14]

Six years have passed since he first published his apostolic exhortation and Pope Francis has yet to respond to the *Dubia*, or even to acknowledge his receipt of them. Nor has he responded to any of the other attempts to seek clarification. However, the Pope's non-responsiveness to these questions has not prevented various writers from using *Amoris Laetitia* to defend what had been heretofore unthinkable, i.e., the reception of Holy Communion in "certain cases" by at least some who live in public, adulterous relationships outside of a valid marriage.[15]

Unfortunately, the profound dismay over *Amoris Laetitia* was not an isolated event. In the years following the election of Pope Francis, many Catholics were concerned at the revelation that a secret group of bishops and cardinals had formed during the pontificate of John Paul II with an agenda to change the Church. This group, which referred to themselves as the St. Gallen mafia, was opposed to Cardinal Josef Ratzinger.[16] In the 2005 conclave, this St. Gallen mafia tried but failed to elect its own candidate.

In 2013, the members of the St. Gallen mafia supported the candidacy of Cardinal Jorge Bergoglio, SJ, who was elected pope and took the name Francis. Accounts of events surrounding the conclave seem to suggest the possibility that members of the St. Gallen mafia had engaged in illegal campaigning for Cardinal Bergoglio before the conclave.[17] In addition, Archbishop Carlo Vigano in his *Testimony* pointed to ex-Cardinal Theodore McCarrick's own account of being asked by an "influential Italian gentleman" to talk up Bergoglio before the conclave.[18] The author has explored these and other conclave oddities on his own blog, *Roma Locuta Est*.[19]

In addition to concerns raised over the orthodoxy of *Amoris Laetitia*, there were other instances where Pope Francis raised doctrinal eyebrows. For example, in 2019, Pope Francis signed a joint statement with the Grand Imam of Al-Azhar Ahmad Al-Tayyeb, the so-called Abu Dhabi statement, wherein it was affirmed that *"The pluralism and the diversity of religions, colour, sex, race and language are willed by God in His wisdom, through which He created human beings."*[20] Various theologians[21] and bishops[22] pointed out the apparent difficulties in the formulation of this statement, which is open to erroneous and heretical interpretations. Pope Francis appears to have come to understand this, but he has not corrected the statement[23] or taken it down from the Vatican website.

Then there were concerns over controversial statements Pope Francis was reported to have made in interviews with Italian journalist Eugenio Scalfari.[24] Many of the statements attributed to Francis are heretical. For example, Scalfari quotes Pope Francis as saying, *"Jesus of Nazareth, once he became a man, although he was a man of exceptional virtue, was not a god at all."*[25] Now, the defense typically given on behalf of Francis is that Scalfari is famous for not recording his interviews and not even taking notes during them. Consequently, they say, we should not trust Scalfari's accounts of his discussion with Pope Francis. However, even accepting the truth of this defense, why would Pope Francis continually grant interviews to one who so habitually misrepresented his views of basic Christian doctrine? Why does Pope Francis not correct the record himself? In other words, why are we blaming Scalfari?[26]

Another event that outraged many Catholics was a strange ceremony that took place in the Vatican Gardens attended by Pope Francis, during which a group of people, including some religious, prostrated themselves before wooden idols.[27] During the synod, the idol was placed inside the Church of Santa Maria in Traspontina, which is near the Vatican. The idols were removed from the Church by a couple of faithful Catholics and tossed into the Tiber. However, Pope Francis apologized for the treatment of

INTRODUCTION

these idols, which were later retrieved from the river. Despite the lame attempts of some to explain away the idols, there were bishops and cardinals who condemned the idols.[28] Then, to top off these events, a Pachamama bowl was placed on the high altar of St. Peter's Basilica during the closing mass of the Amazon synod.[29] Understandably, many observers drew comparisons between this sacrilege and the Abomination of Desolation spoken of in chapter 24 of the Gospel of Matthew.

What we have considered thus far is but a small sampling of the controversies, doctrinal and other, surrounding Pope Francis in the eyes of those Catholics who follow events in Rome closely. Suffice it to say, a long list could be compiled. However, as much as posterity[30] might benefit from such a listing, it is not within the scope of this book to present one.

Rather, the point of all this is to say, Pope Francis has raised many disturbing questions in the minds of many Catholics. How could a true successor of Peter do *any* of these things, especially in view of the teaching on papal infallibility as defined in *Pastor Aeturnus* from Vatican I? "How could a pope do these things?" Or, perhaps better put, "how could a *real* pope do these things?"

Consideration of such questions has led some Catholics to question the legitimacy of Pope Francis and to look for theories that might "explain" *who* or *what* Francis is; i.e., how to explain him away. This search has led some to ultimately conclude that Francis cannot be a valid pope. But, how does one undo a papacy?

Some approached the question by claiming that the resignation of Pope Benedict XVI was invalid. According to their theory, because it was invalid, Benedict remained pope after the supposed effective date of his resignation on February 28, 2013, and since. If Benedict XVI is still pope, then it necessarily follows that Francis could never have been a valid pope. "Problem" solved. Or so it seemed to some. Thus, Benepapism was born.

The Rise of the Benepapists

The "Benedict is (still) pope" theory often denoted by the acronym BiP—as we have already indicated, asserts that Benedict is still pope because his resignation was invalid. The curious thing about Benepapism is that it really isn't a single theory. There are various flavors of the BiP theory which generally fall into the following categories:

(a) Benedict's resignation was invalid because he was forced to resign
(b) Benedict attempted to bifurcate the papacy—to create something of a papal diarchy; but given this is impossible, Benedict's erroneous attempt was invalid
(c) Benedict succeeded in bifurcating the papacy, creating something of a papal diarchy, thus remaining pope in some way
(d) Benedict attempted to detach the Petrine office from the See of Rome; however, given this is not possible, Benedict's erroneous attempt was invalid
(e) Benedict succeeded in detaching the Petrine office from the See of Rome, therefore he is still pope
(f) Benedict intentionally "sabotaged" his *Declaratio* in order that it would be null. Thus, he retained the papacy; thereby protecting it from the modernists who are trying to take over the Church

The list above is not all-inclusive. There might be variations under each of these categories, as well as others not given above. Many of those who believe "Benedict is still pope" have not necessarily committed to any specific one of these theories, even though they may have a favorite or two among them. One will find there are even those open to two or more theories which are mutually contradictory. Given Benepapists are often open to multiple theories, it is difficult to pin them down to admit what possible facts might falsify their belief.

Benepapism first came to my attention in 2017. That was when I first began to look into the arguments for the theory as put forward by Ann Barnhardt[31] and Mark Docherty.[32] Ms. Barnhardt was the first, to my knowledge, to suggest that Pope Benedict XVI attempted only a *partial* resignation of the papacy. The idea here is that Benedict attempted to "bifurcate" the papacy to create a papal diarchy comprised of an *active* and a *passive* member.

INTRODUCTION

Essentially, the general argument appears to be that Pope Benedict XVI had a faulty understanding of the papacy. He believed, erroneously, the papacy could be so divided, and or that he could retain a part of being papal in some way, even after his resignation. Evidence for such a claim was said to be found in the wording of Benedict's *Declaratio*, the text of his last general audience, and in a speech given by Archbishop Georg Gänswein three years after the resignation.

However, one cannot "partially" resign the papacy, and there can be no such thing as a papal diarchy, or a bifurcated papacy. Therefore, argue the Benepapists, Benedict held an erroneous view of the papacy. It is at this point that Canon 188 is cited as proof the resignation was invalid. Canon 188 reads as follows:

> A resignation submitted out of grave fear, which has been unjustly inflicted, or because of fraud, substantial error or simony is invalid by the law itself.[33]

Thus, the Benepapists argue that Benedict committed a "substantial error" by attempting to partially resign the papacy, or bifurcate it, etc. Per Canon 188, they say, his resignation is invalid.

Out of the previously listed half-dozen theories, the *substantial-error* theory is one of the two major Benepapist theories. The other main theory is what might be called the *Plan B* theory. Brother Alexis Bugnolo appears to be one of the first, if not the first, to advance this theory.[34] However, perhaps the one most identified with popularizing this *Plan B* theory, and labeling it, is an Italian journalist named Andrea Cionci, who just released a book advancing the theory titled, *The Ratzinger Code*.[35]

The *Plan B* theory essentially holds that Pope Benedict XVI in his *Declaratio* did not fully resign the papacy. There appear to be variations of this general theory. Some think Benedict "sabotaged" the resignation by including errors in it to make it invalid; while others suggest he resigned only the exercise of his papacy, while retaining the papal office. In doing the latter, he created an "impeded" see, while remaining the true pope.

In either variation, it is believed that Benedict submitted a resignation where it only appeared he resigned the papal office, when in fact he intended to retain it. Benedict did this, these Benepapists argue, in order to keep the papacy out of the hands of the modernists within the Church. We will revisit this theory in more detail later in this book. However, it suffices to say that the proponents of this theory view Pope Benedict XVI as something of a strategic genius for having developed and enacted this *Plan B*.

These last two theories, as stated, are the primary Benepapist theories. One declares Benedict's erroneous views of the papacy led him to attempt a renunciation that was in fact invalid. The other theory suggests Benedict intentionally created a renunciation letter that was null and void, as part of a strategic plan to thwart the enemies of the Church.

Whither Benepapism?

We have briefly surveyed the origin of the *Benedict is (still) pope* movement, as well as its key theories. Unfortunately, it is difficult to gauge how many Catholics either fully accept or seriously entertain such beliefs. However, it does appear Benepapism has gathered steam in recent years. This momentum is directly related to a continuous stream of bad news from Rome, some of which we sampled earlier in this Introduction.[36] It seems with each new papal utterance, decree, appointment, or action, confusion and consternation among the Catholic faithful grows.

Five or six years ago, there were perhaps only a few internet sites seriously engaged in the advancement of the theory.[37] However, over the ensuing years, the controversy has continued to be the subject of articles,[38] various blogs,[39] and has now even appeared in at least four books. In 2019, a well-respected Italian writer, Antonio Socci, published a book *Il Segreto di Benedetto XVI: Perche' ancora e' Papa* (The Secret of Benedict XVI: Why He Is Still Pope).[40] In 2021, Estefania Acosta, a Colombian attorney, wrote and published a book entitled *Benedict XVI: Pope "Emeritus"?* Also in 2021, Fr. Paul Kramer published a work entitled *On the True and the False Pope (The Case Against Bergoglio)*. Then there is the aforementioned Italian journalist, Andrea Cionci, who has recently published in 2022 *The Ratzinger*

INTRODUCTION

Code. In addition to the written word, adherents of the BiP theory have appeared on popular video podcasts[41] to advance their theories.

Yet, the relative success of Benepapism has seemingly bred division between lead proponents of the *substantial-error* and *Plan B* theories. Even if the conclusion of these two opposing theories is the same, i.e., "Benedict is (still) pope," their arguments on how to arrive at that conclusion are mutually exclusive and contradictory. Perhaps division between the two groups was always there, lying beneath the surface. Whatever the case, something of a civil war has recently broken out between these two opposing Benepapist camps.[42]

Many of the lead Benepapists over the last several years could often be heard railing against those opposed to Benepapism, complaining they were being told to "shut up" and "go away," and that their arguments were dismissed out-of-hand with derision. So, it is somewhat amusing to find the two opposing camps now dismissing the other side's arguments as "absurd."[43] Unfortunately, the typical Benepapist in the audience is presented with a conundrum. Is Benedict a strategic genius or is he a theological fool?[44]

That the day would come for the battle for the middle ground within Benepapism was, perhaps, inevitable. Rumors of ill health seem to surround both Benedict and Francis, and speculation is in the air that the next conclave might not be that far off. Soon the decision point will come. However, there is no middle ground. One can only hope that those individuals tempted to believe Benedict is (still) pope might see that, strangely enough, the *substantial-error* and *Plan B* theoreticians, in refuting each other, have only succeeded in refuting Benepapism altogether.

So, to what end is Benepapism heading? Inevitably, it will come to no good end. Following the inevitable logic of their position, some leaders of the movement have already issued a Declaration with an attached Petition earlier this year declaring they "*remain faithful to his Holiness Pope Benedict XVI, who continues to be the Vicar of Christ on Earth until he dies or issues a valid abdication.*"[45] Francis is said not to "*hold any authority as Roman Pontiff.*"[46] Thus, he is in effect an anti-pope.

In addition, this declaration's third point declares the following:

> III. Any future papal election made under any of the following circumstances will lack of canonical validity:
> (a) If it be held during the pontificate of His Holiness Pope Benedict XVI, and / or
> (b) With the participation of the cardinals named by Bishop Jorge Mario Bergoglio, and / or
> (c) In accordance with any provisions issued by Bishop Jorge Mario Bergoglio for the purpose of such election.
>
> Consequently, both the person who is elected under such conditions, as well as his possible successors, will necessarily be anti-Popes.[47]

This declaration, which has already gathered a few thousand signatures,[48] is exceedingly rash. To say this was an imprudent act would be a gross understatement. It is utter folly. The potential for schism is very real. One can only imagine the various scenarios that might emerge depending on which of the two, Francis or Benedict, precedes the other to the grave.

The author is sympathetic to many, if indeed not all of the common critiques of the current pontificate. However, it is not for the leading Benepapists, petitioners, or for any Catholic for that matter to issue declaratory demands upon the Church. Catholics cannot act apart from the judgment of the Church on such weighty questions. Popes of the past have been judged and even corrected by later popes, such as in the cases of Pope Honorius[49] and Pope John XXII.[50] Some future pope may in fact examine the current pontificate, but one should not anticipate any resulting judgment or the nature of it.

However, it appears among the leading Benepapists there are those with neither the prudence nor the patience to await a judgment, particularly one that may not agree with what they have already taken upon themselves to decide. They are painting themselves into a corner—or rather, walling themselves into one from which they and their followers may find it difficult to extricate themselves. One can only hope that some among the luminaries in the BiP movement might try to pull back some of their colleagues from the edge of the abyss that looms before them, and toward which they, like so many pied pipers, are leading those they have convinced to follow them.

The Case against the Benepapists

Along with the author's own blog, *Roma Locuta Est*, there have been several writers who have published articles against Benepapism.[51] However, given several books have by now been published in support of Benepapism, there seems to be a need for a resource in book form to provide the case against the Benepapists. With this in mind, the author set out to adapt a series of his articles, supplemented with additional research, to fill that need.

The first five chapters of this work will focus on the key documents in this controversy which are often cited by the Benepapists in favor of their position, as well as some which they generally pass over or ignore entirely. These will include chapters dedicated to the following:

- The *Declaratio*
- *Normas Nonnullas*
- Benedict's Last Audience
- Benedict's Comments to the Pilgrims from Albano
- Archbishop Gänswein's Speech.

Each chapter will provide an initial discussion of the given document, as well as its relevance to the controversy and to the validity of the resignation of Pope Benedict XVI. Following this opening argument, a section is included for typical objections made by Benepapists, and the author's replies to those objections. Each objection and reply will be referenced first by the chapter in which it is found, and then by its place among the objections in the chapter. For example, "Objection 2.3" refers to the third objection in chapter two, and "Reply to Objection 2.3" is the reply to said objection. The final chapter of this book will provide a summary argument against Benepapism.

The goal of this book is to critically examine the chief evidence provided by the leading Benepapists, and to respond to their objections. It is the author's hope that this work might be of benefit to those who have encountered Benepapist arguments and have either been tempted by them or succumbed to them. Finally, it is the goal of this work that the reader will likewise conclude that Benepapism is false and that the resignation of Pope Benedict XVI was valid.

Chapter 1: The *Declaratio*

In this chapter, we will examine the *Declaratio* of February 11, 2013, in which Pope Benedict XVI announced his decision to renounce the papacy. This document is proof in itself that Pope Benedict XVI fully intended to and actually did resign the papacy. Yet, the *Declaratio* is one of the documents to which the Benepapists appeal to advance their belief that Benedict intended either to resign the papacy only in part in some way,[52] or not *really* to resign at all.[53]

The text of the *Declaratio* is provided in full below, followed by commentary on how it manifests Benedict's true intention to fully resign the papacy. Then, immediately following that commentary, we will consider both objections to the validity of the resignation, and the replies to those objections.

Let's proceed with an examination of the *Declaratio* of Pope Benedict XVI (*italics and parenthetical notations are mine*):

> I have convoked you to this Consistory, not only for the three canonizations, but also to communicate to you a decision of great importance for the life of the Church. After having repeatedly examined my conscience before God, I have come to the certainty that my strengths, due to an advanced age, are no longer suited to an adequate exercise of the *Petrine ministr*y (munus). I am well aware that this ministry (munus), due to its essential spiritual nature, must be carried out not only with words and deeds, but no less with prayer and suffering. However, in today's world, subject to so many rapid changes and shaken by questions of deep relevance for the life of faith, in order to govern the *barque of Saint Peter* and proclaim the Gospel, both strength of mind and body are necessary, strength which in the last few months, has deteriorated in me to the extent that I have had to recognize my incapacity to adequately fulfill the ministry (*ministerium*)

entrusted to me. For this reason, and well aware of the seriousness of this act, with full freedom I declare that I renounce the ministry (*ministerio*) of Bishop of Rome, *Successor of Saint Peter*, entrusted to me by the Cardinals on 19 April 2005, in such a way, that as from 28 February 2013, at 20:00 hours, the See of Rome, the See of Saint Peter, will be vacant and a Conclave to elect the new Supreme Pontiff will have to be convoked by those whose competence it is.

Dear Brothers, I thank you most sincerely for all the love and work with which you have supported me in my ministry and I ask pardon for all my defects. And now, let us entrust the Holy Church to the care of Our Supreme Pastor, Our Lord Jesus Christ, and implore his holy Mother Mary, so that she may assist the Cardinal Fathers with her maternal solicitude, in electing a new *Supreme Pontiff*. With regard to myself, I wish to also devotedly serve the Holy Church of God in the future through a life dedicated to prayer. (February 10, 2013)[54]

Based on the *Declaratio* above, the argument for the validity of Benedict's resignation is straightforward. In the sentence beginning with "*for this reason,*" Benedict declared that "*with full freedom*" he was renouncing "*the ministry of the Bishop of Rome, Successor of Peter…in such a way…the See of Rome, the See of Saint Peter, will be vacant and a Conclave to elect the new Supreme Pontiff will have to be convoked by those whose competence it is.*"

If the "*See of Rome, the See of Peter*" is to be vacant as Pope Benedict XVI declares, then there is no one holding the primacy over the Church as Bishop of Rome, Peter's successor. In short, there is no pope. That this is the effect of the resignation is clear from the fact Benedict immediately states that, as a result of this vacancy, a conclave would be needed to elect "*the new Supreme Pontiff.*"

While no formula for papal resignations is specified by canon law, Pope Benedict XVI's resignation met all the specified requirements of Canon 332§2 for validity.[55] First, Benedict stated his resignation was made "with full freedom." Second, the resignation, made in writing, presented in person before a consistory of cardinals, as well as inserted in the *Acta Apostolicae Sedis*,[56] [57] was "properly manifested."

The validity of this resignation is quite clear. Unfortunately, as discussed in the Introduction, various theories have arisen to call into dispute the obvious. The tenacity of the Benepapists is remarkable, especially given Benedict himself after his resignation has rejected theories which call the validity into doubt as being "absurd."[58] Even before the effective date of his renunciation, Benedict promised his *"obedience"* to the future pope, thereby demonstrating he intended to resign in full.[59] In none of his post-resignation interviews has he affirmed he remained "Supreme Pontiff"[60] or "true pope."[61] Rather, in fact, he has gone out of his way to say he is not.[62]

Furthermore, no cardinal has publicly argued or even suggested the resignation was invalid. Even cardinals that have expressed reservation with regard to papal acts of Pope Francis over the last nine years, such as the *Dubia* cardinals, have rejected the BiP theory.[63] Cardinals Burke and Brandmüller later reaffirmed the validity of Benedict's resignation.[64] Still more recently in June 2022, Cardinal Gerhard Müller reaffirmed the validity of Benedict's resignation,[65] and Bishop Athanasius Schneider spoke forcefully on the issue.[66] No active bishop of any episcopal see has publicly stated he either doubts or rejects the validity of Benedict's resignation.

In sum, the case for the validity of Pope Benedict XVI's resignation is overwhelming. Papal juridical acts are presumed valid. Papal decrees cannot be appealed. Papal resignations do not require acceptance by anyone.[67] The only one who could review and resolve any potential doubts that might be raised is a future pope. Consequently, one should not anticipate a decision for invalidity, as some rashly have, as in the case of the Benepapists' aforementioned declaration.

Nine years have passed since the resignation. Benedict has not asserted he was forced out. He has not asserted he either made or was in "substantial error." He has made no attempt to govern the Church over the last nine years. It is obvious he willed to remain pope no longer, and thus he has vacated the *"See of Rome, the See of Peter.*" The evidence clearly demonstrates that Benedict was no longer pope, in whole or in part, as of 8 p.m., February 28, 2013.

Objections, and Replies to Those Objections

Objection 1.1: Resignation was not freely made

> According to Canon 332.3, a papal resignation must be made "freely" in order for it to be valid. Benedict was forced to resign, therefore Benedict's resignation was invalid.

Reply to Objection 1.1: Although it has been suggested by some that Pope Benedict XVI was forced to resign, perhaps by the St. Gallen mafia, proponents of this theory have offered no evidence which demonstrates this was the case. Some have suggested financial pressure may have been brought to bear against Pope Benedict XVI,[68] while others have suggested there were death threats.[69] However, these theorists have produced no "smoking gun" to prove his resignation was "forced."

Rather, such theories are contradicted by Benedict himself. Pope Benedict XVI in his *Declaratio* specifically states he is renouncing the papacy freely. After his resignation, he called theories that called the validity of his resignation into doubt "absurd." In his interviews with Peter Seewald, the former pope makes it quite clear he resigned freely. For example, speaking of whether pressure of the Vatileaks scandal led to his resignation, Benedict told Seewald:

> …that no one is permitted to step back when things are going wrong. I could resign because calm had returned to this situation. It was not a case of retreating under pressure or feeling things couldn't be coped with.[70]

To suggest that Benedict resigned due to direct threat or pressure is to make a coward and a liar of the man.

Finally, Benedict is not behaving like a man who acted under a threat or coercion. Benedict as former pope has been in communication with old friends, colleagues, and well-wishers; he has entertained guests who have visited him. Not one of them has ever come forward to suggest that Benedict either hinted he resigned because of a threat, or that he appeared to be living under some threat.

In sum, the objection amounts to little more than speculation. There is no evidence Pope Benedict XVI submitted his resignation out of fear or threat. There is no ground on this objection to reject the validity of his resignation.

Objection 1.2: BXVI did not renounce the "munus"

> In the *Declaratio*, Pope Benedict XVI said "I renounce the ministry of the bishop of Rome." The Latin word for "ministry" is "ministerio." Thus, Benedict XVI renounced the "ministerio" (ministry); he did not renounce the "munus" (office) as required by Canon 332§2. Therefore, given Benedict renounced the "ministerio" and not the "munus," as required by the aforementioned canon, Benedict's renunciation is invalid.

Reply to Objection 1.2: The objection is based on a misreading of Canon 332§2. The canon reads:

> If it should happen that the Roman Pontiff resigns his office [*munus*], it is required for validity that he makes the resignation freely and that it be duly manifested, but not that it be accepted by anyone.[71]

As can be seen in the text, the canon in question *specifically* lists only two conditions that are "required for validity." The first is that the resignation is made *freely*. The second is that it be *duly manifested*. That's it. The use of the word *munus* is not given as being among that which is "required" for a valid resignation.

Furthermore, there is no specified formula for a papal resignation that requires a specific word or words be used to convey the reality of the resignation. When some doubt arose over the possibility of a papal resignation in the case of Pope Celestine V, Pope Boniface VIII had both the teaching recognizing the possibility of papal resignations, and a canon on papal resignations placed into the *Liber Sextus*. None of these documents either taught or required the word *munus* be used. The teaching document stated a pope may resign the "*papacy,*" and the subsequent canon said that the "*Roman pontiff may resign freely.*"[72]

The reality is there are various words that might be used to convey the idea of the "papacy," and which can be used to signify the renunciation of it. Thus, Canon 332§2 should be understood in the sense of "*if the Roman pontiff resigns the papacy*" and not in the sense that the exact use of the word *munus* is required to do so. Regardless, it is clear Pope Benedict XVI intended to give up the papacy entirely in saying he renounced "*the ministry of the Bishop of Rome...in such a way...the See of Rome, the See of Peter*" would be vacant.

However, while the points above refute the objection, an additional devastating proof can be made against it. This point was recently made by Fr. John Rickert. Pope Benedict XVI's *Declaratio* was entered into the *Acta Apostolicae Sedis* (AAS), the authoritative, official record of papal acts. As Fr. Rickert points out,[73] the title of this document in the AAS is *Declaratio Summi Pontificis: De Muneris Episcopi Romae, Successoris Sancti Petri Abdicatione*. This is translated "*Declaration of the Supreme Pontiff on the abdication of the office (munus) of the Bishop of Rome, Successor of Saint Peter.*" Regarding the significance of this Latin phrase, Fr. Rickert comments:

> As I argue in my last post, it is not prescribed for the pope to use any particular formula, phrase, or word. But for those who think so, look at the title: De muneris episcopi Romae, successoris sancti Petri abdicatione.
>
> There it is, the second word: munus in the genitive singular, as required by the grammar. But I also draw your attention to the word abdicatio. Lewis and Short make it clear that this is a strong and unequivocal word; when applied to persons, it means to disown them.
>
> Sat est. Benedictus locutus, causa finita.[74]

In sum, Fr. Rickert's argument is devastating to the Benepapist cause. It alone should suffice to defeat it! The title tells us explicitly it is a *"Declaration of the Supreme Pontiff."* The official Latin title in the AAS includes the proper form of *munus* (*muneris*) required by the grammar. This is the very word, *munus*, demanded by the objector. Further, as Fr. Rickert tells us, the title uses "abdication" in the title, which is a form of the Latin *abdicatio*, which in *Lewis and Short* is defined as "a renouncing, disowning."[75]

Therefore, in the official entry for the *Declaratio* in the AAS, the element which the objector claims is required by Canon 332§2 for a valid resignation is, in fact, present. It is clear Pope Benedict XVI did renounce or abdicate the *munus*. It is there in black and white in the AAS. With that, it is appropriate to repeat Fr. Rickert's concluding remarks on this point: "*Sat est. Benedictus locutus, causa finita*," or "It is enough. Benedict has spoken, the case is closed." So it is. The objection fails on its own terms.

Objection 1.3: An appropriate synonym for *munus* was not used

> Not all Benepapists argue the word "*munus*" is specifically required for a valid resignation. However, what is sufficient "for the act to be valid…is that the object to be renounced is precisely said munus or officium, even when expression other than these are used."[76] Expressions such as "I resign the papacy," or "I resign from the office of the Roman Pontiff," etc., can be used.[77] However, the use of ministerium is insufficient for the purpose of resigning the papacy because it represents the function of the office, not the office itself.

Reply to Objection 1.3: In the Reply to Objection 1.2, we have already seen that the word *munus* is not required for a valid resignation. We have also seen there is no specified formula for a valid resignation. At the heart and core of the current objection is that those advancing such an argument make themselves the judges of which words are appropriate synonyms for *munus*, and of what words sufficiently convey—*to the objectors'* *satisfaction*—the sense of what is needed to make a papal act of resignation valid.

However, this is an office in the Church that is *not* held by those who make this objection. Per Canon 332§2, papal resignations need not "be accepted by anyone."[78] Yet, the Benepapists are here declaring their nonacceptance of such a papal act. They have assumed the authority to review and veto a papal act; something which is as outrageous as it is absurd. Papal juridical acts, by their nature, are presumed valid. They cannot be appealed, as per Canon 333§3: *"There is neither appeal nor recourse against a decision or decree of the Roman Pontiff."*[79] One commentary on the canon governing papal resignations states:

> The general provisions on resignation of an office are contained in canons 187-189. These legal regulations are only guidelines since, due to his supreme power, the pope can always pass new laws, and stands above already valid laws *(Papa supra omnes canones)*.[80] [The pope is above all canons.]

As this commentary states, the legal regulations in the code of canon law, for a pope, "are *only* guidelines." "*Papa supra omnes canones*"—the pope is above all canons! Consequently, the resignation must be presumed valid.

However, even if one grants, arguendo, the words may possibly be deficient, only another pope could judge another pope's juridical acts. This fact works against those who make the objection because—given the presumption of validity—one should not anticipate a judgment of invalidity by a future pope in such a manner, especially when there is potential for schism in doing so.

Unfortunately, various leading Benepapists have certainly violated the letter and spirit of the canons—to which they *claim* to faithfully appeal—by declaring the resignation invalid, that "Benedict is still pope," and setting demands and conditions for them to consider a future conclave as valid.[81]

Now, though the comments above are sufficient in reply to the present objection, let us consider the absolute distinction between *ministerio/ministerium* and *munus* which the objection wishes to draw. The objection rests on there being a clear distinction between *ministerio/ministerium* and *munus*. If there is no clear distinction, the Benepapist argument, on their own terms, fails.

So, is there a clear, absolute distinction or difference? In his critique of the Benepapist argument,[82] Ryan Grant argued the two words may be used synonymously.[83] Mr. Grant wrote:

> The argument about a difference between munus and ministerium does not hold water for several reasons. The first is that they are more or less synonymous. Munus can mean a gift, although even there it is not disconnected from the notion that it is a gift that carries responsibility. In ecclesiastical parlance, it typically means an office or duty. Thus, the episcopate, and the papacy, is considered a munus, properly speaking. In this sense, it is roughly synonymous with officium, which is the Roman word for duty. *Ministerium can mean a ministry or service, but it also means office or duty, in the sense of the essence of what the munus entails.*[84]

Separately, Fr. John Rickert, FSSP, Ph.D., makes a similar case, noting the *"distinction attempted is not based on a correct interpretation of the words."*[85] Fr. Rickert further notes *A Latin Dictionary* by Lewis and Short explicitly lists *ministerium* and *munus* as synonyms.[86] If one consults *The Dictionary of Ecclesiastical Latin* by Leo F. Stelten one finds overlapping definitions.[87] For example, both can mean *duty* and *office*.

Furthermore, a theologian quoted by Diane Montagna in a LifeSiteNews article provided a similar analysis to those of Mr. Grant and Fr. Rickert.[88] Also, in the same LifeSiteNews article, Ms. Montagna reported that Cardinal Burke, speaking of Benedict XVI's *Declaratio* said, *"it seems clear he uses interchangeably 'munus' and 'ministerium'"*[89] and that, speaking of Benedict, *"It doesn't seem that he's making a distinction between the two."*[90] Further, speaking of the *Declaratio* of Pope Benedict XVI, Cardinal Burke said it is clear Benedict *"was renouncing the munus."*[91]

Cardinal Burke's opinion on the question carries considerable weight given he is a noted canonist, and is the former Prefect of the Supreme Tribunal of the Apostolic Signatura, and has extensive knowledge of Latin.

In sum, the validity of the objection in this case rests on there being a clear distinction between *ministerium* and *munus*, that is, *ministerium* could not be used in place of *munus*. However, given there is no specific formula mandated for papal resignations, and that the two words are synonyms and used "interchangeably" as Cardinal Burke notes, the objection fails. There is no clear distinction.

In fact, while the arguments above suffice, we might also look at other documentary and historical precedent in recent times. In terms of Church documents, we may look at *Lumen Gentium* 20, which clearly considers *ministerium* and *munus* as synonyms (emphasis added):

> That divine mission, entrusted by Christ to the apostles, will last until the end of the world, since the Gospel they are to teach is for all time the source of all life for the Church. And for this reason the apostles, appointed as rulers in this society, took care to appoint successors. For they not only had helpers in their ministry (*ministerio*), but also, in order that the mission assigned to them might continue after their death, they passed on to their immediate cooperators, as it were, in the form of a testament, the duty of confirming and finishing the work begun by themselves, recommending to them that they attend to the whole flock in which the Holy Spirit placed them to shepherd the Church of God. They therefore appointed such men, and gave them the order that, when they should have died, other approved men would take up their ministry (*ministerium*). *Among those various ministries (ministeria) which, according to tradition, were exercised in the Church from the earliest times, the chief place belongs to the office (munus) of those who, appointed to the episcopate, by a succession running from the beginning, are passers-on of the apostolic seed.*[92]

Lumen Gentium 20 speaks of the Lord appointing the Apostles as rulers of the Church. The Apostles, it is noted, had helpers in their ministry. These helpers, for example, might include deacons, priests, etc. The Apostles, in turn, appointed men to take up their *ministry* (*ministerium*) when they should have died. The text explicitly says that:

> "Among these ministries (*ministerio*) which, according to tradition, were exercised in the Church from the earliest times, the chief place belongs to the office (*munus*) of those who, appointed to the episcopate, by a succession running from the beginning, are passers-on of the apostolic seed."

Lumen Gentium clearly states that "*among these ministries (ministerio)*" the "*chief place belongs to the office (munus) of those*" appointed to the episcopate. Therefore, the text states the office or *munus* of the bishop is a ministry or *ministerio,* for it is "among these ministries." Hence, it is indisputable that the terms are used synonymously here.[93]

Up to and including the election of Pope Paul VI, papacies were officially inaugurated by a papal coronation mass. At this mass, the pope would receive the symbols of his office to symbolize the commencement of his papacy. For example, a new pope would receive the pallium, and the Fisherman's ring, all symbols of his office.

However, Pope John Paul I did not have a coronation mass using the papal tiara because following the council the papacy had moved away from some of the pomp historically associated with the office. So, instead of a papal coronation mass to mark John Paul I's election to the Throne of St. Peter, there was a mass to "inaugurate the Petrine *Ministry* of the Bishop of Rome,"[94] where the new pope received the pallium and the Fisherman's ring. The opening of his homily, which is here translated from Latin, reads:

> In this sacred celebration, which takes place as the solemn beginning of the ministry [ministerii] of the Supreme Pastor of the Church, placed on our shoulders, we turn our minds primarily to adoring and praying to God, the infinite and eternal, who, by his inexplicable design, human arguments, and his most kind condescension, has raised us to the chair of blessed Peter.[95]

VALID? THE RESIGNATION OF POPE BENEDICT XVI

Pope John Paul I speaks of the "solemn beginning of the ministry" (ministerii) of the Supreme Pastor of the Church being placed upon his shoulders. Given the context of the mass, and the reception of the pallium and Fisherman's ring, it is clear he is speaking of the papacy, and not simply the exercise of it.

Soon after his election, Pope Benedict XVI in a homily during a mass in the Sistine Chapel repeatedly used *ministerium* in a reflection on his election.[96] For example, Pope Benedict, in Latin, spoke of *"The Eucharist, the heart of Christian life and the source of the good news of the Church, is an essential, permanent and central part of the Petrine ministry (ministerii) entrusted to us."*[97]

Here Benedict speaks of the Petrine ministry "entrusted" to him. In his *Declaratio*, he uses similar language when he resigned: "I renounce the ministry (*ministerio*) of Bishop of Rome, Successor of Saint Peter, *entrusted to me* by the Cardinals."[98] Thus, Benedict is speaking of his election as Supreme Pontiff because that is what the cardinals entrusted to him, i.e., the papacy.

When we look at the inauguration mass of Pope Benedict XVI's papacy, we find similar language to that used for John Paul I. The mass to mark Benedict's assumption of the papacy was called, in Latin, "*Sollemne Initium Ministerii Summi Eccelesiae Pastoris,*"[99] or the "solemn commencement of the ministry of the supreme pastor of the church."

We have already seen in this Reply to Objection 1.2 that *ministerium* is a recognized synonym for *munus*, both having "service" and "office" in their definitions. In addition, above, we have seen that *ministerium*, contrary to what the Benepapists assert, is shown in a practical, real-life example to be an appropriate word to refer to the papacy. In these examples, we see it used to mark both the inauguration of the papacy by newly elected popes, and, in the case of Pope Benedict XVI in his *Declaratio*, to renounce the papacy.

Also, the reader should refer back to the Reply to Objection 1.2 which details Fr. Rickert's argument based on the title of *Declaratio* as found in the *Acta Apostolicae Sedis*: *Declaratio Summi Pontificis De Muneris Episcopi Romae, Successoris Sancti Petri Abdicatione.*[100] As Fr. Rickert notes, the title uses a form of *munus* and speaks of the *abdication* of the Bishop of Rome.[101] This title alone in the authoritative AAS meets the condition that some Benepapists read into Canon 332§2, albeit incorrectly, i.e., that it is necessary for the pope to specifically renounce the *munus*.

It is clear the title demonstrates that Benedict's use of *ministerium* within the body of the *Declaratio* must be interpreted as a synonym of *munus*. That is to say, given the AAS title is "*Declaration of Supreme Pontiff on the abdication of the office (munus) of the Bishop Rome, Successor of Saint Peter*," then the declaration "*I renounce the ministry (ministerio) of Bishop of Rome, Successor of Saint Peter*" must necessarily and *definitively* be interpreted as synonymous with that title. Consequently, the objection fails.

Objection 1.4: BXVI withdrew only from his function as pope.

> The act performed by BXVI in February 2013 did not exist at all for canon law, so on his part there was only a partial and de facto withdrawal from his function.[102]

Reply to Objection 1.4: Canon law only makes provision for a resignation from the papacy. There is no such provision for a withdrawal from the function or activities of the papacy, while maintaining the papal office. If Benedict had only wanted to withdraw de facto from the functions of his office, he need not have done anything all. There would have been no need to issue a *Declaratio*.

However, his declarations that the See of Rome, "the See of Saint Peter," would be vacant, and that a new conclave was necessary to elect a "new Supreme Pontiff" demonstrate that his intention was to resign the papal office. But let us consider another argument against the Benepapists, as advanced by Fr. Rickert:

> Let us leave aside how proponents of the theory could claim to know Benedict's intentions with greater certainty than the rest of us. We consider, then, a conceptual distinction between an officeholder and an administrator. Often, the officeholder is the administrator: such as a president, general, bishop, or pastor. But

VALID? THE RESIGNATION OF POPE BENEDICT XVI

sometimes the administrator is not the officeholder: e.g. an acting president, or one *pro tempore*, or an administrator of a diocese without a bishop at present. A key point here—and the pun is very much intended: The Supreme Pontiff, in virtue of his office, has a *right to act* pursuant to that office.

> Can. 331 (Latin) — Ecclesiae Romanae Episcopus, in quo permanet munus a Domino singulariter Petro, primo Apostolorum, concessum et successoribus eius transmittendum, Collegii Episcoporum est caput, Vicarius Christi atque universae Ecclesiae his in terris Pastor; *qui ideo vi muneris sui suprema, plena, immediata et universali in Ecclesia gaudet ordinaria potestate, quam semper libere exercere valet* (emphasis added).
>
> Can. 331 (English) — The bishop of the Roman Church, in whom continues the office given by the Lord uniquely to Peter, the first of the Apostles, and to be transmitted to his successors, is the head of the college of bishops, the Vicar of Christ, and the pastor of the universal Church on earth. *By virtue of his office he possesses supreme, full, immediate, and universal ordinary power in the Church, which he is always able to exercise freely* (emphasis added).

If a pope renounces the administration of his office, he necessarily renounces the office itself, because the office *per se* (*vi muneris*)[103] entails the right to act. Thus, Pope Benedict's renunciation of his administration entails renunciation of the papal office. That is why he goes on to express the results, which he is clearly cognizant of: the Chair of St. Peter will be vacant, and a new pope must be elected.[104]

Fr. Rickert argues that even if we assume, arguendo, that Benedict meant to resign the "*ministerium*" in the sense of the "active ministry" of the Petrine office, then this would still result in a valid resignation. This is so, as Fr. Rickert demonstrates, because "Pope

THE DECLARATIO

Benedict's renunciation of his administration entails the renunciation of the papal office."

Perhaps in terms of a baseball analogy, it might be like a player telling the team he will "no longer play second base." In such a case, it is meaningless to ask if he still nonetheless remains the second baseman for the team, even if he no longer plays the position. The point being, if you don't have someone who plays second base, you don't have a second baseman. If a man gives up the exercise of the papacy, he is no longer the pope. Thus, the objection fails.

Objection 1.5: "Substantial error" re "partial" resignation

> Pope Benedict XVI held erroneous views about the papacy even before he was elected pope, by which he erroneously believed the papacy could be "bifurcated" into a papal diarchy, comprised of an active and a contemplative component. Benedict attempted to retain either a part or the whole of the papal *munus* when, in the *Declaratio*, he resigned the Petrine "ministry" (*ministerio*), signaling that he intended to resign only the "active ministry" (*ministerio*) while retaining the Petrine office (*munus*) in whole or in part. However, given it is impossible to split the papacy, Benedict's attempted partial resignation constituted a "substantial error" which invalidated his resignation per Canon 188.[105]

Reply to Objections 1.5: Before proceeding to the reply to this objection, let us recall the wording of Canon 188, as it is the basis to Benepapists' claim that Benedict's resignation was invalid due to "substantial error":

> A resignation submitted out of grave fear, which has been unjustly inflicted, or because of fraud, *substantial error* or simony is invalid by the law itself.[106]

With the above in mind, let us proceed to the reply to the objection.

The objection alleges that even prior to his election Pope Benedict XVI, as theologian Josef Ratzinger, held erroneous opinions regarding the nature of the papacy. Ratzinger's writings, as theologian and then as pope, span decades of work. There are four works that the Benepapists have proffered as evidence. Two of them are Ratzinger's books *Principles of Catholic Theology* and *Theological Highlights of Vatican II*, which we will specifically review in *Objection 1.6*, although the comments in this reply to the current objection apply to them as well.

The other two works, which we will address here, are a dissertation authored by J. Michael Miller, *The Divine Right of the Papacy in Recent Ecumenical Theology,* and a paper written by Cardinal Ratzinger titled *The Primacy of the Pope and the unity of the People of God.*

Given the objection alleges such errors are to be found in Ratzinger's earlier writings, the burden of proof is on the objector to produce the works wherein such statements can be found. Further, this burden requires the evidence demonstrate:

> (1) Ratzinger as a theologian, in fact, *explicitly* and *specifically* held erroneous thoughts on and or confusion over the *munus* as it relates to the papacy specifically; and,
> (2) that any erroneous conclusions Ratzinger drew from any such erroneous premise *explicitly* and *specifically* relate to questions regarding papal resignations, and to a prospective former pope; and, that,
> (3) Ratzinger, once he became pope, continued to believe the same errors.

Let us now consider the first two documents offered as proof that Benedict, as theologian Fr. Ratzinger, posited erroneous opinions regarding the papacy. The first document proffered as evidence of Ratzinger's errors is *The Divine Right of the Papacy in Recent Ecumenical Theology*, which was a dissertation authored by J. Michael Miller in 1979 while at the Gregorian University in Rome. One Benepapist makes the following claim about this document:

> It is a Rosetta Stone-esque synthesis of the massive Teutonic Theological Academy's writings in the mid-20th century on the

"need" to "fundamentally transform" the *irrelevant, illegitimate and expired Monarchical model* of the Papacy by essentially dissolving the Petrine Office into a collegial, synodal Petrine Ministry or Function.[107]

We do not need to debate the *Miller Dissertation*'s outline of the "Teutonic Theological Academy" of the mid-twentieth century, and any bizarre theories that might have arisen from some German theologians within it. We are concerned with the allegations against only one German theologian here, Josef Ratzinger.

It is alleged the *Miller Dissertation* provides *"proof of Joseph Ratzinger, like his German and Nouvelle Theologie colleagues and peers of the day, positing RADICALLY SUBSTANTIALLY ERRONEOUS IDEAS about the Petrine Office."*[108] However, this is simply not the case.

The truth is no one has brought forth from the *Miller Dissertation* a single quote of Fr. Ratzinger's, wherein he proposes or "posits" any error regarding the papacy, let alone the specific error of which he, later as Pope Benedict XVI, is accused by some Benepapists of having made in his *Declaratio*. The *Miller Dissertation* has proved to be a big "nothing burger."

Having disposed of the first document under consideration, let us proceed to the second. Unlike the first document which does not quote him, the second document is a paper written by Cardinal Ratzinger, entitled *The Primacy of the Pope and the unity of the People of God.* It is alleged this paper contains "thermonuclear substantial error:"[109] One Benepapist makes the claim that Ratzinger had:

> ...considered [the] hypothesis that a monarchical Papacy was intrinsically "Arian" in nature, and the Papacy should reflect the Trinity, a "Pope-Troika" consisting of One Catholic, One Protestant and One Orthodox.[110]

The article which produced such "analysis" is based on a partial citation of Cardinal Ratzinger's paper, which perhaps represents only a fifth of the full paper. The full paper certainly does not bear out the conclusion Ratzinger "considered" or entertained such thoughts as his own.[111]

Ratzinger's paper traces the spiritual basis of the primacy and collegiality, the martyrological structure of the primacy, and concludes with a view of the situation in Christendom. Early in the paper, Ratzinger does discuss "collegiality as an expression of the 'we' structure of the faith."

In that context, he briefly discusses thoughts of other theologians without adopting them. Ratzinger advances neither the notion the papacy is "intrinsically Arian" nor that the papacy should reflect the Trinity, as if consisting of a "Pope-Troika." Instead, as Ratzinger states in his paper, it was E. Peterson who suggested that Arianism was favored by the Eastern Roman emperors. Ratzinger wrote:

> Petersen tried to show that Arianism was a political theology favored by the emperors because it ensured a divine analogy to the political monarchy, whereas the triumph of the trinitarian faith exploded political theology and removed the theological justification for political monarchy.[112]

Ratzinger would go on to explain that Petersen's commentary on Arianism was picked up by others who suggested the "exercise of the primacy by a single man, the pope in Rome, actually follows an Arian model."[113] From this, Ratzinger explains, apparently some suggested the papacy should instead follow a Trinitarian model, requiring a *"college of three, and the members of this triumvirate, acting together, would be the pope."*[114]

However, it is clear that Ratzinger was not himself suggesting the papacy was either Arian, or that it should be Trinitarian, i.e., comprised of a college of three. In fact, in footnote 9 of his paper, Ratzinger attributes such speculations to oral remarks of a theologian named H. Mühlen. While Ratzinger charitably compliments Mühlen's scholarship, he pointedly states his arguments "are not free of the danger of a new analogous way of thinking that exaggerates the applicability of the trinitarian doctrine to ecclesiology."[115] Thus, Ratzinger rejects the notion of applying the Trinitarian concept to the papacy, as if to create a synodal papacy of three popes.

In sum, a review of the full article by Ratzinger demonstrates there is nothing there that helps the Benepapist cause. Ratzinger is not "positing" any ideas of his own about either an "Arian" or a multi-member synodal papacy. Neither the much trumpeted *Miller Dissertation* nor Ratzinger's own paper provides any basis to the claim that Pope Benedict XVI held erroneous ideas which would impact the validity of his resignation.[116] Thus, if the objection demonstrates anyone's "thermonuclear substantial error," it is that of the objector.

Additional Thoughts on Canon 188

Apart from the discussion above, there is one other thing to consider. That is whether the Benepapist appeal to "substantial error" in Canon 188 would even apply in Benedict's situation, if we were to assume, arguendo, Benedict held some erroneous opinion about a "partial resignation." One commentary on canon law defines "substantial error" as follows (italics added):

> "Substantial error is a mistaken judgment that is not of minor importance and is *truly a cause* of the consequent decision. This would be the case in which the officeholder judged that he or she had caused serious injury to someone when this was not the case."[117]

Substantial error is *truly a cause* of the consequent decision to resign. With that in mind, reread the example of mistaken judgment given in the quote from the commentary above. Also consider the following example of *substantial error* given by Cardinal Brandmüller: "*If a Pope decided to resign because he thought Islamic troops were invading the Vatican, the resignation would be invalid if the Islamic troops weren't in fact invading.*"[118]

As can readily be seen, these examples have nothing in common with what is alleged in Benedict's case. That is to say, the erroneous opinions of which the Benepapists accuse Benedict were not the *true cause* of his resignation. Even if we assume

Benedict held such an error, and misunderstood what he might retain as a former pope, the evidence still demonstrates he intended to submit a papal resignation. Benedict understood the *"See of Rome, the See of Peter"* would be vacant, and that a new conclave would now be necessary, and that his successor would be a *true pope* (see discussion of *Normas Nonnullas* in Chapter 2). Thus, even if we were to assume, arguendo, that Benedict held some strange opinion, his resignation would still be valid.

Objection 1.6: BXVI believed in a "sacramental papacy"

> Pope Benedict XVI held erroneous views regarding the "Petrine *munus*," believing in a "sacramental papacy." He believed that following his resignation he would continue to keep either the whole or a part the Petrine *munus* in some real, ontological sense as "Pope Emeritus." However, had Benedict understood there was no such thing as a "sacramental papacy," and that when a pope renounces the Petrine office he loses the Petrine *munus* completely, he would not have resigned.[119]

Reply to Objection 1.6: The thesis of the objection is comprised of two linked propositions which must be proven true to conclude that Benedict's resignation was invalid. The objector must demonstrate:

> (1) Benedict believed in a "sacramental papacy" through which he would retain the Petrine *munus* in some way or to some degree even if he resigned; and that
> (2) Benedict would not have resigned the papacy if he understood his view was erroneous, and he would retain nothing at all. This constitutes Benedict's "substantial error" which invalidates his resignation.

The reply to the second part of this objection will be addressed in the Reply to Objection 1.7. Now, with regard to part one of the current objection, to evaluate the case for "substantial error" on these grounds, we must first examine the first proposition as to whether Pope Benedict XVI actually believed in a "sacramental papacy," in which he distinguished between a sacramental *ontological munus* and a canonical *juridical munus*. We need not go too deeply into this. The main distinction here is that while the latter might be lost, the former cannot be.

Essentially, it is alleged, Benedict's erroneous view is that he received an ontological *munus* upon his election as pope which can never be lost. If that were truly the case, one would retain the papacy in some sense even if one resigned it. It seems that some Benepapists argue here that Benedict believed this ontological *munus*, becoming pope, is the ultimate completion of the sacrament of Holy Orders conferred by his papal election. However, to suggest Benedict believed anything of the sort is to make him a heretic, as *Lumen Gentium* 21 explicitly teaches episcopal consecration confers the *fullness* of the sacrament of Holy Orders (italics added):

> And *the Sacred Council teaches that by Episcopal consecration the fullness of the sacrament of Orders is conferred,* that fullness of power, namely, which both in the Church's liturgical practice and in the language of the Fathers of the Church is called the high priesthood, the supreme power of the sacred ministry.[120]

The Church teaches Episcopal consecration, *not papal election*, confers the *fullness* of the sacrament of Holy Orders. So taught Vatican II. Given Benedict XVI, when he was Fr. Ratzinger in the 1960s, was at Vatican II, it would be quite remarkable if this fact either escaped his notice or that he rejected it. There are absolutely no grounds to say Fr. Ratzinger, or Ratzinger as pope, believed the fullness of Orders was only conferred upon papal election. To say he did believe this is to make him a *heretic*. That is problematic because the whole theory of Benepapism was supposedly designed to saved us from one "*heretical pope*," but in trying to so, it has only given us back another.

Still, the evidence which is said to substantiate the objection rests on two quotes from Josef Ratzinger. The first is found in Ratzinger's 1987 book, *Principles of Catholic Theology*, and the second, in his *Theological Highlights of Vatican II*.

VALID? THE RESIGNATION OF POPE BENEDICT XVI

Let us first take a look at the Benepapist argument which is based on Ratzinger's *Principles of Catholic Theology*. The following argument is made by a proponent of the thesis found in the objection (emphasis added):

> But now we get back to the sacramental ontological *munus* vs. the canonical juridical *munus*, if you will. So let me introduce a quote from Josef Ratzinger from *Principles of Catholic Theology* from 1987 available from Ignatius Press...and *basically he says "I disagree with those who teach" that "the papacy is not a sacrament that it is only a juridical institution, but this juridical institution has set itself above the sacramental order."* Let me unpack that. Ratzinger is arguing that what is foremost, what's important foremost, is the sacramental ontological *munus* not the "office" that perhaps comes and goes.[121]

And elsewhere, the proponent says:

> What does Joseph Ratzinger say? He says, "No, no, no. I disagree with those people who say the papacy is not a sacrament, that it's only a juridical institution. That juridical institution has set itself above the sacramental order."[122]

So we see a Benepapist paraphrases Ratzinger in an attempt to show that Ratzinger is arguing *against* those who say "the papacy is not a sacrament." If, as suggested, Ratzinger is in fact saying he "disagrees" with those who say the "papacy is not a sacrament," this would clearly imply Ratzinger believes that the papacy *is* a sacrament. If it is true the papacy is a sacrament, one could never lose it—just like a priest is forever a priest, or a bishop a bishop. That is what the proponent of Benepapism is alleging, and if he is right on this point, it would seem the objection might have some merit.

However, did Ratzinger really say this in his book *Principles of Catholic Theology*? Given this quote is central to the thesis Pope Benedict XVI believed the *"papacy is a sacrament"* we need to examine the original text from Ratzinger's book to determine whether the aforementioned paraphrase is an accurate one. However, as we shall shortly see, such an examination indicates Cardinal Ratzinger is not saying what has been attributed to him.

An extended citation from Ratzinger's *Principles of Catholic Theology* is provided below to demonstrate this point. Ratzinger, in context, is speaking on the subject of ecumenism between East and West. Ratzinger writes (italics added):

> All this, as we have said, is basically true also of the separation between Rome and Constantinople that became the starting point of the division between East and West. Not everyone, it is true, especially on the Orthodox side, would agree with this opinion—which shows how time has served to intensify the gravity of the dispute. For, *from the Orthodox point of view*, at least according to one interpretation, the *monarchia papae* means a destruction of the ecclesial structure as such, in consequence of which something different and new replaces the primitive Christian form. *Because this aspect of the problem is, generally speaking, more or less foreign to us in the West, I should like to indicate in a few words how this impression has arisen in the East. For such a view*, the Church in the West is no longer, under the leadership of her bishops, a nexus of local churches that, in their collegial unity, go back to the community of the twelve apostles; she is seen, rather, as a centrally organized monolith in which the new legal concept of a "perfect society" has superseded the old idea of succession in the community. In her, the faith that was handed down no longer (so it seems) serves as the sole normative rule—a rule that can be newly interpreted only with the consensus of all the local churches; in her, the will of the absolute sovereign creates a new authority. Precisely this difference in the concept of authority grew steadily more intense and reached its climax in 1870 with the proclamation of the primacy of jurisdiction: in one case, only the tradition that has been handed down serves as a valid source of law, and only the consensus of all is the normative criterion for determining and interpreting it. In the other case, the source of law appears to be the will of the sovereign, which creates on its own authority (ex sese) new laws that then have the power to bind. *The old sacramental structure seems overgrown,*

> even choked, by this new concept of the law: the papacy is not a sacrament, it is "only" a juridical institution; but this juridical institution has set itself above the sacramental order.[123]

Recall, the proponent of Benepapism said Ratzinger wrote that he disagreed with those who say "*the papacy is not a sacrament.*" Thus, implicitly, he is saying Ratzinger believes the "papacy *is* a sacrament." This is central and essential to his Benepapist thesis.

However, what should be immediately evident from the extended quote above from *Principles of Catholic Theology* is that Ratzinger is not arguing anything of the sort. Rather, Cardinal Ratzinger is simply explaining how the Eastern Church views the Western Church, and the papacy in particular. He says so himself:

> Because this aspect of the problem is, generally speaking, more or less foreign to us in the West, I should like to indicate in a few words how this impression has arisen in the East. For such a view…[124]

To briefly sum up Ratzinger's presentation of the Eastern view, it proceeds generally as follows. The East sees that the West, through such developments as the doctrine of papal infallibility, the pope as "absolute sovereign," etc., has turned the papacy into something of a sacrament, or tantamount to one. Such a view the East rejects. This is the East's straw man view of the West, which the East rejects, essentially saying through Ratzinger's presentation of the East's view: "*the papacy is not a sacrament, it is 'only' a juridical institution; but this juridical institution has set itself above the sacramental order.*"

Ratzinger was obviously describing the Orthodox Church's critical view of the Western Church, not his own, and without suggesting he personally "disagrees with those who say the papacy is not a sacrament." For that matter, he expresses no opinion on the question at all. There is nothing in this citation from Ratzinger's book to support the thesis that Ratzinger believed in a sacramental papacy. Let us consider the second citation offered as proof.

THE DECLARATIO

Immediately following the Benepapist's attribution of these Eastern beliefs to Ratzinger, the proponent of Benepapism introduced a second quote to support his view Ratzinger believed the papacy is a sacrament:

> Here's another quote from Ratzinger right after the council and it is from his book *Theological Highlights of Vatican II* published in 1966 by Paulist Press, again another money line, "the ministry of the bishop—meaning *munus* in Latin—is not an externally assigned administrative power but rather is itself sacramentally based. The ruling of the Church and its spiritual mystery are inseparable."[125]

As we did above, let us first examine the original source material before commenting on its relevance. Beginning earlier in the text for more context from the source material, *Theological Highlights of Vatican II* reads (emphasis added):

> The eucharist is there to build man up for the body of Christ, and conversely the building up of the Church is accomplished through the eucharist. Each of these penetrates the other. Whoever has, as a priest, the privilege of presiding over the eucharist not only transforms the substance of the bread into that of the body of Christ, but is also performing a ministry for the Church of God, which lives from this eucharist. In the eucharistic office, both the sacrament and the "ruling power" interpenetrate one another, and it becomes at once clear how inappropriate the words "rule" and "power" are with regard to the Church. We have no more right to speak of a quasi-profane ruling power, neatly separated from the sacramental ministry, than we have a right to speak of a separation between the mystical and eucharistic body of Christ.
>
> But this means that the pluralism of the sacramental communities and the unity of the Church's ministries safeguarded by the pope likewise interpenetrate one another. It is precisely this that is the actual content of collegiality. Its reference to the sacramental definition of the office of bishop ultimately comes from a sacramentally defined image of the Church. The ministry

> of the bishop is not an externally assigned "administrative power," *but rather arises from the necessary plurality of the eucharistic communities (i.e., of the Churches in the Church) and, as representing these,* is itself sacramentally based. The ruling of the Church and its spiritual mystery are inseparable.[126]

First, Ratzinger, as the extended quote manifests, was not speaking of the papacy exclusively or even primarily. That is not the subject of his discussion. Second, the Benepapist's reading of Ratzinger from this source emphasizes that the "ministry of the bishop is not an *externally* assigned 'administrative power'," but is sacramentally based. This, at first glance, might appear to have some relation to the Benepapist thesis. However, the Benepapist's paraphrase leaves out an important point found in the original source text in the italics below:

> The ministry of the bishop is not an externally assigned "administrative power," *but rather arises from the necessary plurality of the eucharistic communities (i.e., of the Churches in the Church) and, as representing these,* is itself sacramentally based. The ruling of the Church and its spiritual mystery are inseparable.[127]

The reader will see Ratzinger is not suggesting the bishop's office cannot be lost! He is speaking of how the "*administrative power…arises from the necessary plurality of eucharistic communities.*" Earlier in the extended quote from *Theological Highlights of Vatican II*, Ratzinger said that "*In the eucharistic office, both the sacrament and the 'ruling power' interpenetrate one another.*" Thus, if we must force a theological conclusion here from this construction, it is not one favorable to the Benepapist thesis.

That is, there is nothing here to suggest the Petrine *munus* or office cannot be lost. Rather, Ratzinger more likely would say the "ruling" power "*necessarily arises*" from a bishop being set over, or "representing," a eucharistic community (i.e., a local Church); and given that "*in the eucharistic office, both the sacrament and the 'ruling power' interpenetrate one another,*" if a bishop should cease being over that eucharistic community as its head, he would lose his "ruling power" or jurisdiction over that local Church (i.e., there would no longer be an interpenetration of the "ruling power"). But here, "sacramentally-based" refers to the community as a eucharistic one; it does not refer to the sacrament of Holy Orders, and certainly not to the papacy as a sacrament.

In sum, there is nothing here to support the notion Benedict believed the Petrine *munus* is sacramental in the sense intended by the objection, i.e., something once received that cannot be lost. There is no evidence to be found in either of these Ratzingerian texts to suggest Ratzinger either believed the papacy is a sacrament, or that the Petrine *munus* is not lost or surrendered in full upon resignation.

Objection 1.7: Deficient consent due to "substantial error"

> Had Benedict understood there was no such thing as a "sacramental papacy," and that when a pope renounces the Petrine office he loses the Petrine *munus* completely, he would not have resigned.[128]

Reply to Objection 1.7: In the earlier Reply to Objection 1.5, it was argued that the Benepapist appeal to Canon 188 and "substantial error" was insufficient to establish the invalidity of Benedict's resignation. This was so, as the given examples showed, because Benedict's alleged errors regarding a "partial resignation" were not "truly a cause" of the resignation.

Now, with regard to the current Objection 1.7, the objector appears to understand the deficiency of his fellow Benepapist's argument (see Objection 1.5), and thus attempts to rectify the weakness in her argument. The objector does this, as hinted in the second part of Objection 1.6, by claiming Benedict's "substantial error" consisted of the following: *Benedict would not have resigned had he realized that (1) his view of a sacramental papacy was in error, and that (2) he would not retain the Petrine* munus *in any way after his resignation.* As one leading Benepapist put it:

VALID? THE RESIGNATION OF POPE BENEDICT XVI

> ...Had he known that the truth of the matter is there is no such thing as a sacramental papacy and that when you renounce the office that's it, you're not papal in any way shape or form any more, I honestly believe based on everything he said over the last sixty years, he would not have resigned...[129]

And, again:

> ...he only resigned because he thought he was going to be papal, he was still going to share in the shadow of Peter...[130]

The suggestion here is pure speculation as to what Benedict would or would not have done under a set of assumed circumstances. It is an attempt at guessing what Pope Benedict XVI would or would not have done had he realized there is no such thing as a "sacramental papacy."

Yet, guessing cannot be a valid approach to determining whether a papal resignation is invalid. When interviewed on the specific question of what Benedict XVI intended in his resignation, Cardinal Brandmüller said, *"You always have to keep in mind that the law speaks of verifiable facts, not of thoughts."*[131]

Yet, the same Benepapist assumes Benedict "stipulated"[132] he would not have resigned if he had known he would lose the *munus* upon his resignation and assumption of the role of "pope emeritus." This stipulation is only in the mind of the Benepapist here, who himself admits: *"I honestly believe based on everything he said over the last sixty years, he would not have resigned."*[133] What this Benepapist "honestly believes" Benedict would or would not do is irrelevant. We need verifiable facts, not speculation.

The truth is we know why Benedict resigned. *He told us.* First, in the *Declaratio,* Benedict cited his weakness and lack of strength. He said so twice, and he said it was *"for this reason"* he was renouncing the papacy. Furthermore, we know from a Peter Seewald interview from 2010, a few years before the resignation, that Benedict said that if he ever lacked the strength to continue, then he would have a *moral obligation* to resign. Benedict said (italics added):

THE DECLARATIO

> Yes. If a pope clearly realizes that he is no longer physically, psychologically, and spiritually capable of handling the duties of his office, then he has a right and, *under some circumstances, also the obligation to resign.*[134]

After his resignation, Benedict said pretty much the same thing. Speaking of the many responsibilities of the papal office, Benedict as Pope Emeritus said, "*Even if you say a few of these things can be struck off, there remain so many things which are essential, that, if the capability to do them is no longer there—for me anyway; someone else might see it otherwise—now's the time to free up the chair.*"[135]

Given his lack of strength, Benedict believed he had a *moral obligation* to resign. His inadequacy to fulfill the *munus-ministerium* was the true cause of his resignation. As he said to Seewald above, "*if the capability to do*" the things a pope must is no longer there, "*now's the time to free up the chair.*"

As this was a moral obligation in Benedict's judgment, it obliged regardless of any condition or status he believed he may or may not have retained relative to the Petrine *munus* after his resignation. Thus, Benedict's resignation would have been valid *even if* we assume, arguendo, he believed in a sacramental papacy as alleged by the Benepapist.

Thus, the objection fails.

Another Argument against the Objection

In addition to the arguments against the objection thus far made, there are other grounds to reject the notion that Benedict believed he somehow retained something of the Petrine *munus* after his resignation.

In the section of canon law dealing with the Roman Pontiff, Canon 331 says of the Bishop of Rome that the *munus* is given in a "special way by the Lord to Peter...and transmitted to his successors," and resides in him uniquely (cf. Canon 331). Therefore, if one is not the bishop of Rome, one does not hold the Petrine *munus* in any size, shape, or form.

VALID? THE RESIGNATION OF POPE BENEDICT XVI

Given Benedict XVI did in fact resign *"the See of Rome, the See of Peter"*—and thus was no longer the Bishop of Rome, it cannot be said that the Petrine *munus* resides in him any longer. As Pope, Benedict was surely aware of the specific canons related to the papacy; it defies credulity to suggest Benedict could possibly believe he could retain anything of the Petrine *munus* following his resignation. The objection fails on this ground as well.

Reductio ad Absurdum

Finally, there is yet another flaw in the objection. The objection rests on the belief that Benedict XVI's understanding of the Petrine *munus* was erroneous. If this was so, then it would seem Benedict XVI could *never* resign the papacy validly even if he had explicitly renounced the *munus* in the *Declaratio*, as the Benepapists require. Moreover, we might wonder, if Benedict's understanding of the papacy was so erroneous that we could never be sure he had properly resigned from it, should we then wonder too, whether his acceptance of his election was valid?

Again, the objection fails.

Objection 1.8: BXVI intentionally "sabotaged" his resignation

> "The Pope assembled in this way what could strategically be defined as a 'planned ruse.'"[136] Pope Benedict XVI intentionally worded the *Declaratio* in such a way that it would necessarily be invalid or meaningless with regard to resigning the *munus*. He did this by renouncing the *ministerium* ("practical exercise") but not the required *munus*. Such a renunciation is canonically and juridically meaningless. However, even if, arguendo, the renouncing of the Petrine *ministerium* were possible, Benedict still retained the Petrine *munus*, and thus remains the true pope.[137]

Reply to Objection 1.8: This objection proposes, essentially, that Pope Benedict XVI sabotaged his own resignation. This theory, called Benedict's "Plan B" by its lead proponents, suggests Benedict willfully submitted a deficient resignation in order to retain the Petrine *munus*, i.e., the papacy. We will address the alleged motives attributed to Pope Benedict XVI in formulating *Plan B* in a bit.

However, first, a quick look at the core premise of the objection, which is that Benedict's renunciation of the *ministerium* rather than the *munus* renders that renunciation invalid. This objection and other forms of it were addressed in the Replies to Objections 1.2, 1.3, 1.4, and 1.5. In sum, there is no canonical formula for a resignation regarding what word or words can be used, and which cannot. Even setting that aside, *ministerium* is a synonym of *munus*. The text and logic of the *Declaratio* make it evident Benedict used the terms "interchangeably."

Further, the validity of Benedict's resignation is clear when he declares he renounced the "*ministry of the bishop of Rome...in such a way...that the See of Rome, the See of Saint Peter will be vacant.*" If the "See of Rome, the See of Saint Peter" is vacant, there is no one holding the Petrine *munus*. This is further supported by Benedict stating that as a result, a conclave would now be necessary to elect a new Supreme Pontiff—something that can happen only if there is no true pope.

The objection also appears to suggest that if Benedict validly resigned anything, it was only the "practical exercise" of the papacy, but not the *munus*. However, as Fr. Rickert argued, as quoted in the Reply to Objection 1.4: "*If a pope renounces the administration of his office, he necessarily renounces the office itself, because the office per se* (vi muneris) *entails the right to act.*"[138] Thus, even assuming the clear distinction of *ministerium* and *munus* demanded by the objection, the resignation of the *ministerium* would entail the resignation of the *munus*, i.e., one cannot resign one without resigning the other.

Having addressed the central premise, it is worthwhile now to take a broader look at this objection. The standard Benepapist theory claims Benedict's resignation was invalid due to a "*substantial error*" per Canon 188. However, there is another branch of Benepapism that asserts Benedict intentionally *sabotaged* his own resignation with the purpose of rendering it invalid. In such a view, Benedict intentionally issued a juridically flawed renunciation, using *ministerium* in place of *munus*, in order to make it invalid. Why on earth would Benedict do such a thing? Here is how one lead proponent explains the theory (italics added):

> With a Church completely infected with the metastasizing globalist modernism subject to and placed under international pressure, Benedict decided upon a definitive *maneuver*, undertaken "to clean out not only the small world of the Curia, but rather the Church in Her totality", as he will explain to the journalist Peter Seewald in 2016.
>
> A "Plan B" worked out over many years precisely in view of an aggression against the Papacy from within the Church, and announced in many prophecies and in the Third Secret of Fatima, according to which Ratzinger was one of the few to be set apart by God for a special mission.
>
> The Pope assembled in this way what could strategically be defined as a *"planned ruse"*, with a *"false target"* and a *"feigned retreat"* to cause the morale of the authentic Catholic population to be recharged and to definitively annihilate the antichristic forces in the bosom of the Church."[139]

Above, it is claimed that Benedict, by implementing this "Plan B," essentially sabotaged his own resignation for a greater purpose, such as to "cause the morale of the authentic Catholic population to be recharged," and to "definitely annihilate the antichristic forces in the bosom of the Church." Essentially, all of this was done by Benedict to *"bring about the definitive cancellation of the 'false Church', along with great purification from heresy and corruption, to open up a new epoch of Christian renewal."*[140]

On my blog *Roma Locuta Est*, I provided rebuttals of this thesis entitled *Benedict's Plan "B" from Outer Space*[141] and *Benedict's Plan B from Outer Space – the Sequel.*[142] There is no more charitable way to say it lest poor souls fall for this *Plan B* theory. It is utterly ridiculous and absurd. I said so before on my blog, and say it again here. While this may appear to be an overly harsh assessment, I am not the only one saying this. Leading Benepapists who support the *"substantial error"* theory have more recently publicly rejected the *Plan B* and/or its associated *Ratzinger Code*[143] theory as "deluded,"[144] or as "categorical nonsense."[145]

Consider what one must believe to accept the reality of the Plan B theory. According to it, Pope Benedict XIV essentially pretended to renounce the papacy via a resignation he knew to be flawed. However, thinking the resignation was valid, the unsuspecting College of Cardinals held a conclave that was actually invalid, and elected a pope who is actually an anti-pope. Thus, the man who the great majority of Catholics accept as true pope is actually an anti-pope. All of this brought to you by Pope Benedict XVI, according to the proponents of Plan B.

Consequently, if Benedict XVI intended to fake his resignation, this would necessarily mean he was both instrumental in and directly responsible for clearing the way for (1) the election of a man the same Benepapists tell us is an antipope, as well as (2) the creation of a "false church" of which the great majority of Catholic are blithely unaware.

Indeed, given nearly all Catholics were unaware of Benedict's master plan, millions of Catholic were put in danger of being led into perdition through the false doctrines of the antipope and of the "false church." How many millions of Catholics have died between Benedict's faux-resignation and today, and have already faced judgment?

Though not stated by the *Plan B* proponents, such a theory would in fact make Pope Benedict XVI a liar, responsible for a great deception, both evil in themselves, and for their consequences. *Plan B* makes Benedict a true monster. Benedict would be morally responsible for the effects of such an ill-considered plan. How could he reasonably justify this ruse? Certainly, it is Catholic moral doctrine that "the end does not justify the means." If Plan B is true, Benedict would be morally responsible for allowing the wolves of the "false church" to ravage the Lord's flock. Indeed, per the logic of the theory, stated or not, the flock is effectively without the protection of their chief shepherd here on earth, Benedict himself!

If one accepts the Plan B thesis, there really is no justification for his behavior after his supposed resignation. Benedict has remained essentially silent, without offering any real resistance to the anti-pope and false Church which has arisen. He has offered no real resistance.

Therefore, whether the proponents of the *Plan B* thesis care to admit it or not, Benedict would be a most horrible monster of a man. It might be one thing to suggest a shepherd might lie in wait, hiding in the dark to ambush a wolf when it prowls among the flock. However, it is quite another thing to suggest a good shepherd would allow the wolf free rein to maul, molest, and eat the sheep—and for the last nine years plus!

The reality is Benedict is neither a monster nor an idiot to have thought up such an absurd thing like *Plan B*. There is no gentler way to put it without veiling the truth of the matter. The objection and the *Plan B* thesis lack common sense and logic. Indeed, such a plan requires the suspension of all common sense to suggest that pretending *not* to be pope is a wiser and more preferable course of action than *actually remaining as the visible and active pope.*

Surely, one can do more good for the Lord's flock by *being* the shepherd and *doing* precisely what the Lord commanded, "tending" and "feeding" the flock (cf. Jn 21:15-17), rather than pretending not to be that shepherd.

The Plan B thesis defies common sense. Yet, one proponent of it asserts in one of his articles that "Benedict allowed the antipope to nominate about 80 cardinals who make the next conclave invalid, precisely: a master's game."[146] A master's game!? What sort of "master's game" can that be? How can Benedict letting an ostensible anti-pope create eighty something cardinals and counting,[147] as well as countless bishops, be better than simply remaining unambiguously the pope, and naming your own cardinals and bishops, and reforming the Church? The Plan B proponent's unbelievable answer was that *"If Bergoglio had not named any, paradoxically, the next conclave could be valid."*[148]

Let us assume, arguendo, that Benedict was concerned over the future of the Church to the extent imagined in the *Plan B* thesis. If he feared the next conclave might elect an unworthy successor, there are far more rational courses of action to follow other than the *de facto* handing over of the Church to an anti-pope due to a fake resignation. Surely, there would be more rational things to

THE DECLARATIO

try, far more reasonable, and far saner alternatives for Benedict to save the Church, other than pretending not to be pope, and leaving the Church at the mercy of an antipope.

Pope Benedict XVI might have tried a couple of different solutions. For example, he might have (1) greatly expanded the College of Cardinals, taking greater care in whom he picked; or alternatively, he might have (2) restricted voting eligibility in a conclave to only a select handful of cardinals in whom he had utmost trust.

But let us not indulge this absurd objection. To propose for *whatever reason* that Benedict XVI *intentionally* misled the Catholic world into thinking he resigned when he really had not—and that such an intentional act is somehow morally neutral or even morally good with respect to the hundreds of millions of Catholics left without a papal shepherd and in the hands of an antipope—is absolutely ridiculous and absurd. There is no way to sugarcoat it.

Objection 1.9: The *Declaratio* contained errors in the Latin

> Pope Benedict XVI's *Declaratio* contains three errors in the Latin. "For centuries it was a constant principle of interpretation, that if a canonical act in Latin contained errors it was not to be construed as valid, but had to be redone,"[149] and further, that "It is a principle of traditional canon law that every rescript, brief or papal bull containing a fault in the Latin is null."[150] Therefore, the resignation of Pope Benedict XVI is invalid.

Reply to Objection 1.9: The errors cited by objectors do not obscure the intent of Pope Benedict to resign. The supposed Latin errors do not impact or substantially alter the meaning of this *Declaratio*.

In response to this objection, I point the reader to an article found on the website of canonist Dr. Edward Peters.[151] In his article, Dr. Peters addressed the question of the relevance of Latin errors in papal documents, such as Benedict's *Declaratio*, and any impact they might have on the documents' validity. Having observed that none of the canons on incorrect Latin were included in either the 1917 Code of Canon Law or the 1983 Code,[152] Dr. Peters references Canon 10 from the Code, which reads:

> Can. 10 Only those laws must be considered invalidating or disqualifying which expressly establish that an act is null or that a person is effected.

Dr. Peters then explains the relevance of the exclusion of laws on the quality of Latin from the code of canon law:

> Because no canon of the 1983 Code, under which Benedict XVI submitted his resignation (c. 332 § 2), addresses the quality of the Latin used in papal documents, let alone does any canon make the Latinity of papal documents go to their validity, I say, odd question answered: bad Latin does not mean that one must remain pope.[153]

Thus, in summary, none of the alleged Latin errors in the *Declaratio* impact the evident intent of Pope Benedict to renounce the papacy. More specifically, as Dr. Peters argued, the presence of Latin errors in the text of the *Declaratio* would not invalidate the resignation.

Objection 1.10: Effective date of resignation was deferred

> Benedict read his *Declaratio* on February 11, 2013, but his resignation, per this document, did not become effective until February 28, 2013, at 8 p.m. "A renunciation of the papacy, in fact, ought to be simultaneous and could never be deferred for 17 days."[154] Therefore, the renunciation was invalid.

Reply to Objection 1.10: The objector wishes to create a requirement for papal resignations not supported by the relevant papal canon. As shown in the Reply to Objection 1.2, per Canon 332§2, there are only two requirements for a valid papal resignation. It must be "free" and it must be "duly manifested." There is no third requirement that it must go into effect

THE DECLARATIO

immediately, and nothing prevents the Supreme Pontiff from setting other conditions.

While Pope Benedict XVI formulated a resignation conditioned on the arrival of a predetermined date and time, it is not unheard-of that previous popes had provided for their own resignations conditioned on the presence of certain predetermined conditions. For example, Pope Pius XII made provisions for his resignation should he be taken prisoner by the Germans during World War II,[155] and Pope Paul VI provided for his resignation should he fall seriously ill.[156]

It may also be noted that Canon 189§4 reads as follows (italics added):

> A resignation can be withdrawn by the one resigning *as long as it has not yet become effective*; once it has become effective it cannot be withdrawn, but a person who has resigned can obtain the office by some other title.[157]

As is apparent in the text above, the canon envisions the possibility of there being a period of time between when a resignation is submitted and when it becomes effective.[158] Therefore, there is no real basis to reject the validity of Pope Benedict XVI's resignation on the grounds alleged in the objection. The objection fails.

Chapter 2: *Normas Nonnullas*

Catholics following the Benepapism controversy are undoubtedly familiar with documents such as the *Declaratio,* Benedict's last audience, and Archbishop Gänswein's speech. However, there is a *"forgotten"* document promulgated by Pope Benedict XVI on February 22, 2013, only six days before the effective date of the resignation.

This "forgotten" document was a *motu proprio* titled *Normas Nonnullas*. Through *Normas Nonnullas*, Pope Benedict XVI made certain changes to the conclave rules last updated by Pope John Paul II in *Universi Dominici Gregis* (UDG). Published only six days prior to the effective date of his resignation, Benedict clearly made these changes in preparation for the March 2013 conclave necessitated by his resignation.

Given this document touches upon the papacy and conclaves, one might think the leading Benepapists would take an active interest in what changes Benedict did or did not make to the conclave rules. However, they have shown no interest in what Pope Benedict XVI said about the conclave precipitated by his resignation, or what rules he did or did not change, and more importantly, what this might mean to their own claims.

After all, any changes made by *Normas Nonnullas* to the then-existing conclave rules in UDG might reveal something about how Benedict understood the papacy, e.g., regarding the *munus* and *ministerium*, or the creation, as some Benepapists suggest, of an "*active*" and "*contemplative*" diarchy in the papacy, or about whether he detached the Petrine succession from the bishopric of Rome.

Similarly, sections of UDG which were left untouched by *Normas Nonnullas* might likewise reveal something of Benedict's thought with regard to the papacy. If a section was left unchanged, for example, then we would presume Pope Benedict XVI was satisfied with the existing state of affairs.

Before looking at one example of how *Normas Nonnullas* changed the UDG, as well as one example of something left untouched by it, let us recall the timeline. Benedict announced his resignation on February 11, 2013. *Normas Nonnullas* was promulgated on February 22, just five days before Benedict's last general audience (February 27), and six days before the effective date of Benedict's resignation (February 28).

From this timeline, one can see *Normas Nonnullas* is contemporaneous to the other key events and documents, such as the *Declaratio* and the last general audience. So, clearly, *Normas Nonnullas* is important to understanding Pope Benedict XVI's mindset at that time. Whatever changes are found in it and whatever was left out of it and thus unchanged were officially promulgated after Benedict announced his resignation, and thus these changes speak directly to the questions of Pope Benedict XVI's intent and his understanding of the papal office as Supreme Legislator in the Church.

Therefore, it may seem odd to the reader, upon first hearing of this document—that some Benepapists have not bothered to examine and comment upon the full record of Pope Benedict XVI's acts in the final days of his papacy, including *Normas Nonnullas*. In Chapter 1, we saw how some Benepapists scoured various long-ago sources, such as the *Miller Dissertation* and several books and essays of Josef Ratzinger, all in the hopes of discovering some "substantial error." Yet, they could not be bothered to review *Normas Nonnullas*?

Indeed, at first blush, this may seem a curious oversight. However, it is not so curious once one reviews *Normas Nonnullas*. The Benepapists have no interest in it because it undermines their entire case for "substantial error."

As noted earlier, *Normas Nonnullas* made various changes to UDG. For example, one of the key changes was to enable a conclave to be called sooner than previously allowed if all the cardinals were in Rome. The prior conclave rule required a period for mourning, funeral rites, etc., for the deceased Roman Pontiff, and travel time for the cardinals.

However, the provision for funeral rites, obviously, did not apply in the case of Benedict's resignation. Consequently, via *Normas Nonnullas,* Pope Benedict XVI altered the rules to allow for the possibility, as in the case of resignation, for the conclave to commence much earlier under certain conditions. So again, and this is a key point to keep in mind: Benedict *specifically* intended these changes for the impending March 2013 conclave.

Now, let us consider a matter more relevant to Benedict's intent that undermines the Benepapist argument. Among the conclave modifications made by Pope Benedict XVI in *Normas Nonnullas* was a change to UDG 87. Of particular note, having changed UDG 87, Benedict made *no* change at all to UDG 88. These two paragraphs—the updated UDG 87 and untouched UDG 88—read together as follows (italics added):

> 87. When the election has canonically taken place, the junior Cardinal Deacon summons into the hall of election the Secretary of the College of Cardinals, the Master of Papal Liturgical Celebrations and two Masters of Ceremonies. Then the Cardinal Dean, or the Cardinal who is first in order and seniority, in the name of the whole College of electors, asks the consent of the one elected in the following words: *Do you accept your canonical election as Supreme Pontiff?* And, as soon as he has received the consent, he asks him: By what name do you wish to be called? Then the Master of Papal Liturgical Celebrations, acting as notary and having as witnesses the two Masters of Ceremonies, draws up a document certifying acceptance by the new Pope and the name taken by him.[159]

> 88. After his acceptance, the person elected, if he has already received episcopal ordination, is *immediately Bishop of the Church of Rome, true Pope and Head of the College of Bishops. He thus acquires and can exercise full and supreme power over the universal Church.*[160]

Both the changed portions and unchanged portions of UDG represent Benedict's official thoughts and teaching on the election of his successor, the "new Supreme Pontiff," and the papal office insofar as UDG and *Normas Nonnullas* touch upon them.

Benedict's motu proprio in conjunction with UDG make clear the one accepting his election as "*Supreme Pontiff*," if already a bishop, "is immediately *Bishop of the Church of Rome, true Pope and Head of the College of Bishops*" and thus "*acquires and can exercise full and supreme power over the universal Church.*"

These declarations are devastating to *Declaratio*-based BiP theories. First, in the *Declaratio*, Benedict explicitly intended a conclave and the election of a "new Supreme Pontiff" after he vacated the "See of Rome, the See of Peter." He knew he would no longer be the Supreme Pontiff as of 8 p.m., February 28, 2013.[161] Second, Benedict understood his immediate successor would be the *Supreme Pontiff* (*Normas Nonnullas* 87), elected by the conclave necessitated by his resignation, and would *immediately* be the *Bishop of Rome* and *true pope,* thereby receiving *full* and *supreme* power over the universal Church.

It cannot be any more obvious, Benedict understood his successor would be the "*true pope*" (singular in the Latin), and would be both the *Bishop of Rome* and the *Supreme Pontiff,* having full and supreme power over the universal Church. Benedict makes no provision for a "bifurcated" papacy. He makes no provision for a papal diarchy. He makes no provision for a "synodal papacy" with an "active" and "contemplative member." There is no provision for the detachment of the Petrine office from the bishopric of Rome.[162] Surely, if Benedict had intended any of these monstrous entities in a state of "substantial error," he would have made provision for them in the conclave rules in *Normas Nonnullas*. Yet, he did no such thing, and the reason why he did no such thing is obvious. Pope Benedict XVI did not hold to any of the monstrous papal errors of which the Benepapists accuse him.

In sum, it is clear there was no intent on Benedict's part to bifurcate the papacy, or to create a papal "diarchy," or to detach the Petrine *munus* from the See of Rome. There is no allowance to be found in UDG or *Normas Nonnullas* for such contrivances imagined by the Benepapists.

Only the *Bishop of Rome*, the *true pope*, holds the Petrine *munus* (cf. Canon 331).[163] Benedict renounced the Petrine ministry "in such a way" that the *"See of Rome, the See of Peter"* would be vacant. Thus, given Benedict resigned the See of Rome, he does not hold the Petrine *munus* in any way. Benedict did not believe he would be Bishop of Rome, Successor of St. Peter, or true pope, following his resignation on February 28, 2013. If he had believed any of the errors the Benepapists claim, he would have changed UDG 88. This he did not do when he issued *Normas Nonnullas* and, consequently, the Benepapist argument fails. Benedict's resignation was valid. He is no longer pope.

Objections, and Replies to Those Objections

Objection 2.1: *Normas Nonnullas* is irrelevant

> Pope Benedict XVI believed when he resigned that he would have a successor. Therefore, *Normas Nonnullas* has no relevance to the debate over the validity or invalidity of Benedict's resignation. The problem remains that his resignation was based on an erroneous premise that he could either "bifurcate" the papacy, or some other error, like that he could maintain the Petrine *munus* in some way after his resignation. Consequently, the resignation was invalid.

Reply to Objection 2.1: In response to the objection above, we would note a few things. The objectors keep alluding to an error that they have not demonstrated. We examined such claims in our Replies to Objections in Chapter 1. Various dissertations, papers, and books were advanced to demonstrate Josef Ratzinger as a theologian held some fundamental error regarding the Petrine office. However, a close examination of each of them in turn demonstrated this was not the case. The Benepapists, as charitably as we can state it, misread and/or misunderstood the source materials before them.

After having searched these sources spanning a fifty- to sixty-year period in the vain hopes of finding some sign that Benedict might have later harbored some error, the Benepapists tell us a more recent document, *Normas Nonnnullas*, is not relevant in revealing the mind of Benedict. They maintain this even though this document is contemporaneous to the resignation period, and speaks on the conclave and the papacy.

Now, the objectors want us to accept that Benedict wanted, albeit erroneously, to either (1) bifurcate the papacy into some sort of diarchy of an "active" and "contemplative member," or (2) detach the Petrine succession from the bishopric of Rome,[164] or (3) believe he would maintain all or a part of the Petrine *munus* after his resignation. Given all this, they say, "of course Benedict expected" a successor, but his base premise was in error, and thus *Normas Nonnullas* is not relevant.

However, this Benepapist counter argument is utter nonsense. Had Benedict really and erroneously intended any of the monstrous entities, such as a bifurcated or synodal papacy, etc., he would have made provision for it in *Normas Nonnullas*. However, as proven in the opening argument of this chapter, this is not the case. There is no such provision for any of these things.

What *Normas Nonnullas* changed or left unchanged in UDG does reveal the mind of the Supreme Legislator of the Church at the time, Pope Benedict XVI. As we saw earlier in the discussion of UDG 87 and 88, the one elected in the upcoming conclave of 2013 is the "*Supreme Pontiff,*" and if already a bishop, "is immediately *Bishop of the Church of Rome, true Pope and Head of the College of Bishops*" and thus "*acquires and can exercise full and supreme power over the universal Church.*" In UDG and *Normas Nonnullas* the terms are singular, e.g., *Supreme pontiff, bishop of Rome, true pope*. There is only *one*.

There is no "partial" resignation in these words. There is no bifurcation of the papacy into an "active" and "contemplative" synodal papacy. There is no detachment of the Petrine succession from the bishopric of Rome. There is no keeping of the Petrine *munus,* in whole or in part.

Again, as the Latin uses the singular, the one elected is the only *Supreme Pontiff*. He is the only *true pope*. Only he "*acquires and can exercise full and supreme power over the universal Church.*" Those who argue Benedict held some "substantial error" related to the papal office simply cannot reconcile these words to their theories. And that, of course, is why they ignore the clear import of *Normas Nonnullas*.

To sum up this discussion surrounding *Normas Nonnullas*, Pope Benedict XVI understood his successor would be *the* Bishop of Rome, *the* Supreme Pontiff, and *the* true pope, who could exercise full and supreme power in the Universal Church. The *Declaratio* makes clear Benedict understood he would no longer be the Bishop of Rome, the Supreme Pontiff, and the true pope. The evidence demonstrates Benedict understood someone else would be the true pope, in the full sense, following the conclave, necessitated by his resignation, for which *Normas Nonnullas* amended the existing rules.

Chapter 3: Benedict's Last Audience

On February 27, 2013, Pope Benedict XVI gave his last general audience. Amongst his comments, Benedict provided a touching reflection on his relationship to the faithful upon his election to the papacy, as well as on that relationship after his resignation from it.

Unfortunately, those who believe Benedict remained pope from February 28, 2013, to this day have tried to make much hay out of the text of this audience. They say Benedict's comments substantiate their arguments that Benedict did not intend to resign the papacy, or perhaps only intended to do so partially by "bifurcating" it into a synodal papacy comprised of one "active" member, and one "contemplative."

The Benepapists point to the fact Benedict spoke of "the 'always' is also a 'forever;'" and of his resignation "not revoking this." The main proponents of Benepapism frequently appeal to these words in their arguments and writings. For example, the phrase "the 'always' is also a 'forever'" appears on the cover of a book written by a leading Benepapist.[165]

For some Benepapists,[166] this reference to the "always" and the "forever" demonstrates that Benedict believed he had received an "indelible mark" upon his election to the papacy. And thus Benedict believed he would always be pope, at least in some *bifurcated* or "partial" way, *sharing the ministry* with his successor. For other Benepapists,[167] the "always" and "forever" refers to their view that Pope Benedict XVI never resigned the *munus*, and that he intended to retain it.

The Benepapists say such an understanding of the papacy is all nonsense because the papacy cannot be bifurcated. To think one could do so is a clear error. Therefore, they argue, Benedict committed a "*substantial error*" by trying to "partially" resign the papacy. This "substantial error" they say, per Canon 188, would invalidate his resignation. Voila! Having invalidated Benedict's resignation, the Benepapists believe they have solved the Francis problem: *Benedict is pope, therefore, Francis cannot be.*

The Benepapists are right inasmuch as the papacy cannot be truly bifurcated or shared in a multi-person papacy. The fundamental question is, is that what Benedict intended to create? We have already reviewed the evidence in the prior two chapters. A review of the *Declaratio* does not support the case that Benedict intended any such thing, and it is clear *Normas Nonnullas* made absolutely no provision for any change to the papacy. None.

The question of this chapter is: does the last audience have anything to say on that question. As indicated in the Preface of this work, from the moment I became aware of the "Benedict is (still) pope" theory and its claims relative to the last audience, I was intrigued and hoped the evidence would establish this was in fact the case. Yet, after reading it through the first time, and many more times again since, my initial impression and conclusion have neither changed nor waivered. The last audience says nothing of what the Benepapists have read into it regarding "bifurcation" or "indelible marks," or any intent to keep the *munus*. Rather, they have grossly misunderstood and warped the meaning of Pope Benedict XVI's use of the phrase "the 'always' is also a 'forever.'"

What Did Pope Benedict XVI Mean by the "Always"?

Let's examine the key part of Benedict's last general audience in which he reflected on his election to the See of Peter:

> Here, allow me to go back once again to 19 April 2005. The real gravity of the decision was also due to the fact that from that moment on I was engaged *always and forever* by the Lord. Always – anyone who accepts the Petrine ministry no longer has any privacy. He belongs always and completely to everyone, to the whole Church. In a manner of speaking, the private dimension of his life is completely eliminated. I was able to experience, and I experience it even now, that one receives one's life precisely when one gives it away. Earlier I said that many people who love

the Lord also love the Successor of Saint Peter and feel great affection for him; that the Pope truly has brothers and sisters, sons and daughters, throughout the world, and that he feels secure in the embrace of your communion; because he no longer belongs to himself, he belongs to all and all belong to him.

The "always" is also a "for ever" – there can no longer be a return to the private sphere. My decision to resign the active exercise of the ministry does not revoke this. I do not return to private life, to a life of travel, meetings, receptions, conferences, and so on. *I am not abandoning the cross, but remaining in a new way at the side of the crucified Lord.* I no longer bear the power of office for the governance of the Church, but in the service of prayer I remain, so to speak, in the enclosure of Saint Peter. Saint Benedict, whose name I bear as Pope, will be a great example for me in this. He showed us the way for a life which, whether active or passive, is completely given over to the work of God.[168]

Benepapists, focusing on the second paragraph above, say Benedict's comments prove he intended to create an *expanded* Petrine office comprised of an "active" pope, and a "contemplative" pope. Here they borrow the terms "active" and "contemplate" from a 2016 speech by Archbishop Gänswein. We will defer discussion of Gänswein's speech until a later chapter devoted to it. Here, it suffices to say that for the Benepapists the text of the general audience substantiates their claim that Benedict XVI made a "*substantial error*" which invalidates his resignation per Canon 188.

However, a closer look at what Pope Benedict XVI said will make clear that the Benepapists are taking the "*always and forever*" grossly out of context. To demonstrate this, let's look at each of the two relevant sections of the general audience where "always" and "forever" are used. Again, Benedict begins (italics added):

> Here, allow me to go back once again to 19 April 2005. The real gravity of the decision was also due to the fact that from that moment on I was engaged *always and forever* by the Lord. *Always* – anyone who accepts the Petrine ministry no

> *longer has any privacy. He belongs always and completely to everyone, to the whole Church.* In a manner of speaking, the private dimension of his life is completely eliminated. I was able to experience, and I experience it even now, that one receives one's life precisely when one gives it away. *Earlier I said that many people who love the Lord also love the Successor of Saint Peter and feel great affection for him; that the Pope truly has brothers and sisters, sons and daughters, throughout the world, and that he feels secure in the embrace of your communion; because he no longer belongs to himself, he belongs to all and all belong to him.*[169]

Benedict speaks of what his life became when he accepted his election to the papacy. First, he talks about being "*always*" and "*forever*" engaged "by the Lord." What does he mean by this? He tells us. By "*always*" he speaks of anyone who is elected pope losing his "*privacy.*" He says of him who is elected pope, meaning here himself especially: "*He belongs always and completely to everyone, to the whole Church.*" It is because of *this*, he says, "*in a manner of speaking,*" his privacy is eliminated.

Benedict is speaking of his own *privacy* being forever lost, but *only in a sense*—not due to some *indelible mark* of papal office, *munus*, or ministry he cannot lose or freely surrender, as the Benepapists wrongly claim. By "loss of privacy" Benedict means "*he belongs always and completely to everyone, to the whole Church.*" How? Again, he tells us. Benedict says when he became pope, he "truly" gained "*brothers and sisters, sons and daughters, throughout the world.*" Thus, Benedict's use of "always" refers to "always belonging to the whole Church" when one *becomes* pope.

This is what the "*always*" refers to, when Benedict speaks of being engaged "always and forever" by the Lord. He *becomes* a *father* to the "*sons and daughters*" he gains upon becoming pope. As he says, the Successor of Peter is loved by the whole Church: "*he belongs to all, and all belong to him.*" He forms a bond of charity with his "sons and daughters" that he feels deeply.

It might do well here to pause and reflect on other times where Benedict used similar imagery of the "loss of privacy" and of "no longer belonging to ourselves." Soon after the death of Pope Paul VI, Cardinal Josef Ratzinger in August 1978 gave a homily on the deceased pope, in part saying (italics added):

> Moreover, we can imagine how heavy the thought must be of *no longer belonging to ourselves*; *of no longer having a single private moment*; of being enchained to the very last, with our body giving up and with a task that day after day demands the total, vigorous use of a man's energy.[170]

Archbishop Ratzinger was reflecting on the life of a recently deceased Pope Paul VI. He spoke of Paul VI as having to bear the "heavy" thought of *"no longer belonging to [himself]"* and of *"no longer having a single private moment."*

Furthermore, twenty-seven years later, during his homily at the mass inaugurating his own Petrine ministry, Pope Benedict spoke of the reciprocity of the bond of charity of himself also *belonging to others*. Speaking of the weight of the papacy, the new pope said:

> I am not alone. I do not have to carry alone what in truth I could never carry alone. All the Saints of God are there to protect me, to sustain me and to carry me. And your prayers, my dear friends, your indulgence, your love, your faith and your hope accompany me.[171]

Consequently, we see in Benedict's thoughts over many years the consistent theme that a pope "no longer belongs to himself," "no longer having a private moment," but also of the Church loving him in return—"accompanying" him with their faith, hope, and love. This reciprocal bond of charity is key to understanding Benedict's thought in his last audience.

What Did Pope Benedict XVI Mean by the "Forever"?

In their use of the last audience for their purposes, the Benepapist do not place much, if any, attention on the paragraph above in their discussion of "always" and "forever." That is unfortunate, as it sets the context which is necessary to understand the depth of what Benedict is conveying. Neglecting this previous paragraph, the Benepapists focus instead on the subsequent paragraph and what Benedict meant with regard to the "always."

In that paragraph, Benedict speaks of how the "*'always' is also a 'forever'*" and "*there can no longer be a return to the private sphere.*" Benedict continues on to say "*my decision to resign the active ministry does not revoke this.*" For the Benepapist, these words are proof Benedict is speaking of an indelible mark of the papacy, i.e., "always…forever" and "*does not revoke this*," which he will always carry.

However, the Benepapists have misunderstood what Benedict is really saying. Let's continue with Benedict's address, picking up immediately where the paragraph we reviewed earlier ends (italics mine):

> *The "always" is also a "for ever" – there can no longer be a return to the private sphere. My decision to resign the active exercise of the ministry does not revoke this.* I do not return to private life, to a life of travel, meetings, receptions, conferences, and so on. *I am not abandoning the cross, but remaining in a new way at the side of the crucified Lord.* I no longer bear the power of office for the governance of the Church, but in the service of prayer I remain, so to speak, in the enclosure of Saint Peter. Saint Benedict, whose name I bear as Pope, will be a great example for me in this. He showed us the way for a life which, whether active or passive, is completely given over to the work of God.[172]

As noted, the Benepapists typically use this paragraph as evidence without reference to the prior paragraph where Benedict speaks in detail about the "always." However, to properly understand the text, one must read both of Benedict's "always and forever" paragraphs together.

In the first section we analyzed, Benedict speaks of when he was elected and how the "always" referred to the loss of privacy. That is, of how he gained brothers and sisters, and sons and daughters upon his election. He specifically speaks of "*belonging always and completely to everyone, to the whole Church.*" He is most assuredly not speaking of an indelible mark of the papacy. He is speaking of a loving attachment, a loving *relationship*. A *bond of charity* of the pope, as a father, for his "sons and daughters," and in turn, the love of the "sons and daughters" for their father, the pope.

Now, in the second paragraph, Benedict continues with this same theme! Benedict says:

> The "always" is also a "forever" – there can no longer be a return to the private sphere. My decision to resign the active exercise of the ministry does not revoke this.

Here, Benedict speaks of the "forever" mentioned in the first paragraph, but of which he has not yet spoken in detail. He says, the "*always*" which is a *bond of charity*—is "*also a forever*," and by this he explains himself—"*there can be no return to the private sphere.*" The "*always*" and the "*forever*" reference the same thing, i.e., the bond of charity we discussed earlier. Just as in Cardinal Ratzinger's homily from 1978, he speaks of the pope's heavy thought of "*no longer belonging to ourselves*" and "*of no longer having a single private moment.*"

Benedict is *not* saying he cannot *return* to a status in which he is not pope. Rather, he *is* saying there is no returning to the "private sphere," that is, to the time when he didn't yet have the bond of charity, the "belonging" to the Church, i.e., his belonging to his "sons and daughters," etc. In other words, there is no return from the bond of charity. One does not stop loving the "sons and daughters" one gained upon becoming pope, even if one stops being pope. The bond of charity persists.

By no means does Benedict say, or intend to say, there is no giving up of the office of the papacy. In fact, he immediately says that his "*decision to resign the active exercise of the ministry does not revoke this.*" However, contrary to what the Benepapists claim, Benedict is neither speaking of an indelible mark, nor of the Petrine *munus* as not being revoked.

Rather, when he says the resignation "*does not revoke this*," the "*this*"—grammatically and in context—necessarily refers to the impossibility of returning "*to the private sphere.*" And, by "no return to the private sphere", we have already seen he means there is no revoking this *bond of charity* with the "brothers and sisters, sons and daughters" he gained upon his election.

Thus, reading both paragraphs in context, Benedict's meaning is clear. His bond of charity with his "sons and daughters" gained at election is a "permanent" one (i.e., a "forever"); and, thus, his resignation will not revoke this bond. Even though he is resigning the papacy, this does not mean his love for his "sons and daughters" is also at an end. It is this bond of charity which will endure, even though he is no longer pope. This is how the "always" is also a "forever," a love which a resignation cannot revoke.

Benedict then explains what this means in practice. He says "I am not abandoning the cross, but remain in a *new way* at the side of the crucified Lord." He is remaining in a *"new way,"* not the "same way"—i.e., not as pope. He concludes for us: *"I no longer bear the power of office for the governance of the Church, but in the service of prayer I remain, so to speak, in the enclosure of Saint Peter."* Here, Benedict tells us again he will no longer be pope and that his life will now be devoted to praying for the whole Church, i.e., for those who became his sons and daughters, sisters and brothers.

It is in this way that Benedict *"so to speak"* remains in the enclosure of Peter, praying for the whole Church. But note closely, Benedict says he remains *"in the enclosure of Peter"* only in a sense ("so to speak"), i.e., *not in fact.* He is speaking metaphorically. Figuratively. Not literally. [*NB: I will return to the meaning of the "enclosure of Peter" in one of the replies in this section.*]

Benedict's logic in the general audience may be summarized as follows: (1) one who is elected pope belongs to the Church and the Church to him, the private dimension of his life in a *"manner of speaking"* is thus lost; (2) yet, one receives one's life when one gives it away, i.e., the pope truly gains brothers and sisters, sons and daughters, throughout the world, i.e., the pope becomes a "father;" (3) a pope "always" carries within himself this "bond of charity," feeling secure in this embrace because he *"no longer belongs to himself, he belongs to all and all belong to him*;" (4)

resigning the papacy *"does not revoke"* this bond of charity, this loving attachment, as he will *"forever"* retain that love for all (i.e., for us in the Church)—just as a father *"always and forever"* loves his sons and daughters; and thus, (5) after his resignation, he will continue to pray in *service* for his "sons and daughters," the Church; and it is in this *qualified* sense—*"so to speak"*—he remains in the "enclosure of Peter," but *not in fac*t. [*NB: As will be seen in the objections section, a Benepapist objected to this interpretation, saying the "enclosure of Peter" is simply the Vatican. That alternative explanation is entirely reasonable, however, such a literal understanding is even less helpful to the Benepapist interpretation of the last audience.*]

What I wrote above is a rather straightforward interpretation of Benedict's words in his last audience. There are no leaps of logic. There are no attempts to stretch the meanings of words, or to read into it some hidden intent, or to impose—or rather concoct—a layer of erroneous theology upon it to explain it—all to prove that the last audience bears proof of "substantial error" within it.

Pope Benedict XVI saw that he became a "father" to the Church, i.e., to "sons and daughters." He both deeply felt and welcomed this "belonging," but he assured us, his decision to resign did not revoke this bond of charity. He may no longer be pope but he will continue to pray for us, his sons and daughters. It is unfortunate, indeed, and it is a shame that the Benepapists have so tortured and warped the former pope's words, as they were quite a beautiful reflection.

Now, my interpretation of Benedict's last audience preceded my familiarity with Peter Seewald's various interviews with the Pope Emeritus. However, the interpretation offered above is consistent with what Benedict has said in the course of his interviews with Peter Seewald after the resignation. For example, speaking of the origin of the bishop emeritus, Benedict told Seewald (italics added):

> Earlier, bishops were not allowed to resign. There were a number of bishops who said "I am a father and that I'll stay", because you cannot simply stop being a father; stopping is a functionalization and secularization, something from the sort of

concept of public office which shouldn't apply to a bishop. To that I must reply; even a father's role stops. *Of course a father does not stop being a father, but he is relieved of concrete responsibility. He remains a father in a deep, inward sense*, in a particular relationship which has responsibility, but not with day-to-day tasks as such. It was also this way with bishops. *Anyway, since then it has become generally understood on the one hand the bishop is bearer of a sacramental mission which remains binding on him inwardly, but on the other hand this does not have to keep him in his function forever.* And so I think it clear that also the Pope is no superman and his mere existence is not sufficient to conduct his role; rather, he likewise exercises a function. *If he steps down, he remains in an inner sense within the responsibility he took on, but not in the function.* In this respect one comes to understand that the office of the Pope has lost none of its greatness, even if the humanity of the office is perhaps becoming more clearly evident."[173]

Benedict's remarks to Seewald echo what we have outlined in our argument about the last audience. Benedict, making an analogy to himself, says of the bishop who resigns: "*a father does not stop being a father.*" Of a bishop who has resigned his office, Benedict says that while "*he is relieved of concrete responsibility,*" the bishop "*remains a father in a deep, inward sense, in a particular relationship which has responsibility, but not with day-to-day tasks as such.*"

Thus, Benedict echoes what he said in his last audience, i.e., his understanding that he is still a "father" who has an inward sense of responsibility to his "sons and daughters" owing to the bond of charity. This responsibility of love leads him, as he says in the last audience, to continue on in the "*service of prayer*" for the Church even after his resignation.

In Benedict's mind, there is no idea of maintaining the Petrine *munus/ministerium* in any real sense. In fact, when Seewald asks about Benedict's use of the honorific title "emeritus," Benedict explicitly says:

> In this formula both things are implied: no actual legal authority any longer, but a relationship which remains even if it is invisible. This legal-spiritual formula avoids any idea of there being two popes at the same time: a bishopric can only have one incumbent. But the formula also expresses a spiritual link, which cannot ever be taken away.[174]

Here again we find from the former pope the expression of the continuance of the bond of charity already seen in our discussion of the last general audience above. The "*'always' is also a 'forever'*" refers to a relational *bond of charity* and not a continuance in the office of the papacy in any sense. It is unfortunate the Benepapists have obscured Benedict's beautiful reflection. One day, when the present controversy has passed, let us hope that Benedict's words will be more fully appreciated.

Objections, and Replies to Those Objections

Objection 3.1: BXVI said the "always is also a forever"

> In the final general audience, when Benedict says the "'always' is also a 'forever' – there can no longer be a return to the private sphere,"[175] this is proof of his erroneous notions of the indelible nature of election to the papacy. That is to say that in Benedict's mind, "the papal coronation indelibly anoints the pontiff in a distinct way, which is different from, and more profound than, the priestly or episcopal ordination/consecration."[176]

Reply to Objection 3.1: Pope Benedict XVI never said or wrote anything about the election to the papacy leaving an "indelible" mark, or an "indelible anointing" that is "more profound" than any priestly or episcopal ordination or consecration! To find such a meaning in Benedict's last audience, one must read it *into* the text, rather than *from* it.

As argued in the beginning of this chapter, Benedict's references to the "always" and "forever" refer to the "loss of privacy" and the "private sphere." This is in context of the discussion of gaining "sons and daughters" and "brothers and sisters" upon his election to the papacy, and of their belonging to him, and his belonging to them. He is speaking of a bond of charity. Benedict is in no way referring to an indelible mark of the papacy. Also, as noted in the opening argument, Benedict as Cardinal Ratzinger spoke on the same theme during his homily upon the death of Pope Paul VI. That is, he spoke of Pope Paul VI *"no longer belonging"* to himself, and *"of no longer having a single private moment."* The "belonging to others" and no longer having a "private moment," are thematically linked.

With the above in mind, for the purpose of responding to this objection, let us briefly revisit the argument by recalling Benedict's explanation of the "always," as found within the text of the last audience. He says:

> "Always – anyone who accepts the Petrine ministry no longer has any privacy. He belongs always and completely to everyone, to the whole Church. In a manner of speaking, the private dimension of his life is completely eliminated. I was able to experience, and I experience it even now, that one receives one's life precisely when one gives it away. Earlier I said that many people who love the Lord also love the Successor of Saint Peter and feel great affection for him; *that the Pope truly has brothers and sisters, sons and daughters, throughout the world, and that he feels secure in the embrace of your communion; because he no longer belongs to himself, he belongs to all and all belong to him."*[177]

Benedict explicitly defines *"no longer having privacy"* in terms of belonging *"always and completely to everyone,"* i.e., the whole Church. He tells us that in a manner of speaking the private dimension of his life was completely eliminated when he was elected.

The text goes on to say that what he gains is the love of those who *"love the Lord"* who *"also love the Successor of Saint Peter and feel great affection for him."* As he says, *"the Pope truly has brother and sisters, sons and daughters, throughout the world."* Benedict said when becoming pope, *"he no longer belongs to himself, he belongs to all and all belong to him.*" This is the "always" he took on when becoming pope, a bond of charity.

Benedict says the "always" refers to a real relationship between him and the Church, and vice versa, not in some abstract sense, but that he feels love for the people of the Church, his true "sons and daughters," etc. He feels himself a father.

As with Benedict's use of the "always," the objector misunderstands the former pope's use of "forever." Here, too, Benedict explains himself (italics added):

> *The "always" is also a "for ever" – there can no longer be a return to the private sphere. My decision to resign the active exercise of the ministry does not revoke this.* I do not return to private life, to a life of travel, meetings, receptions, conferences, and so on. *I am not abandoning the cross, but remaining in a new way at the side of the crucified Lord.* I no longer bear the power of office for the governance of the Church, but in the service of prayer I remain, so to speak, in the enclosure of Saint Peter. Saint Benedict, whose name I bear as Pope, will be a great example for me in this. He showed us the way for a life which, whether active or passive, is completely given over to the work of God.[178]

As I believe the reader will find evident, the objector has misunderstood the meaning and context of "forever" in Benedict's text. Benedict has already told us the "always" refers to the "loss of privacy" when he entered into a bond of charity with the Church upon being elected. He told us that this new "belonging to others" means the "*private dimension of his life is completely eliminated.*" This explains why he says this "always" bond or "loss of privacy" is also a "forever" one, where he is *no longer able "to return to the private sphere."*

This is because of the fact we are talking about love and a relationship. Even though he is resigning, he cannot simply forget or walk away from a relationship of love, his sense of "*belonging always and completely to everyone.*" He is explaining that even though he is resigning, we should not think he had abandoned this love of his "sons and daughters," the Church. This bond of charity will persist beyond his resignation from the papacy.

In sum, in our opening analysis of the last audience, we argued the "always is also a forever" ultimately refers to a personal and relational bond of charity with the Church, formed upon the election of Benedict XVI, one which cannot be revoked even though he is resigning the papacy. That is, he cannot walk away from this bond of charity even though he has renounced the papacy. He is speaking of a spiritual relationship of love which he cannot forsake, and not of a papacy from which he cannot fully resign. The objection fails.

Objection 3.2: BXVI said the resignation "does not revoke" his office

> Continuing on with Benedict's text spoken of in Objection 3.1, Benedict immediately adds "My decision to resign the active exercise of the ministry does not revoke this." That is to say, the 'indelibility of the papal ministry is irrevocable—Benedict thinks he is pope forever, but he will now exercise only a part of the Petrine ministry.'[179]
>
> "Therefore, in his mind, Benedict remains pope even after he 'resigns' the governing office and passes the throne to the next 'pope.' This is SUBSTANTIAL ERROR."[180]

Reply to Objection 3.2: The objector reads his premise into the text when he claims the words "*My decision to resign the active exercise of the ministry does not revoke this*" proves Benedict is saying the "*indelibility of the papal ministry is irrevocable—Benedict thinks he is pope forever, but now exercising only part of the Petrine ministry.*"

In response to the objection, let us recall the full context of Benedict's statement. He said:

> The "always" is also a "for ever" – there can no longer be a return to the private sphere. My decision to resign the active exercise of the ministry does not revoke this.

BENEDICT'S LAST AUDIENCE

As demonstrated, the *"always" and "forever"* refer to Benedict's loss of privacy with relation to a bond of charity with the "sons and daughters" he gained upon his election. *When he says "there can no longer be a return to the private sphere,"* Benedict is merely affirming that he cannot abandon, or walk away from this bond of charity.

We have already seen Benedict's sense of fatherly responsibility along this same line expressed in the Seewald interview quoted earlier in this chapter. In sum, he is indicating there can be no return from the real sense of "fatherhood" he has come to feel toward his "sons and daughters" after becoming pope. That is way the *"always"* is also a *"forever,"* and there is no longer a return to the "private sphere."

How then to understand what Benedict means when he says, *"My decision to resign the active exercise of the ministry does not revoke this"*? When Benedict says the resignation *"does not revoke this,"* the *"this"*—*grammatically and in context*—necessarily refers back to the impossibility of returning *"to the private sphere."* And, by "no return to the private sphere," we have already seen he means there is no revoking this *bond of charity* with the "brothers and sisters, sons and daughters" he gained upon his election. He will "forever" love them.

Although he is resigning the papacy, Benedict cannot just walk away as if nothing had happened, as if he had never formed a bond of charity with his "sons and daughters." He feels a father's responsibility. Although he is resigning, he carries that sense of the responsibility of that bond of charity with him. He explains what this ultimately means in practice for his life post-resignation (italics mine):

> *I am not abandoning the cross, but remaining in a new way at the side of the crucified Lord.* I no longer bear the power of office for the governance of the Church, but in the service of prayer I remain, so to speak, in the enclosure of Saint Peter. Saint Benedict, whose name I bear as Pope, will be a great example for me in this. He showed us the way for a life which, whether active or passive, is completely given over to the work of God.

Having explained his resignation does not revoke this bond of charity, he explains he will remain by the cross in a *"new* way"—not the *same* way, i.e., *not as pope*. He is not abandoning the Church but in the "service of prayer" he remains, "so to speak, in the enclosure of Saint Peter."

Thus, we can understand Benedict's meaning of "the always is a forever" and why it is not "revoked." He has a true bond of charity, like a father, for his "sons and daughters." His resignation does not "revoke" this bond, as he still loves his "sons and daughters." He does not walk away from the love. He will not forsake "us." Though he no longer bears the "power of governance of the Church" because he is no longer pope, Benedict will remain in the "service of prayer" to the Church.

Objection 3.3: The "forever" suggests BXVI kept the *munus*

> Let us note, first of all, that, in the context of the discourse under analysis the words "always" and "forever" appear in the first place linked to the commitment "assumed with the Lord" as a consequence of the acceptance, by Benedict, of the election to the pontificate. But also, let us note that the public dimension and the bond of love with the Church, of which Benedict speaks, completely related with the "always" and only partially with the "forever." In light of the "forever," Benedict alludes to something else, the services (function, *ministerium*), that according to the *Declaratio*, make up the charge (*munus*) of the Roman Pontiff: "acting" (governing the boat of St. Peter"), "speaking" (announcing the Gospel"), "suffering" and "praying," and this is done to corroborate that he will stop exercising only the first two alluded services, and will keep the rest (which obviously means his "resignation" did not fall on the *munus*, it was not a total resignation as it should be).[181]

Reply to Objection 3.3: The objection states the *"words 'always' and 'forever' appear in the first place linked to the commitment 'assumed with the Lord' as a consequence of the acceptance, by Benedict, of his election to the pontificate."*

I do not wish to deny this point. But here we are speaking of their link to the commitment "assumed with the Lord." Yet that alone does not speak to what Benedict means by the "always" and "forever" in his last audience. We already addressed his meaning in the commentary that began this chapter and in the Replies to Objection 3.1 and Objection 3.2 above.

Still, let us continue with the objector's argument, which proceeds:

> But also, let us note that the public dimension and the bond of love with the Church, of which Benedict speaks, completely relate with the "always" and only partially with the "forever."[182]

First, I am glad to note that the objector agrees with me that the "bond of love" or "bond of charity" of which Benedict speaks is "*completely* related with the 'always.'" That is what I have argued throughout this chapter. Unfortunately, the objector's analysis goes amiss, falling into error, by claiming the bond of love is only *partially* related with the "forever." Let us see the objector's explanation:

> In light of the "forever," Benedict alludes to something else, the services (function, *ministerium*), that according to the *Declaratio*, make up the charge (*munus*) of the Roman Pontiff: "acting" ("governing the boat of St. Peter"), "speaking" ("announcing the Gospel"), "suffering" and "praying," and this is done to corroborate that he will stop exercising only the first two alluded services, and will keep the rest (which obviously means his "resignation" did not fall on the *munus*, it was not a total resignation, as it should be).[183]

First, keep in mind, the objector has admitted Benedict's reference to a bond of love is *completely* related to the "always" and at least *partially* linked to the "forever." This is an admission not conceded by the other objectors we have considered up to this point.

Unfortunately, seemingly wanting to minimize the acknowledged link between "forever" and the bond of love, the objector stresses that Benedict "*alludes* to something else." However, the objector quickly passes over and obscures what is otherwise quite clear. Let us reconsider the context again. Benedict said:

> The "always" is also a "forever" – there can no longer be a return to the private sphere. My decision to resign the active exercise of the ministry does not revoke this.

Benedict explicitly says "The 'always' is *also* a 'forever' – *there can no longer be a return to the private sphere*" clearly linking the "forever" to Benedict's references to the "private sphere," i.e., his discussion of the bond of charity or the bond of love. Furthermore, Benedict's text is clear, the "always" and "forever" are both linked *fully* and *only* to his discourse on this bond of charity. Consider the structure of his comments and compare the two references:

1. "Always – anyone who accepts the Petrine ministry no longer has any privacy."
2. "The 'always' is also a 'forever' – there can no longer be a return to the private sphere."

In both instances, Benedict wants us to understand the "always" and "forever" are in reference to the "loss of privacy," which, as we have already demonstrated from the text of the last audience, refers back to the bond of charity he feels toward his "sons and daughters" (i.e., the members of the Church). This is clear.

The first reference to "always" is in the context of first *accepting* the Petrine primacy, and how that acceptance leads to the "loss of privacy," i.e., the gaining of "sons and daughters," the sense of "belonging," etc.

In the second reference, "*the always is also a forever,*" Benedict is speaking of *resigning* the Petrine primacy, and here he speaks of there not being a return to the "private sphere,"— meaning he does not forsake the bond of charity in his resignation. That is why he says in the very next sentence the resignation does not "revoke this." He is assuring us his resignation does not "revoke" the bond of charity. That is why the "always is a forever."

Still, there is more to say about the objector's claim the "forever" only partially refers to the bond of love but also "alludes to something else." The "something else" the objector seems to want the reader to focus on is Benedict's reference to the "active exercise of the ministry"—as if she means to say his resignation does not fully revoke his papacy in some way, i.e., that he retains the papacy either wholly or partially. However, such an interpretation is unwarranted in both the text and in context. The objector's interpretation does violence to Benedict's clear meaning. Consider Benedict's words once more:

> The "always" is also a "forever" – there can no longer be a return to the private sphere. My decision to resign the active exercise of the ministry does not revoke this.

Benedict says his "decision to resign the active exercise of the ministry *does not revoke this.*" The *"this,"* as we have argued already in the chapter, grammatically refers back to the prior sentence, as argued in Reply to Objection 3.2. He is not speaking of a papacy that cannot be "revoked." No, he is speaking of the "loss of privacy" that cannot be revoked. Therefore, Benedict's use of the meaning is apparent. Benedict's decision to resign does not revoke the bond of love, the bond of charity! No other interpretation makes sense here. The *"this"* does not refer back to anything else. The objection fails.

Objection 3.4: Admits to resigning only the "active" ministry

> Benedict had erroneous ideas about the *potestas iurisdictionis* (power of jurisdiction) and *potestas ordinis* (power of order) with regard to the Petrine *munus*, believing he could retain the *potestas ordinis* of the Petrine *munus*, even when he surrendered the *potestas iurisdictionis*. He believed he could give up one, the power of jurisdiction, or the "active exercise" of the *munus*. Thus he can say "I no longer bear the power of the office for governance for the Church." Yet, at the same time, he believed

he would maintain the power of order, and thus could immediately add "…but in the service of prayer I remain, so to speak, in the enclosure of Saint Peter."[184]

Reply to Objection 3.4: The objection is based on the premise that Benedict, as theologian Joseph Ratzinger and then as pope, held erroneous ideas about the Petrine *munus*, e.g., the papacy as a sacrament, etc. This portion of the objection was refuted in the Replies to Objection 1.6 and 1.7.

Given I have addressed the premise previously, there is no need to do so again here. I refer the reader to the replies referenced above. However, I offer a couple of brief comments on some of the references in the objection.

First, let us briefly look at Benedict's statement "I no longer bear the power of office for the governance of the Church." It stretches credulity to look at this statement and find support for Benepapism. Surely, on its face and absent any Benepapist assumption, a former pope can verily make this statement, as it is perfectly consistent with a valid resignation. That is certainly the natural way to read the text, given Benedict's *Declaratio* states he renounced the "ministry of the Bishop of Rome" in "such a way" that the "see of Rome, the See of Peter" will be vacant. One must bring a pre-existing assumption in opposition to the facts to suggest this is a definite proof of anything in support of Benepapism.

However, in saying he no longer has the "power of governance" or the power of administration of his office, Benedict is admitting he is no longer pope. As Fr. Rickert argued,

> If a pope renounces the administration of his office, he necessarily renounces the office itself, because the office *per se* (*vi muneris*)[185] entails the right to act. Thus, Pope Benedict's renunciation of his administration entails renunciation of the papal office. That is why he goes on to express the results, which he is clearly cognizant of: the Chair of St. Peter will be vacant, and a new pope must be elected.[186]

Consequently, in line with Fr. Rickert's argument, even if we assume Benedict intended to resign the "active ministry" or that he lacks the "power of governance" as he says in the last audience, then Benedict would be admitting he is no longer pope. This is so, as Fr. Rickert demonstrates, because *"Pope Benedict's renunciation of his administration entails the renunciation of the papal office."*[187]

The objector's interpretation of the "enclosure of St. Peter" as referring to the power of order, the *"potestas ordinis,"* suggesting Benedict believed in a sacramental papacy, is not only a bit of a stretch, it is unfounded (*see Reply to Objection 1.6*). However, it might be worthwhile to consider some of the differences of opinion on the phrase "enclosure of St. Peter." I do believe it possible that Benedict's use of *"enclosure of St. Peter"* may refer to the ministry of St. Peter. However, even if so, Benedict only said he "remains, *so to speak*, in the enclosure of St. Peter." That is to say, *"so to speak"* means one is speaking figuratively, and or metaphorically—i.e., not in a literal sense. To say Benedict was figuratively still participating in the ministry of Peter is consistent with the interpretation first offered in my opening commentary to this chapter, as well as with the Replies to Objections 3.1, 3.2, and 3.3.

How so? Benedict told us his resignation does not revoke his bond of charity for his "sons and daughters," the Church, and that he will remain "in the service of prayer" for her. In this mission, Benedict is, in an extended, metaphorical, and figurative sense, continuing the ministry of Peter in a *personal* mission of prayer which encompasses the entire Church with whom he spoke of sharing a bond of charity. His self-appointed, non-official mission here is "Petrine" in the metaphorical sense that his "bond of charity" into which he first entered upon becoming pope, and continues even after his resignation, extends uniquely as a former pope to the universal Church.

However, here I take note of another interpretation of the *"enclosure of Saint Peter."* When I first offered my interpretation of the last audience and the figurative sense of the "enclosure of Saint Peter" in my blog, a Benepapist offered a refutation of this interpretation. The Benepapist said that "so to speak, in the enclosure of Saint Peter" referred to the Vatican. After all, he argued, the Vatican is "so to speak" the "enclosure of St. Peter," and it is where Benedict still lives.

Yes, the Benepapist could very well be right, and his reading might be the probable one. Indeed, it may be the more probable one. I don't contest that. However, if it is, that does not help the Benepapist case at all. Further, such an interpretation refutes Objection 3.4.

Objection 3.5: BXVI bifurcates the papacy into "active or passive" parts

> In his last audience, Benedict speaks of resigning the "active exercise of the ministry," clearly indicating he does not intend to surrender his entire Petrine ministry, otherwise he would not have qualified "exercise of the ministry" with the word "active." Later in the audience he draws the distinction between a life that is "active or passive," again showing he draws a distinction within. The above demonstrates Benedict erroneously tried to bifurcate the papacy into an active and passive (or "contemplative") component, of which he believes himself to be the "contemplative" member of a papal diarchy. As there can be no real bifurcation of the papacy, Benedict's attempt to do so manifests he was in "substantial error" per Canon 188. Therefore, his resignation was invalid. Benedict is still pope.

Reply to Objection 3.5: The objector observes that Benedict speaks of resigning the "active exercise of the ministry." The objector then claims Benedict's insertion here of the word "active" qualifies the "exercise of the ministry," showing Benedict intended to resign only the "active" ministry while retaining the *passive* ministry.

The objector supports his claim above by further arguing Pope Benedict XVI made clear this distinction between an "active or passive" Petrine ministry, when he said (italics added):

> Saint Benedict, whose name I bear as Pope, will be a great example for me in this. He showed us the way for a life which,

whether *active or passive*, is completely given over to the work of God.

In reply to the objection, Pope Benedict XVI did not split his renunciation into an active and passive component. Benedict literally declared, "I renounce *the ministry* of the Bishop of Rome, Successor of Peter." Benedict did not say "I renounce the *active* ministry of the Bishop of Rome, Successor of Peter." Further, Benedict said he resigned in such a way the "See of Rome, the See of St. Peter" would be vacant. If the See of Peter is vacant, there is no pope. Consequently, Benedict, in his last audience, could not have intended to suggest he retained some sort of "passive" or "contemplative" exercise of the Petrine *munus* or *ministerium*.

But what does Pope Benedict XVI mean when he speaks of St. Benedict *"showing us a way for a life which, whether active or passive"* is given over to the Lord? To be clear, Pope Benedict quotes St. Benedict as speaking of a *way of life* which is *active* or *passive;* and not of a *papacy* which is either *active* or *passive*.

Consequently, Pope Benedict XVI was speaking of his life that will now be devoted to prayer, after he resigns the Petrine ministry. This is clear when he says he no longer has the *power of governance* in the Church. Benedict XVI is giving up the papacy, the *active* part of his life, and will now devote his post-resignation life to a *passive* one of prayer.

Finally, when evaluating the Benepapist claim Benedict spoke of retaining the "passive" or "contemplative" *ministerium* or *munus*, we should remember the previously cited Canon 331 (italics mine):

> Canon 331—The bishop of the Roman Church, in whom *continues* the office (*munus*) given by the Lord *uniquely* to Peter, the first of the Apostles, and to be transmitted to his successors, is the head of the college of bishops, the Vicar of Christ, and the pastor of the universal Church on earth. By virtue of his office he possesses supreme, full, immediate, and universal ordinary power in the Church, which he is always able to exercise freely.[188]

The canon explicitly states the Catholic teaching that it is the bishop of Rome, in whom *continues* the "office (*munus*) given by the Lord *uniquely* to Peter." Therefore, if one is not the bishop of Rome, one does not have the *munus* in any size, shape, or form—it does not, and cannot "*continue*" in him. Not a supposed *active* Petrine *munus*. Not a supposed *passive* or *contemplative* Petrine *munus*.

To say that Benedict denied this through his words and actions of the *Declaratio* or the general last audience is to accuse him not only of "*substantial error*," but *to accuse him of formal heresy*. The objectors throughout this discussion make Benedict into something of a heretic, one gravely mistaken about the nature of the papacy. The objectors set out under the pretense of saving the Church from the possibility of following one heretical pope, but have only compounded the confusion by giving us another.

Chapter 4: Pilgrims from Albano

We have already considered in chronological order some of the last acts of Pope Benedict XVI in the days leading up to the effective date and time of his resignation, 8 p.m., February 28, 2013. The three documents thus far reviewed are the *Declaratio*, *Normas Nonnullas*, and Benedict's last general audience.

Let us now examine words spoken by Pope Benedict XVI to a group of Catholic pilgrims in the last couple of hours of his papacy. These words further demonstrate his true intent to fully resign the papacy. These are words that Benepapists, if they are even aware of them, generally ignore, or for which they have no credible explanation.

On February 28th, 2013, the very day on which his resignation would become effective, Pope Benedict XVI spoke to a group of Catholic pilgrims from the Italian Diocese of Albano. He briefly addressed them in these words (italics mine):

> *Thank you. Thank you all.*
> *Dear Friends,*
>
> I am happy to be with you, surrounded by the beauty of Creation and your kindness, which does me so much good. Thank you for your friendship and your affection. You know that this day is different for me from the preceding ones. *I am no longer the Supreme Pontiff of the Catholic Church, or I will be until 8:00 this evening and then no longer. I am simply a pilgrim beginning the last leg of his pilgrimage on this earth.* But I would still, thank you, I would still—with my heart, with my love, with my prayers, with my reflection, and with all my inner strength—like to work for the common good and the good of the Church and of humanity. I feel greatly supported by your kindness. Let us go

forward with the Lord for the good of the Church and the world. Thank you. I now wholeheartedly impart my blessing.

May Almighty God bless us, Father, Son, and Holy Spirit. Good night! Thank you all![189]

Pope Benedict, mere hours before his resignation took effect, explicitly stated he will *"no longer"* be the *"Supreme Pontiff of the Catholic Church"* as of 8 p.m. that evening. After that hour comes, he said he would become *"a simple pilgrim"* who is *"beginning the last leg of his pilgrimage on this earth."*

Needless to say, these are not the words of someone who believed he would remain pope in any sense of the word after 8 p.m. that evening. This, of course, is consistent with what Benedict wrote in his *Declaratio:*

> For this reason, and well aware of the seriousness of this act, with full freedom I declare that I renounce the ministry (*ministerio*) of Bishop of Rome, *Successor of Saint Peter*, entrusted to me by the Cardinals on 19 April 2005, in such a way, that as from 28 February 2013, at 20:00 hours, the *See of Rome, the See of Saint Peter, will be vacant* and a Conclave to elect the new Supreme Pontiff will have to be convoked by those whose competence it is.[190]

Benedict renounced the *"ministry of the Bishop of Rome...in such a way...that the See of Rome, the See of Peter, will be vacant"* and that a *"conclave to elect the new Supreme Pontiff"* would now be *necessary*. Of course an election for a *"new Supreme Pontiff"* would be necessary, because—as he would later tell the pilgrims from Albano—he *"will no longer be supreme pontiff of the Catholic Church."*

Pope Benedict XVI's use of the canonical term "supreme pontiff" clearly includes within it the idea of the *munus* or office of the papacy. Indeed, the man elected to the papacy is asked, *"Do you accept your canonical election as Supreme Pontiff?"* (cf. *Normas Nonnullas*); then, per *Universi Dominici Gregis*:

> After his acceptance, the person elected, if he has already received episcopal ordination, is immediately Bishop of the Church of Rome, true Pope and Head of the College of Bishops. He thus acquires and can exercise full and supreme power over the universal Church.[191]

Note closely, upon his acceptance of his election, the one elected as Supreme Pontiff is *"immediately Bishop of the Church of Rome,"* and *"true pope."* Therefore, by saying to the pilgrims from Albano that he "will no longer be supreme pontiff," Benedict is clearly saying he will *no longer* be the Bishop of Rome, and he will *no longer be "true pope."* Only the Bishop of Rome uniquely bears the Petrine *munus*, as per Canon 331. It is clear Benedict understands he will not only no longer be Supreme Pontiff, but he will no longer be Bishop of Rome, and thus, no longer hold the Petrine *munus*.

We have established that Benedict, as per his *Declaratio,* understood his successor would be the new "supreme pontiff" elected by the conclave necessitated by his resignation. He also understood this *"new supreme pontiff"* would be the "true pope," as per *Normas Nonnullas*[192] and *Universi Dominici Gregis*. Clearly, he understood he would no longer be Supreme Pontiff, someone else would be. He understood he would no longer be true pope, someone else would be. He understood he would no longer be Bishop of Rome, someone else would be. He understood he no longer would hold the Petrine *munus*, someone else would.

Benedict saying *"I will no longer be the Supreme Pontiff of the Catholic Church"* does not fit *credibly* into the various Benepapist theories. Perhaps that is why the great majority of them have avoided discussion of this address. For example, while one Benepapist book does cite Benedict's words to the pilgrims, it does so without providing any commentary or explanation of his words, *"I will no longer be the Supreme Pontiff of the Catholic Church."* That book's author passes over this sentence in complete silence.[193] Instead, the author discusses other phrases and words from Benedict's brief speech to the pilgrims in order to make a point regarding a separate, erroneous thesis about "parallelism."[194]

This lack of any explanation is quite noteworthy. It is all the more remarkable when one considers that only twelve pages later in that same book, after quoting an entire passage in her manuscript of Benedict's words including, "*I will no longer be the Supreme Pontiff of the Catholic Church,*" the author titled a section of the book: *Has BXVI explicitly denied his status as "Roman Pontiff"?*[195] That author's answer to that question is "no." However, given *Supreme Pontiff* is essentially synonymous with *Roman Pontiff*, it is clear that Benedict did in fact implicitly deny it. Regarding his "status," Benedict said he would "no longer be *Supreme Pontiff*" after 8 p.m. on February 28, 2013; and thus, he implicitly denied his status as *Roman Pontiff* would continue beyond that same date and time.

So, the leading lights of the BiP theory haven't offered plausible, public explanations.[196] They may search dusty old theology texts written by Fr. Josef Ratzinger from forty to sixty years ago, trying to find a phrase here or there, albeit unsuccessfully, that they hope might show "substantial error."[197] Yet, they cannot be bothered to comment on texts contemporaneous to the resignation, like *Normas Nonnullas* and the brief remarks to the pilgrims.

By saying "*I will no longer be the Supreme Pontiff of the Catholic Church*," it is undeniable that Benedict fully intended to resign *all* associated with the papacy. The very office of "*Supreme Pontiff*"—the office *explicitly* accepted in a conclave by the one elected—*undoubtedly* bears within it the notion of *munus* which the Benepapists claim to hold so dear. Yet, here, Benedict essentially said he will no longer bear that Petrine *munus*; but the Benepapists cannot be bothered to give a plausible answer. The reason is clear. There is no plausible answer.

Objections, and Replies to Those Objections

Objection 4.1: Irrelevant due to "substantial error"

> Given Benedict XVI is in "substantial error" as to the nature of the papacy, with regard to being able to partially resign, his

reference to "Supreme Pontiff" does not harm the "substantial error" theory.

Reply to Objection 4.1: Contrary to the objector's assertion, the reference to Supreme Pontiff does have relevance to the Benepapist claim of "substantial error." Per the rule for conclaves set forth by John Paul II in *Universi Dominici Gregis*, and amended by Pope Benedict XVI in *Normas Nonnullas* the one elected by the conclave accepts his election as "Supreme Pontiff." UDG 88 makes it explicitly clear that the elected Supreme Pontiff, singular in the Latin, is Bishop of Rome (singular) and is the "true pope," again singular. In the face of these facts, there is no room here for the *substantial-error* Benepapists to plausibly argue Benedict thought there could be a multiple member 'synodal papacy,' or that he could still share the papacy in some way after a 'partial' resignation, etc.

Benedict XVI clearly understood the one Supreme Pontiff is the one "true pope." Further, the Supreme Pontiff, as Bishop of Rome, per Canon 331 uniquely holds the *munus*. If one is not, or no longer Bishop of Rome, one does not hold the *munus*. Therefore, in saying he would no longer be the Supreme Pontiff, Benedict is admitting he will no longer be "true pope," or Bishop of Rome, and thus, will no longer hold the *munus*, unique to the Bishop of Rome.

Benedict's statement to the pilgrims from Albano cannot be reconciled with the "substantial error" theory. Therefore, it is clear that the Benepapists have misunderstood Benedict's meaning in the *Declaratio* and the last general audience.

Objection 4.2: BXVI is speaking in a "Ratzinger Code"

> Pope Benedict XVI engaged in a "strategic ruse." His words above must be understood as having a surface meaning, and then an underlying meaning. He is speaking in a cryptic code, which some have named the "Codice Ratzinger" in Italian, or "Ratzinger Code."[198] Benedict, speaking in Italian, did not use the proper title of "Sommo Pontefice" (Supreme Pontiff) for the Latin *Summus Pontifex*. Instead, Benedict used the words

"Pontefice Sommo," which strictly translated to the English is "Pontiff Supreme." Thus, literally, Pope Benedict XVI said:

> I am no longer the Pontiff Supreme of the Catholic Church, or I will be until 8:00 this evening and then no longer. I am simply a pilgrim beginning the last leg of his pilgrimage on this earth.

"Thus, Pope Benedict makes it clear that 'he will no longer be a pontiff supreme,' that is, he will no longer be a pontiff placed in the highest and largest place, but will remain a hidden pontiff, a hermit, hidden under the nonexistent institution of the papacy emeritus. There will be someone else who will occupy the highest and largest place. To be precise, an antipope."[199]

Reply to Objection 4.2: The objection above is associated with Objection 1.8 which advances the *Plan B* thesis, which was addressed in the Reply to Objection 1.8. By claiming Benedict is speaking in a cryptic code, or *Ratzinger Code*, those who support this thesis obscure the plain meaning of Benedict. After all, how much clearer can one say, "*I am no longer the Supreme Pontiff of the Catholic Church, or I will be until 8:00 this evening and then no longer*"?

Yet, some Benepapists believe that having "willfully"[200] formulated an invalid resignation with respect to the Petrine *munus*, Benedict remains as pope and continues to communicate to the faithful through a cryptic *Ratzinger Code*. One Italian journalist recently published a book, titled the *Codice Ratzinger*,[201] to advance and explain this thesis. Another leading Benepapist author appears to share something of a similar view, having written elsewhere that Benedict has been speaking "*...more or less in a veiled way*" in both "*verbal language*" and "*deeds.*"[202]

The belief that Benedict is using something of a cryptic code rests entirely on the absurd *Plan B* theory, which we have already reviewed in the Reply to Objection 1.8. Despite protestations to the contrary by its lead purveyors, the Plan B theory makes Benedict into a *monstrous liar;* a man *derelict in his duties*, who abdicated his responsibility, though not his office, to *"tend and feed"* the Lord's sheep (cf. Jn 20:15-17); leaving them prey for the last nine years to an anti-pope and a "false church." Incredibly, the theory implicitly argues that Benedict concluded it was better to pretend not to be pope, than to actually serve as pope! It is an unbelievable theory, and it is utterly ridiculous. However, this was noted earlier in Reply 1.8, so we need not review again.

Instead, let us look more closely at the idea of a *Ratzinger Code*. Some Benepapists believe Benedict has been speaking a *cryptic language* all along, as if to lay bread crumbs for those wise enough to follow them, and that it is possible to interpret him and understand what he has been up to since his pretended resignation. One proponent of this theory writes:

> As always happens for the messages in the Ratzinger Code, there are TWO READING PLANS: the first is the superficial one, good for non-believers, the indifferent and all those who detest Pope Benedict, modernists or traditional-sedevacantists. There is always, however, some inconsistency that intrigues those who "have ears to hear", as we have seen HERE and that pushes the Logos to work, the reason that discovers the truth.[203]

Yes, and as you might have guessed, this cryptic *Ratzinger Code* can *only* be deciphered by those who *"have ears to hear."* So, apparently, if you're a Catholic who finds this theory absurd, you are just not with the "reading plan" and must be among the *"indifferent and all those who detest Pope Benedict, modernists or traditional-sedevacantists."*[204]

The reality is this branch of Benepapism is devolving here into something of a *gnostic cult,*[205] speaking of hidden knowledge, and "people who know"—and those who do not. How convenient! Only the Benepapists who can interpret this cryptic code are the ones who really understand what is going on. There is much written on the subject, but the reader is cautioned not to waste their time on deciphering it, as its proponents will take you as far down into the proverbial Rabbit Hole as you will let them.

Let us review one example by returning to the topic of this chapter, the words of Pope Benedict XVI to the pilgrims from

Albano. As we asked at the beginning of this reply, how does a proponent of the *Ratzinger Code* explain the plain and evident meaning of Benedict's words: "*I am no longer the Supreme Pontiff of the Catholic Church, or I will be until 8:00 this evening and then no longer*"? These words clearly indicate Benedict knew that after 8 p.m. on February 28, 2013, he would no longer be *Supreme Pontiff*. He knew he would no longer be *true pope*. He would no longer be *Bishop of Rome*. He no longer would hold the Petrine *munus*.

So, how does a Benepapist explain these self-evident words away by using the Ratzinger Code? This is how:

> *Pope Benedict XVI*: "*I am no longer the Pontiff Supreme of the Catholic Church*, or I will be until 8:00 this evening and then no longer. I am simply a pilgrim beginning the last leg of his pilgrimage on this earth."[206]
>
> *Ratzinger Code translation*: "The inversion between adjective and complement therefore prevented Pope Benedict – although he had already prevented him for 17 days – from lying by saying that from 8.00 pm he would renounce his canonical title of pope, which he never did…But beware: the construct of the sentence also takes on another meaning…Thus, Pope Benedict makes it clear that *'he will no longer be a pontiff supreme'*, that is, *he will no longer be a pontiff placed in the highest and largest place, but will remain a hidden pontiff, a hermit, hidden under the nonexistent institution of the papacy emeritus. There will be someone else who will occupy the highest and largest place. To be precise, an antipope.*"[207]

The objector tries to make much out of Benedict's "inversion" of the title, which in Latin is *Summus Pontifex*. That is, according to the objector, Benedict did not use the proper title of *Sommo Pontefice* in the Italian, but instead reversed the words to say "*Pontefice Sommo*," which strictly translated into the English is "Pontiff Supreme." Thus, the plausibility of the *Ratzinger Code* here rests on whether it is true to say it is unheard-of and improper to use "Pontefice Sommo" in reference to the office of *Summus Pontifex (i.e., the pope)*, and that, indeed, it cannot be so used.

What to say of this *Ratzinger Code* argument? Certainly, to the ear accustomed to English, "*Pontiff Supreme of the Catholic Church*" does indeed stick out as very strange. However, in Italian, the placement of adjectives is more flexible than it is in the English language. Consequently, a native Italian speaker like the author of the *Ratzinger Code* book[208] would be hard-pressed to say the average Italian (1) would not know exactly what the native-German, Pope Benedict XVI, was speaking of when he said "*Pontefice Sommo della Chiesa Cattolica*;" or that the average Italian (2) would discern a *different* meaning or office depending on whether one uses "*pontefice sommo della Chiesa Cattolica*" or "*sommo pontefice della Chiesa Cattolica.*"

Furthermore, it is not unheard-of for the pope to be referred to as "*Pontefice Sommo.*" For example, on *Sapere.It,* the second entry under "pontefice" reads (italics added):

> 2) Titolo attribuito al vescovo di Roma. Usato un tempo anche per altri vescovi, con il sec. V divenne la denominazione ufficiale del papa: Gregorio Magno fu il primo a essere chiamato *pontefice sommo.*[209]

The entry translated reads (emphasis added):

> 2) Title attributed to the bishop of Rome. Also used once by other bishops; with the 5th century it became the official title of the pope: Gregory the Great was the first to be called Pontiff Supreme ('*pontefice sommo*')[210]

Other examples can be found. A brief survey of just a few sources over the course of 165 years will suffice to drive the point home. A pamphlet containing a poetic homage commemorating the visit of Pope Pius IX to Modena in the summer of 1857 was entitled "*Quando II Luglio MDCCCLVII La Santita Del Pontefice Sommo Papa Pio IX Letificava Di Sua Sacra Augusta Presenza La Citta di Modena.*" Roughly translated it becomes, "When in July 1857, the Holiness of the Supreme Pontiff (Pontefice

Sommo) Pope Pius IX by his sacred, august presence made joyous the city of Modena."[211]

In 1870, in the midst of the debate over papal infallibility, Bishop Tommaso Michele Salzano published a piece on the topic titled: "*Brevi Riflessioni sul modo di Risolvere e Sull'Opportunita di Definire l'Infallibilita del Pontefice Sommo.*"[212] This title may be translated as, "Brief reflections on the way to resolve and on the opportunity of defining the infallibility of the Supreme Pontiff (*Pontefice Sommo*)." Aside from the title, there are multiple instances in this work of the use of *pontefice sommo* to signify the office of *supreme pontiff*.

In 1909, within the *Acta Apostolicae Sedis* (AAS), the Encyclical *Communion Rerum* by Pope Pius X was published in Latin. There also appears in the AAS along with the official Latin of the text, the official Italian translation of the same encyclical. This official Italian translation uses "*pontefice sommo*" for supreme pontiff in section 3 of the translation from the Latin.[213]

In May 1959, on the occasion of bringing forth the relics of St. Pius X and St. John Bosco, Pope John XXIII, speaking in Italian, uses the term *pontefice sommo* for supreme pontiff. Speaking of Pope Pius X he says: "Pio X è tutta una glorificazione dei compiti pastorali; e ad osservare minutamente gli undici anni del suo governo di *Pontefice Sommo*...". Here, Pope John XXIII speaks of the great pastoral works of Pope Pius X, and "*...the eleven years of his government as Supreme Pontiff* (Pontefice Sommo)." The above words of Pope John XXIII appear in the *Acta Apostolicae Sedis*.[214] Other instances appear in the AAS where *pontefice sommo* is used by a pope for supreme pontiff. John XXIII, on another occasion speaking of Pope Pius X used *pontefice sommo* for supreme pontiff.[215] On still another occasion, Pope John XXIII, speaking in Italian, uses *pontefice sommo* to refer to Pope John XXII.[216] There is no reason to doubt other examples could be found.

In summary, a brief search yields over a half dozen examples of pontefice sommo being used for the office of supreme pontiff, among them a theological work written by a bishop. We have two popes (Benedict XVI and John XXIII) who used *pontefice sommo* when speaking of the office of supreme pontiff, and one who approved the translation of his encyclical from Latin to Italian where the title *pontefice sommo* appears.

These few examples demonstrate *pontefice sommo* has been used in Italian for the office of supreme pontiff, and indeed has been used by popes. Perhaps *"Sommo Pontefice"* is the more common usage in the Italian; but that is a question I leave to the native Italian speakers to debate and decide amongst themselves. However, it is indisputable that *Pontefice Sommo* has been used to refer to the pope and his office of *Summus Pontifex* (Supreme Pontiff). The Ratzinger Code argument is clearly a pile of rubbish.

Furthermore, Benedict's use of *"Pontefice Sommo della Chiesa Cattolica"* is not some meaningless, bizarre turn of phrase that requires one to open a box of *Cracker Jack* to find one's secret *decoder ring* to decipher it! Benedict was clearly referring to his office as *Supreme Pontiff of the Catholic Church*. The attempt to appeal to a "Ratzinger Code" to deny the clear import of Benedict's words, or to assign another meaning to them, is both *desperate* and *absurd*.

Benedict said that after 8 p.m. that day he would *"no longer be the Supreme Pontiff of the Catholic Church."* Thus, whether "Sommo Pontefice" or "Pontefice Sommo," if he would no longer be *it* after 8 p.m. on February 28, 2013, then obviously, he was *it* at the moment he spoke those words. Benedict could only have been referencing the one and the same thing, that is, the office he accepted upon his election as *Summum Pontificem or* "Supreme Pontiff."

This office he clearly intended to resign at the hour of 8 p.m. on February 28, 2013, as he indicated in his *Declaratio*, when he renounced the *"ministry of the Bishop of Rome…in such a way that the "See of Rome, the See of Peter" would be vacant*. If the See of Rome, the See of Peter is vacant, there is no pope. If the See of Peter is vacant, there is no *Supreme Pontiff of the Catholic Church*. Hence, Benedict's words to the pilgrims of Albano, a few short hours before 8 p.m.: *"I will no longer be Supreme Pontiff of the Catholic Church."* There is no other reasonable and credible conclusion. The *Ratzinger Code* crumbles like the house of cards that it is. *Falsus in uno, falsus in omnibus.*

Chapter 5: Gänswein's Speech

Thus far in this book, we have considered documents or remarks either written or spoken by Pope Benedict XVI prior to the effective date and hour of his resignation. These documents and or remarks have been more than sufficient to establish the validity of Benedict's resignation.

In this chapter, we will now consider a document that was not authored by Benedict. This document is a speech given by Archbishop Georg Gänswein at the Gregorian University in Rome on May 20, 2016.[217] Both before and after the resignation of Pope Benedict XVI, Gänswein served as Prefect of the Papal household, as well as Benedict's personal secretary.

Background to Gänswein's Speech

Archbishop Gänswein's speech played a significant role in jumpstarting the Benepapist controversy, and continues to energize it to this day. Those desperate to find a solution to the "*Francis problem*" believed they found in his speech proof that Benedict really did try to bifurcate the papacy and intended to create an "*expanded Petrine ministry*." This speech, probably more than any other one thing or document, provided the match to light the controversy over the resignation of Pope Benedict XVI. This is unfortunate, because a close examination of the speech as well as its context will show it has been greatly misunderstood.

Gänswein's speech was given three years *after* Benedict's resignation in February 2013. This is important to keep in mind. The previously referenced "Benedictine" sources, the subjects of the last four chapters, are all dated to within seventeen or fewer days before Benedict's resignation on February 28, and one of them given that very day, a few short hours before it became effective.

Therefore, to best understand Benedict's thinking on the subject of the resignation, these earlier documents and remarks must take precedence over Gänswein's speech. In other words, we should interpret Benedict through *Benedict*, and not Benedict through *Gänswein*. Unfortunately, the Benepapists have done the latter, and have consequently gone awry.

Reading *Benedict through Benedict*, what is it we understand about the resignation? From the *Declaratio*, we know that he stated he was resigning the *"ministry of the Bishop of Rome...in such a way...that the See of Rome, the See of Peter will be vacant,"* and that a new conclave would be necessary to elect a new Supreme Pontiff (see Chapter 1). If there is no occupant of the See of Rome, the See of Peter—there is no pope. Benedict said a conclave would then be required to elect a "new Supreme Pontiff." Clearly, this is because he knew he would no longer be Supreme Pontiff as of February 28, 2013, at 8 p.m.

Benedict made changes to the rules for the conclave necessitated by his resignation, via the motu proprio *Normas Nonnullas* (see Chapter 2). Had he intended a partial resignation, a papal diarchy, or intended to separate the Petrine *munus* from the See of Rome, or intended to maintain something of the Petrine *munus* for himself, he would have included such changes in *Normas Nonnullas*. However, this he did not do, proving that he fully understood his immediate successor would be *Supreme Pontiff, Bishop of Rome*, and *true pope* with the *full* powers of the papacy. There is "partial resignation." There is no "shared" papacy.

Benedict admitted in his last audience that he will no longer have the *"power of governance"* in the Church, and spoke of his resignation (see Chapter 3). He spoke of a continuation of his bond of charity with the faithful during his pontificate, which he would carry with him after his resignation, devoting himself to a life of prayer for his "sons and daughters," the Church.

Benedict—just a couple of hours before the end of his pontificate—told a group of Catholic pilgrims from the Italian Diocese of Albano (see Chapter 4) that:

VALID? THE RESIGNATION OF POPE BENEDICT XVI

> I am no longer the Supreme Pontiff of the Catholic Church, or I will be until 8:00 this evening and then no longer. I am simply a pilgrim beginning the last leg of his pilgrimage on this earth.

Reading *Benedict through Benedict*, it is abundantly clear that he fully intended, and in fact did, fully and validly, resign the papacy, effective on February 28, 2013, at 8 p.m. Benedict understood that as of that moment he would no longer be *Supreme Pontiff*; he would no longer be *Bishop of Rome*; he would no longer be *true pope*, and that he would no longer hold the *Petrine office* within the Church.

Let us return for a moment to Pope Benedict XVI's words in his last audience about the "always" and "forever." In Chapter 3, we considered the Benepapist interpretations of those words, based on tortuous theories read into the text, as well as a failure to understand the plain meaning of words. I put forth a simpler, more natural interpretation of Benedict's words than the one offered by the Benepapists, one which is consistent with the intent to fully resign the papacy. There is no need to assume Benedict held erroneous or heretical opinions of the papacy. There is no need for a *Ratzinger Code* decoder ring.

Benedict's last audience does give us a sense of how he sees himself as a *"former pope"*—just as he called himself in his letters to Cardinal Brandmüller.[218] Benedict nowhere claims to be pope in any sense any longer. Rather, he sees himself as a former pope or "pope emeritus" who still retains the bonds of charity for his "sons and daughters" he came to know as pope—this is his "spiritual mandate," his "spiritual link" spoken of in the Peter Seewald interview.[219]

In that Seewald interview, Benedict compares himself, as a former pope, to a father who has given up his worldly responsibilities as he grows old. Though Benedict resigned his office as universal pastor of the Church, the bonds of charity he felt and had for the flock, i.e., his "sons and daughters" and "brothers and sisters," remain, just like the "spiritual side of the fatherhood" remains for the father in the analogy in the Seewald interview.

This sentiment is presented in Benedict's last audience as pope as I argued in Chapter 3. Below, I provide a summary of Benedict's logic and meaning, as it will be useful background and key to understanding Gänswein's comments on "pope emeritus" and "an expanded ministry." Benedict's logic regarding the "always" and "forever" may be summarized as follows:

> (1) one who is elected pope belongs to the Church and the Church to him, the private dimension of his life in a *"manner of speaking"* is lost;
> (2) yet, one receives one's life when one gives it away, i.e., the Pope truly gains brothers and sisters, sons and daughters, throughout the world, i.e., the pope becomes a "father";
> (3) a Pope feels secure in the Church's embrace because he "no longer belongs to himself, he belongs to all and all belong to him"—this is the "always";
> (4) but this "always is also a forever" in that resigning the papacy *does not revoke* this bond of charity, this "loss of privacy," this loving attachment which has been gained by the loss of the private dimension of one's life;
> (5) thus, even after his resignation, he will always retain that love for all (i.e., for us the Church)—just as a "father" would for his sons and daughters, he will continue to pray in *service* for his "sons and daughters, etc."—the Church.

Having now recalled some of our prior points offered as proof of Benedict's intent to resign, and the validity and fullness of his resignation, we can now move on to consider Gänswein's speech.

Archbishop Gänswein's Speech

In May 2016, three years following Benedict's resignation, Archbishop Gänswein, Prefect of the Papal Household under Pope Benedict, and under Pope Francis as well, gave a speech at the Gregorian in the Rome. It was a speech which at the time raised some eyebrows. As one Benepapist rightly observed: *"musings left many veteran Vatican commentators non-plussed."*[220]

VALID? THE RESIGNATION OF POPE BENEDICT XVI

There are phrases in Gänswein's speech[221] that indeed seem curious. For example, Gänswein speaks of Benedict's resignation to become *pope emeritus* as a "spectacular and unexpected step," and then likens this decision to what John Duns Scotus had posited about the Immaculate Conception. Here is the core of the most problematic passages (italics added):

> And I, too, a firsthand witness of the spectacular and unexpected step of Benedict XVI, I must admit that what always comes to mind is the well-known and brilliant axiom with which, in the Middle Ages, John Duns Scotus justified the divine decree for the Immaculate Conception of the Mother of God:
>
> *"Decuit, potuit, fecit."*
>
> That is to say: it was fitting, because it was reasonable. God could do it, therefore he did it. I apply the axiom to the decision to resign in the following way: it was fitting, because Benedict XVI was aware that he lacked the necessary strength for the extremely onerous office. He could do it, because he had already thoroughly thought through, from a theological point of view, the possibility of popes emeritus for the future. So he did it.
>
> The momentous resignation of the theologian pope represented a step forward primarily by the fact that, on February 11, 2013, speaking in Latin in front of the surprised cardinals, he introduced into the Catholic Church the new institution of "pope emeritus," stating that his strength was no longer sufficient "to properly exercise the Petrine ministry." The key word in that statement is *munus petrinum*, translated—as happens most of the time—with "Petrine ministry." And yet, *munus*, in Latin, has a multiplicity of meanings: it can mean service, duty, guide or gift, even prodigy. *Before and after his resignation, Benedict understood and understands his task as participation in such a "Petrine ministry."* He has left the papal throne and yet, with the step made on February 11, 2013, he has not at all *abandoned* this ministry. *Instead, he has complemented the personal office with a collegial and synodal dimension, as a quasi-shared ministry* (als einen quasi gemeinsamen Dienst); as though, by this, he wanted to reiterate once again the invitation contained in

the motto that the then Joseph Ratzinger took as archbishop of Munich and Freising and which he then naturally maintained as bishop of Rome: *"cooperatores veritatis,"* which means "fellow workers in the truth." In fact, it is not in the singular but the plural; it is taken from the Third Letter of John, in which in verse 8 it is written: "We ought to support such men, that we may be fellow workers in the truth."

Since the election of his successor Francis, on March 13, 2013, there are not therefore two popes, but de facto an expanded ministry—with an active member and a contemplative member. This is why Benedict XVI has not given up either his name, or the white cassock. This is why the correct name by which to address him even today is "Your Holiness"; and this is also why he has not retired to a secluded monastery, but within the Vatican—as if he had only taken a step to the side to make room for his successor and a new stage in the history of the papacy which he, by that step, enriched with the "power station" of his prayer and his compassion located in the Vatican Gardens.[222]

Before addressing some of the elements of Gänswein's speech above, I draw the reader's attention to the concluding remarks of one Benepapist's position paper, which were also echoed in an appearance on a popular podcast.[223] I think the Benepapist's remarks nicely summarize the Benepapist take on the speech:

> Or as Archbishop Gänswein (quoting Scotus on Mary's Immaculate Conception) said: *"Decuit, potuit, fecit."* It was fitting…God could do it, therefore he did it. In this case, so did Pope Benedict. If he truly separated Peter's Primacy from the Roman See, then Gänswein's gushings over Benedict's maneuver, at last, appear apt: "profoundly transformed," "extraordinary courage," "daring," "spectacular," "unexpected," "a new phase," "turning point," "historic," "entirely different," "never been a step like it," "unprecedented," terms that fall flat describing a simple bishop's retirement—even a pope's! Only a "Captain Kirk" *"Kobayashi Maru"* solution by Pope Benedict could justify the use of such superlatives while simultaneously answering all the

criticisms of his "renunciation" and satisfying all the parameters of the "Pope Emeritus" controversy.[224]

This commentary pithily crystallizes the point.[225] But is what it asserts really true? Is it really true to say (italics added):

> *Only* a "Captain Kirk" "Kobayashi Maru"[226] solution by Pope Benedict could justify the use of such superlatives while simultaneously answering all the criticisms of his "renunciation" and satisfying all the parameters of the "Pope Emeritus" controversy.

Above, the reference to a *"solution by Pope Benedict"* refers to that writer's theory that Benedict intended to separate the Petrine *munus* from the See of Rome.[227] Now, my understanding is this particular Benepapist writer has since discarded this theory, and moved on to a different species of Benepapism.[228] Even so, the general point probably still applies. That is, we have all these superlatives, and according to most Benepapists, this can only be explained if Benedict did something unique, and different, such as attempting to create a papal diarchy, or synodal papacy, etc.

But is the only true explanation for Gänswein's *"superlatives"* and comments about Benedict and the *"Petrine ministry"* or *"expanded ministry"* that *Benedict believes himself to still be pope in some way*? Is that the *only* possible explanation here that makes sense?

The reality is, a great many of the critics of Gänswein's speech, Benepapists and non-Benepapists alike, have lost sight of the forest for the trees, focusing as they do on the *seemingly* problematic phrases and passages apart from the full context of the speech. I, for one, do believe there is another explanation. It is one that doesn't require the accusation Benedict concocted a potentially heretical theory of a "papal diarchy," or "synodal papacy" or that he changed or somehow altered the Petrine Primacy, all without telling us beforehand.

Unfortunately, Gänswein's speech has been the launching pad into the realm of the Benepapists. Benedict's actions and words are often interpreted—*or rather misinterpreted*—through

Gänswein's speech. However, the Benepapists have things backwards. As suggested earlier, if we are to understand both what Benedict XVI did in his resignation and his use of "pope emeritus," then we must understand Benedict through Benedict, and *not Benedict through Gänswein*.

Understanding Gänswein

With that introduction, we can now address Gänswein's superlatives and his references to the "Petrine ministry" and an "expanded ministry." To understand Gänswein, we must first understand the context of his speech—something I have not seen any Benepapist address.

Keep in mind that Gänswein's speech was *not* given at some theological forum. At such a forum, we might expect special care and precision in language and expression. Instead, Gänswein spoke "at the presentation of a new book by Roberto Regoli. Regoli's book was titled *Beyond the Crisis of the Church—The Pontificate of Benedict XVI.*"[229]

Such retrospectives on a pope's life and papacy are usually written after the pontificate when its subject is dead—something noted by Gänswein in his speech. However, on this occasion, the subject involved a still-living, former pope, Benedict. Thus, in this regard, the event was quite exceptional and unique.

Given Gänswein was quite close to Benedict, and still served him, it should not be a surprise that this retrospective on Benedict's life and work should be excessively flowery, effusive, over the top, and even full of the sort of *panegyrical* language of praise we might expect to hear at a eulogy at a memorial service.

However, here, the speaker's task was unique in that the subject was not yet dead. Further, Gänswein was certainly aware and mindful that Dante had consigned Benedict's prototype of a resigning pope, Celestine V, to the Inferno. Further, Gänswein was surely well aware that many of Benedict's closest friends and associates were deeply disappointed in his resignation. He said as much in his speech.

In this light, it is not difficult to understand Gänswein. On the one hand, he wanted to sing glowing praise of his friend, the pre-resignation *Pope* Benedict and his papacy. On the other hand, he hoped to also paint a flattering, panegyrical description of a still living, but *resigned* Benedict, ascribing some purpose to a post-resignation life as *pope emeritus.*

Thus, we might understand—even if we roll our eyes as we groan—Gänswein's application of Duns Scotus' axiom (*"Decuit, potuit, fecit"*) to Benedict's decision to resign and become *pope emeritus.* Gänswein says explicitly that Benedict "*introduced into the Catholic Church the new institution of 'pope emeritus.'*" But here, I think we might take note that Gänswein has exaggerated the case to some degree, or simply was not aware of Benedict's thinking on the use of "emeritus."

First, we may note that Canon 185 states that anyone who "loses an office due to resignation" may use the title "emeritus."

> Canon 185: *The title of emeritus can be conferred upon the person who loses an office by reason of age or by a resignation which has been accepted.*[230]

Granted, the context in the Code of Canon Law does not explicitly apply this to the Roman Pontiff, but certainly the text provides an appropriate title for Benedict to find in his own case, as he would "lose his office" due to resignation.

Further, one of Benedict's letters to Cardinal Brandmüller after his resignation clearly suggests Benedict believed prior popes who had resigned had been "emeritus" in fact, though they had not been so explicitly by name.[231] Still, it can be said Benedict introduced the title of "pope emeritus."

Regardless, even in saying this, Gänswein still affirms a true resignation occurred from the Petrine office (e.g., "it was fitting, because Benedict XVI was aware that he lacked the necessary strength for the extremely onerous office"—clearly implying that he surrendered that office, that *munus*). Furthermore, Gänswein affirms Benedict has "left the papal throne." That is, there is no question: Benedict is no longer pope.

How then should we understand Gänswein when he says: "*Before and after his resignation, Benedict understood and understands his task as participation in such a 'Petrine ministry?'"*

As we have already seen in Chapter 3, and summarized again earlier, Benedict as pope described the "always" of the bond of charity towards the "sons and daughters" he gained when elected pope. Benedict added this "always is also a forever," that his resignation would not revoke this bond. Benedict said of himself in his last audience he remains *"in a new way at the side of the crucified Lord"*—i.e., in a new way, not the same way—not as pope. He said he "no longer bear(s) the power of office for the governance of the Church"—i.e., he will no longer be pope. However, Benedict did say in the "service of prayer" he remains "so to speak, in the enclosure of Saint Peter."

One could say that Benedict's continued "service of prayer" as pope emeritus is "Petrine" in a certain sense. This is so because the bond of charity of which he spoke in his last audience encompasses *all* the faithful, i.e., the "sons and daughters" he gained upon his election as pope. After the resignation, as pope emeritus, he continues in service to *all* the faithful, i.e., the Church, through prayer. Thus, in this limited, metaphorical sense, Benedict can be said to participate in a "Petrine ministry" of sorts, as this "service of prayer" is "Petrine-like" in that it encompasses *all* the faithful, i.e., the whole Church. In this way we should understand Gänswein when he says *"Before and after his resignation, Benedict understood and understands his task as participation in such a 'Petrine ministry.'"*

Next, Benepapists point out that Gänswein says Benedict *"has complemented the personal office with a collegial and synodal dimension, as a quasi-shared ministry,"* suggesting Benedict intended to be some sort of "co-pope" with his successor. However, Gänswein speaks only of a *"quasi-shared ministry,"* i.e., shared in a qualified sense only. We have already seen how it can be said in a qualified way Benedict "participated" in the "Petrine ministry"—understood in something of a *figurative* or *metaphorical* sense.

But what is this "synodal dimension" and this "shared" dimension? Gänswein explains in his speech by referencing Benedict's coat of arms and the inclusion of the following words

VALID? THE RESIGNATION OF POPE BENEDICT XVI

from a letter of the Apostle John: *"fellow workers in the Truth"* (cf. 3 Jn 1:8). Keep in mind, one can share a ministry of the truth, or be "fellow workers in the truth" without sharing the same office in any real sense. For example, a layman can be a "co-worker of the truth" with a priest, bishop, or pope—while not being in any of these offices.

St. Paul makes an even stronger reference to being God's "*co-workers*" and "*fellow workers*" (cf. 2 Cor 3:9, 6:1) without suggesting any sort of equivalency or sharing of an office! Thus, Francis and Benedict may be spoken of, in a sense, as sharing a "Petrine-like" ministry in that both focus on the *whole* Church. Francis does so as the true pope, while Benedict as a former pope, owing to the bonds of charity formed at his election between him and his "sons and daughters," whereby he continues to pray for the whole Church.

Gänswein also affirms Benedict hasn't "*abandoned this ministry*" similar to when he says of Benedict that "*he has not abandoned the Office of Peter.*" Both references are consistent with Benedict's last audience, wherein Benedict said:

> I am not abandoning the cross, but remaining in a new way at the side of the crucified Lord. I no longer bear the power of office for the governance of the Church, but in the service of prayer I remain, so to speak, in the enclosure of Saint Peter.

However, again, Benedict is remaining in a "new way," not the same way—i.e., not as pope, as he no longer bears the "power of office" to govern. However, in the "service of prayer" he remains, as described before, in relation to the bond of charity with his "sons and daughters," the Church.

So, in this way, we can understand Gänswein when he speaks of an "expanded ministry" immediately after saying "*there are not therefore two popes.*" There is, for Gänswein, Pope Francis who is the real pope with authority over the Church as Supreme Pontiff; and there is Benedict who continues to pray for the "sons and daughters" he gained when he became pope but does not abandon or forsake when he resigns. That is, he continues to pray for the Church, but not as pope. Indeed, Gänswein refers to Benedict as having "stepped to the side" to "make room for his successor," and as a "power station" of prayer.

Benepapists want to focus on such seemingly controversial passages as we have just reviewed. However, Gänswein makes clear Benedict is no longer pope at all. He affirms Benedict "*left the papal throne,*" and speaks of him as having "*stepped down,*" and refers to Francis as "his successor." Other references in his speech also make it clear Benedict is no longer pope. For example, Gänswein says, "*I was present when Benedict XVI, at the end of his mandate, removed the Fisherman's ring, as is customary after the death of a pope, even though in this case he was still alive!*" Also, he specifies in his speech that Benedict's pontificate had a beginning and an end: "*Benedict XVI, at the helm of the barque of Peter in the dramatic years 2005–2013.*"

Beneath the superlatives and rhetorical flourishes of the speech, Gänswein, in describing Benedict as "emeritus," was neither speaking of a real expansion nor even a real change in the "Petrine ministry" or "Petrine *munus*" properly, and strictly understood. While Gänswein might be criticized for potentially troublesome, unguarded, or exaggerated *panegyrical* praise of Benedict as pope and as "emeritus," he might be forgiven that others took him quite so literally on the occasion of a book release event covering the papacy of his close friend, Benedict.

However, for those people who want to interpret Gänswein's talk of an "expanded ministry," or a continued "participation" in the "Petrine ministry" in a strict non-exaggerated sense, how do they interpret Gänswein's description of Roberto Regoli, whose book was the reason for the presentation and speech? Gänswein says of Regoli at the end of his speech (italics added):

> Thus, this book once again throws a consoling gaze on the peaceful imperturbability and serenity of Benedict XVI, at the helm of the barque of Peter in the dramatic years 2005–2013. At the same time, however, through this illuminating account, *Regoli himself now also takes part in the* munus Petri *of which I spoke. Like Peter Seewald and others before him, Roberto Regoli—as a priest, professor, and scholar—also thus enters into that enlarged Petrine ministry around the*

successors of the Apostle Peter; and for this today we offer him heartfelt thanks.

Gänswein says the author Roberto Regoli now takes part in the *munus Petri*! Gänswein even goes further saying Regoli, Peter Seewald, and others enter into that *"enlarged Petrine ministry."* Where are our Benepapist interpreters on this? Is Gänswein speaking literally or figuratively of Regoli taking "part in the *munus Petri*"? Is Gänswein speaking literally or figuratively when he says of Regoli, Seewald, and others that they have entered into that "enlarged Petrine ministry"? Clearly, Gänswein is speaking figuratively of Regoli taking part in the *"munus Petri,"* and also when he says Regoli and others have entered *"into that enlarged Petrine ministry around the successors of the Apostle Peter."* But that of course is the point. This is how Gänswein should be understood throughout his speech! He is speaking figuratively and extravagantly of Benedict's *post-resignation* participation in the "Petrine ministry."

Objections, and Replies to Those Objections

Objection 5.1: BXVI wears white; still called Your Holiness

> Gänswein says Benedict created the "pope emeritus." Further, he speaks of a now "expanded ministry" of which Benedict is the contemplative member, and that this is "why Benedict XVI has not given up either his name, or the white cassock," and "why the correct name by which to address him even today is 'Your Holiness.'" Given Benedict's adopted title of "pope emeritus," his style of address, and his manner of dress, it is clear—both to Gänswein and Benedict—that Benedict still believes himself to be pope in some way.

Reply to Objection 5.1: The objection centers on Benedict's title, "pope emeritus," his style of dress (wearing white), and his style of address ("Your Holiness"), and suggests these are indications that Benedict believes himself still pope. What Archbishop

Gänswein meant by "expanded ministry" will be addressed in the Reply to Objection 5.4.

Benedict was the first pope since Celestine V to resign due to an incapacity to fulfill his role as pope. Benedict spoke of this weakness in his *Declaratio* and in his interviews with Peter Seewald. It is apparent that by his resignation Benedict intended to establish a precedent for future pontiffs to follow in a similar circumstance of weakness. Thus, Gänswein speaks of Benedict's resignation as an "act of courage" that strengthened the papacy. That is, by stepping aside when weak, a physically weak or enfeebled pope allows potentially for a more vigorous successor. This, Benedict seemed to believe, and Gänswein argued, would actually make the papacy stronger.

Certainly, Benedict appears to have been the first pope to try to establish a precedent for other weakened popes of the future to follow. As he described in his last audience, Benedict said his mission as a former pope was to continue in the "service of prayer" for the Church (see Chapter 4). As he devoted some thought to what service a former pope might still render even in his weakness, it should not then be surprising he would also devote some attention to the externals such as dress and even where he might live. Perhaps, he did this to make the life of a former pope somewhat more appealing to future popes than it was for Celestine V following his imprisonment by Boniface VIII!

Now, it is suggested in the objection that Benedict by wearing white, being called "Your Holiness," and by using the title "pope emeritus," believes himself to still be pope in some way. Leaving aside the practical wisdom of Benedict's decisions over these externals, such a conclusion does not follow upon examination of the evidence and application of some common sense.

With regard to "your holiness," this is an honorific title. It is commonplace for someone who once held high office to be referred to by their former position. Former American presidents are regularly addressed as "Mr. President." Similar examples are found in cases of former governors, senators, military officers, etc. "Your Holiness" may seem odd, but that's probably because it is not common for there to be a living former pope, so we are not accustomed to it.

Some also make a big deal out of the pope still wearing white. Again, I am not defending Benedict's choices. The issue is only whether the clothing necessarily means that Benedict is still pope. However, here again, the reality is not what the Benepapists would have one believe. Following his resignation, Benedict does not wear the same style of dress as he did as pope. Benedict wears a simple cassock but *without the mozetta*, which is a symbol of authority.[232] He no longer wears the red shoes he wore as pope, which are also a symbol of authority. In addition, Benedict no longer wears the Fisherman's ring which he received at the mass officially inaugurating his papacy.[233] Gänswein said in his speech that he witnessed the removal of the ring. In sum, these changes are themselves an indication that Benedict no longer sees himself as pope.

Objection 5.2: BXVI created the "pope emeritus"

> Gänswein says Benedict created the "pope emeritus." Further, he speaks of a now "expanded ministry" of which Benedict is the contemplative member, and that this is "why Benedict XVI has not given up either his name, or the white cassock," and "why the correct name by which to address him even today is 'Your Holiness.'" Given Benedict's adopted title of "pope emeritus," his style of address, and his manner of dress, it is clear—both to Gänswein and Benedict—that Benedict still believes himself to be pope in some way.

Reply to Objection 5.2: The Benepapists have a big problem with the title *pope emeritus*. This, they say, is without any historical precedent. Certainly, in the past, popes who resigned returned to their former rank and title, for example, "cardinal." Again, it is fair to wonder whether this would have been a better choice for Benedict. However, it is clear he was not bound by former precedent as to the choice of an honorific title.

Certainly, in common parlance, "emeritus" is applied as an honorific title to an office or position which is no longer held. One example here should suffice to prove the point. A former professor might have the title of and be referred to as "professor emeritus."

The very point of adding "emeritus" is to underline that the individual is no longer a professor, while at the same time honoring him for his former position.[234] Thus, "professor emeritus" refers to an individual who once was a professor, but no longer is.[235]

It is true, *pope emeritus* is a title without precedent. However, as discussed in the opening of the chapter, Benedict implies in a letter to Cardinal Brandmüller that the resigned popes of the past were each an emeritus *in fact*, if not in name. Regardless, the use of "emeritus" does have a basis in canon law.

> *Canon 185: The title of emeritus can be conferred upon the person who loses an office by reason of age or by a resignation which has been accepted.*[236]

Granted, the context in the Code of Canon Law does not explicitly apply this canon to the Roman Pontiff but certainly the text provides an appropriate title for Benedict to find for his own case. In this regard, it is said the "title of emeritus" may be conferred on him who "loses an office" due to resignation. The significance of this fact is relevant to the argument over whether Benedict still believed he held his papal office. The answer here must be no, as emeritus connotes the reality of a *"loss of office"*—which in itself clearly demonstrates Benedict recognized his "loss of office," i.e., his papal office, owing to his resignation.

As a final note, it is clear from his interviews with Peter Seewald that Benedict does not see that a pope emeritus bears any authority. When Seewald asks about Benedict's use of the honorific title "emeritus," Benedict says:

> In this formula both things are implied: no actual legal authority any longer, but a relationship which remains even if it is invisible.[237]

Indeed, Benedict told Seewald explicitly this "legal-spiritual formula avoids any idea of there being two popes at the same time: a bishopric can only have one incumbent. But the formula also expresses a spiritual link, which cannot ever be taken away." He is not speaking of any legal office remaining.

Objection 5.3: BXVI still gives "apostolic blessings"

> One thing that Archbishop Gänswein does not mention in his speech is that Benedict still gives apostolic blessings. He did this in a letter to Cardinal Brandmüller in November 2017, and on at least another occasion in a letter to Cardinal Sarah, saying that he imparted "my Apostolic Blessing." However, only popes have the authority to give apostolic blessings. Therefore, Benedict must still believe himself to be pope in at least some way to think that he can still give apostolic blessings. By using the possessive "my" in imparting "my Apostolic Blessing," Benedict clearly indicates he believes himself to still be papal in some way. This either demonstrates Benedict did not intend to resign the papacy at all, or that if he did that he committed a "substantial error" which invalidates his renunciation.

Reply to Objection 5.3: It is true that in at least a couple of private letters to at least Cardinal Brandmüller and Cardinal Sarah, the pope emeritus concluded "with my Apostolic Blessing."

The Benepapists claim that only a pope can give an apostolic blessing. This is partly true. The authority to give apostolic blessings does rest in the pope; however, the pope can and does delegate this authority to others.[238] On some occasions a certain solemn rite and formula are prescribed, but for others this is not the case.

By what authority does Benedict give apostolic blessings? It may be the case that Pope Francis delegated the right to his predecessor, the Pope Emeritus Benedict, either with or without certain conditions attached to this right. Per Canon 1167§1, Pope Francis certainly would have had the authority to do so. That he might do so should not be a surprise. Bishops are accorded the right to give a certain number of apostolic blessings each year, thus it is fitting that a former pope should be granted this privilege to an even greater extent in view of the dignity of his former office.

There is another way in which Benedict might have received the delegated authority to give apostolic blessings. It may be that Benedict, while he was still pope, granted to any future *pope emeritus* the delegated authority to give apostolic blessings. Obviously, this would apply to himself when he renounced the papacy. Again, that Pope Benedict XVI could do this is granted by Canon 1167§1[239] which reads: *"The Apostolic See alone can establish new sacramentals, authentically interpret those already received, or abolish or change any of them."*[240] As stated above, it is fitting a pope emeritus would be accorded the delegated authority to give apostolic blessings in view of the dignity of his former office.

But, what of Benedict's use of the possessive "my" when imparting the apostolic blessing, i.e., *"with my Apostolic Blessing"*? Doesn't that mean he must be asserting he has the *inherent* authority to give an apostolic blessing, and thus believes he is still fully pope, or at least pope in some partial way? The answer is a clear "no."

Per the relevant portion of Canon 1168 which applies to this question, *"the minister of sacramentals is a cleric who has been provided with the requisite authority."*[241] Thus, Benedict, even as pope emeritus, is the *"minister of the sacramental"* on the basis of having been *"provided the requisite authority"* via delegation. Consequently, even in giving the apostolic blessing in an informal setting of a private letter, he is a true *"minister of the sacramental."*

Thus, Benedict's use of the possessive "my" refers to the apostolic blessing being *his* to give, to whom *he* chooses to give it, on those occasions *he* chooses to do so as the true "minister of the sacramental" for which *he* has been *"provided the requisite authority."* He is using *"my"* in this delegated sense of being a true "minister of the sacramental," and not in the intrinsic, inherent sense that would apply only in the case of a pope. As a final point, to my knowledge Benedict has not given the apostolic blessing in public settings. He has done so only in private letters between friends and associates, so the lack of precise formula for the blessing is not surprising.

Whatever the specific arrangement that was made which allows Benedict as *pope emeritus* to give apostolic blessings, the point is, there are more mundane explanations available to account for it than to wildly assert Benedict must still believe himself to be pope in some way. The real point is that the Benepapists would have to show the canons were violated here.²⁴² The burden is on the Benepapists to demonstrate there is no other solution but their own. This they have failed to do. So, in summary, if Benedict still gives apostolic blessings, that is not a proof that he still believes himself to be pope.

Objection 5.4: Gänswein spoke of an expanded Petrine ministry

> Gänswein speaks of a now "expanded ministry" of which Benedict is the contemplative member. He says Pope Francis and Benedict represent one "expanded" Petrine office with "an active member" and a "contemplative." Indeed, Gänswein says since February 11, 2013, "the papal ministry is not the same as before." This certainly means Gänswein must have recognized Benedict attempted to change the papacy into a synodal one, or a diarchy. Indeed, Gänswein underlines this by speaking of Benedict's "participation in such a 'Petrine ministry.'" Therefore, Gänswein, as a close confidante of Benedict and familiar with his thought, demonstrates that Benedict still considers himself to be pope in some way.

Reply to Objection 5.4: Let us go straight to the heart of the question. At first glance, it does sound odd to pious ears to read that Archbishop Gänswein said that Pope Francis and Pope Emeritus Benedict together comprise an "expanded ministry." The question of course is: did Gänswein really mean to suggest there was now, somehow, an official, legal, or structurally "expanded" papacy? That Benedict was still "papal" in some real way?

To this question, we know the answer given by the Benepapists. They demand we interpret Gänswein in a very strict sense, a sense that is consistent with the alleged "substantial error" necessary to overturn the resignation of Pope Benedict XVI. The Benepapists will allow no other explanation, one must be a "liar" or have some "financial interest" to suggest otherwise, as one of them suggested.[243]

However, such protestations are nonsense. Reading the whole of Gänswein's speech in context, it is clear he is not speaking of an "expanded" ministry in the strict sense as interpreted by the Benepapists. Rather, he is speaking in a looser, metaphorical sense. Consider the following passage from the speech (italics added):

> Before and after his resignation, Benedict understood and understands his task as participation in such a "Petrine ministry." He has left the papal throne and yet, with the step made on February 11, 2013, he has not at all abandoned this ministry. Instead, he has complemented the personal office with a collegial and synodal dimension, as a *quasi-shared* ministry (als einen quasi gemeinsamen Dienst); as though, by this, he wanted to reiterate once again the invitation contained in the motto that the then Joseph Ratzinger took as archbishop of Munich and Freising and which he then naturally maintained as bishop of Rome: "cooperatores veritatis," which means "fellow workers in the truth." In fact, it is not in the singular but the plural; it is taken from the Third Letter of John, in which in verse 8 it is written: "We ought to support such men, that we may be fellow workers in the truth."
>
> Since the election of his successor Francis, on March 13, 2013, there are not therefore two popes, but *de facto* an expanded ministry—with an active member and a contemplative member. This is why Benedict XVI has not given up either his name, or the white cassock. This is why the correct name by which to address him even today is "Your Holiness"; and this is also why he has not retired to a secluded monastery, but within the Vatican—as if he had only taken a step to the side to make room for his successor and a new stage in the history of the papacy which he, by that step, enriched with the "power station" of his prayer and his compassion located in the Vatican Gardens.

First, one can see that Gänswein recognizes Benedict is no longer pope. He explicitly says he *"left the papal throne."* He also states that since the election of Francis *"there are not therefore two popes."* Thus, Gänswein is most definitely not speaking of a new sort of papacy with two men who are somehow each pope. There is only one "legitimate" pope—one true pope, and in context this is clearly Francis, and not Benedict. Gänswein would later reiterate this years later in an interview with Diane Montagna, affirming there is "one legitimately elected and incumbent Pope, and that is Francis."[244] Benedict is no longer the true pope. Gänswein clearly affirms this and has done so consistently.

Second, when he speaks of complementing the personal office with a "collegial and synodal dimension," Gänswein is speaking of what he calls a *"quasi-shared* ministry." Note, Gänswein speaks only of a *"quasi"* shared ministry. To say "quasi" is to speak of a likeness to something without being the thing itself. Thus, the archbishop is speaking of a shared ministry in a qualified sense not in a true sense. We know this because Gänswein has affirmed, as in the examples cited earlier, that Benedict is no longer pope. He cannot truly share the ministry. Consequently, when Gänswein speaks of Benedict continuing to "participate" in the "Petrine ministry"—he is speaking of a "participation" and "sharing" in a looser, *figurative*, or *metaphorical* sense.

Third, as I noted in the opening argument of this chapter, Gänswein spoke of Benedict's coat of arms and its inclusion of a phrase from a letter of the Apostle John, i.e., "fellow workers in the truth" (cf. 3 Jn 1:8). Gänswein made this reference immediately following, and in the context of explaining, his use of the term "quasi-shared ministry." What is apparent in St. John's expression "fellow workers in the truth" is that he is speaking of a shared ministry of a sort. But one can share a ministry or be "fellow workers of the truth" without sharing the same office in any real sense. For example, a layman can be a "co-worker of the truth" with a priest, bishop, or pope —while not holding any of these offices. St. Paul, for example, makes an even stronger reference to being God's "co-workers," and God's "fellow workers" (see 2 Cor 3:9, 6:1) without suggesting any sort of equivalency of office to God!

GÄNSWEIN SPEECH

Thus, we see that Gänswein is speaking of Benedict sharing in an "expanded" Petrine ministry in a loose, figurative, or metaphorical sense. He is not speaking of a true papal office that Benedict shares with Pope Francis. What then is this quasi-shared office?

Well, it is as Benedict explained in his last audience, as was argued in Chapter 3. As was summarized in this chapter's opening, even though Benedict resigned the papacy, he does not simply walk away, forgetting the bond of charity he formed towards his "sons and daughters," i.e., the Church. That bond persists even after his resignation, and so he will continue in the "service of prayer" for the Church. That is the purpose, mission, or ministry that Benedict set out for himself as pope emeritus.

Few pastors of souls in the history of the Church can have the same sort of unique, spiritual relationship toward the *whole* Church as "sons and daughters" as a pope does. We might say this spiritual relationship, this bond of charity, is "Petrine" in the sense it encompasses the *whole* Church. Benedict told us in his last audience that the bond of charity persists for him after his resignation. Even though he is no longer pope, he continues to love his "sons and daughters," the Church.

This bond of charity for Benedict, even though he is no longer pope, remains Petrine-*like* in a sense because it encompasses the *whole* Church. In this, there is something of a *remote* similitude or analogy, by which we should understand Gänswein when he says (italics mine):

> Since the election of his successor Francis, on March 13, 2013, there are *not* therefore two popes, but *de facto* an expanded ministry—with an active member and a contemplative member.

That is to say, Francis, now in office as pope, is responsible with the actual care of *the whole Church*. Benedict, as a former pope, has a "spiritual relationship"[245] and thus a felt responsibility to continue on in the "service of prayer"[246] for his "sons and daughters," the *whole* Church. This "spiritual relationship" is Petrine-like for that reason, it encompasses the *whole* Church.

Thus, in a sense, the two men are *"fellow workers of the truth"* (cf. 3 Jn 1:8) as they both have a ministry to care for the whole Church. But again, not in the same way, or by virtue of sharing the same office. Gänswein is clear on that point, as he says, *"there are not therefore two popes, but de facto an expanded ministry."* Gänswein explicitly says he is not speaking of two popes. Instead, he refers to this "expanded ministry" as a "de facto" one. It is *de facto*, meaning it is not a legal structure. It is not a ministry as if it were an institutional one. He is not talking about a legal or theological change to the papacy.

What Gänswein calls a *de facto* expanded ministry, he also calls a *"quasi"* shared ministry earlier in his speech. It is clear he is speaking of a likeness to something without being the thing itself. Francis, as the reigning pope, is the "active member" of this expanded ministry. He has, in virtue of his office, the true responsibility to care of the *whole* Church. Benedict, as the former pope, is the "contemplative" member and, not forsaking his bond of charity for the whole Church, continues in the "service of prayer" for her.

Gänswein is not asserting an equivalency of the two, as if each participates or shares in the same Petrine office in a true sense. Indeed, Archbishop Gänswein on at least two occasions has strenuously rejected any controversial interpretations of his speech.[247] For example, the Catholic News Agency provided the following on Gänswein's reaction to various Benepapist interpretations of his speech:

> "Any talk of two popes, one legitimate, one illegitimate, is therefore incorrect." What he did in fact say, Archbishop Gänswein added, was that Benedict continues to be present in prayer and sacrifice, which bears spiritual fruit.[248]

Separately, Diane Montagna queried Gänswein regarding the controversy over Pope Benedict XVI, i.e., whether he had resigned the *munus*, "or just the public actions that pertain to that *munus*?"[249] Gänswein responded that he had "already cleared up the 'misunderstanding' several times,"[250] and that "It makes no sense at all, no, even more, it is counterproductive to insist on this 'misunderstanding' and to quote me again and again."[251]

Therefore, it should be sufficiently clear that Archbishop Gänswein is not talking about a true expansion of the papal office or ministry. He is speaking in a loose sense of Benedict's sense of mission, his "spiritual responsibility," to continue in the "service of prayer" for the Church. It is in this sense that Gänswein speaks of a quasi-shared ministry, and a de facto expanded ministry. Gänswein is speaking in the sense of Benedict being a "fellow worker in truth" with Francis: Francis as true pope governing the whole Church; Benedict as a former pope praying for the whole Church.

That Gänswein is speaking in a figurative sense in his speech is also clear when we consider the conclusion to it. In the last paragraph of his speech at the presentation of Regoli's book on the papacy of Pope Benedict XVI, he speaks of Regoli and Seewald and others entering into the "expanded ministry" as well:

> Thus, this book once again throws a consoling gaze on the peaceful imperturbability and serenity of Benedict XVI, at the helm of the barque of Peter in the dramatic years 2005–2013. At the same time, however, through this illuminating account, Regoli himself now also takes part in the *munus Petri* of which I spoke. Like Peter Seewald and others before him, Roberto Regoli—as a priest, professor, and scholar—also thus enters into that enlarged Petrine ministry around the successors of the Apostle Peter; and for this today we offer him heartfelt thanks.

Gänswein says the author, Regoli, now also "*takes part in the munus Petri*" of which he spoke, i.e., the "expanded ministry." Clearly, Gänswein is speaking here of Regoli in a loose, metaphorical, or figurative sense. He is not meaning to say Regoli and Seewald, who have each written extensively about the papacy of Benedict, are taking part in the *munus Petri* in a real, true, and strict sense. No. Rather, we understand that Gänswein has been speaking in a similar sense about Benedict all along.

VALID? THE RESIGNATION OF POPE BENEDICT XVI

Objection 5.5: BXVI "has not abandoned the Office of Peter"

Gänswein said of Benedict that: "He left the Papal Throne and yet, with the step he took on 11 February 2013, he has *not abandoned* this ministry." Gänswein's words merely echo what Pope Benedict XVI said in his last general audience: "*I am not abandoning the cross, but remaining in a new way at the side of the crucified Lord.*" Also, later on in his speech, Gänswein again affirmed Benedict "has *not abandoned* the Office of Peter—something which would have been entirely impossible for him after his irrevocable acceptance of the office in April 2005." According to Gänswein, Benedict has not "*abandoned the office of Peter*" and he speaks of an "*irrevocable acceptance*" of this office at the time of his election. Therefore, Gänswein, as a close confidante of Benedict and familiar with his thought, demonstrates that Benedict still considers himself pope in some way.

Reply to Objection 5.5: In one place in the speech, Gänswein says Benedict has not "*abandoned this ministry,*" and in another he has not "*abandoned the office of Peter.*" Benepapists want to interpret these expressions as if to say, "Because Benedict did not abandon his office, that this is either an implicit or direct assertion Benedict still retains the Petrine office (*munus*)." However, such an interpretation is unwarranted. To see why this is so, let us take each of these expressions in turn.

When Gänswein first says Benedict has not "*abandoned this ministry*" he says so immediately after saying Benedict "*has left the papal throne.*" Yet, here, Gänswein explicitly affirms Benedict is no longer on the papal throne. He is no longer pope. This statement leads directly into Gänswein's treatment of an "expanded ministry" we just reviewed in the Reply to Objection 5.4. There, we saw the sort of ministry Benedict lives as a former pope; i.e., a life dedicated to the "service of prayer" for the Church (also, see discussion in Chapter 3 on this point). This is what Benedict believes is his *spiritual mandate*: he will continue to serve the Church in prayer following his resignation.

GÄNSWEIN SPEECH

That this is Benedict's thinking is seen during his last Angelus as pope, on February 24, 2013—just three days before his last audience. Reflecting on the reading about Peter and the Transfiguration, and in the context of his imminent departure from papal office, Pope Benedict XVI said in part (italics added):

> Moreover, prayer does not mean isolating oneself from the world and from its contradictions, as Peter wanted to do on Mount Tabor; rather, prayer leads back to the journey and to action. "The Christian life", I wrote in my Message for this Lent, "consists in continuously scaling the mountain to meet God and then coming back down, bearing the love and strength drawn from him, so as to serve our brothers and sisters with God's own love".
>
> Dear brothers and sisters, I hear this word of God as addressed to me in particular at this moment of my life. Thank you! *The Lord is calling me "to scale the mountain", to devote myself even more to prayer and meditation. But this does not mean abandoning the Church; indeed, if God asks me this it is precisely so that I may continue to serve her with the same dedication and the same love with which I have tried to do so until now, but in a way more suited to my age and strength.*

Pope Benedict XVI, only a few days before the effective date of his resignation, tells us that his decision to resign and live a life a prayer "*does not mean abandoning the Church.*" His point is that he is not abandoning the Church, as he will now serve it in prayer. This is "more suited" to his age and strength, which were the reasons given in the *Declaratio* for his resignation.

Because Benedict continues to serve the Church through prayer, he is not "abandoning" her, as he says in the Angelus reflection. There is no talk of remaining a pope in some partial way, or retaining the *munus*! No.

The sense in which Benedict spoke at the Angelus, is quite apparently the same sense in which Gänswein spoke, saying Benedict has not "*abandoned this ministry*" and it is in this sense "*he has not abandoned the Office of Peter.*" Gänswein knows Benedict does not abandon those who "belong" to him, and to whom he "belongs," i.e., the Church. This is his spiritual mandate—to pray for the Church—which he has not abandoned. And indeed, in his last audience, Benedict said:

> I am not abandoning the cross, but remaining in a new way at the side of the crucified Lord. I no longer bear the power of office for the governance of the Church, but in the service of prayer I remain, so to speak, in the enclosure of Saint Peter.

Benedict says by his resignation he is not "abandoning the cross," but remains "in a new way" by the crucified Lord, not the same way, not as pope. Benedict's spiritual mandate as a former pope, pope emeritus, is to pray for the Church.

Consequently, we can see why Gänswein rejects the view that Benedict has "abandoned" anything. Instead, Gänswein clearly wants to cast the resignation in a positive light. After all, as he notes at this point in the speech, there were those who opposed the resignation. Surely, some viewed the resignation then and possibly to this day as an irresponsible act, indeed, even as an act of "abandoning" one's duty.

Gänswein rejects such characterizations. For Benedict, such abandonment is *"something which would have been entirely impossible for him after his irrevocable acceptance of the office in April 2005."* In saying "irrevocable acceptance," Gänswein is not suggesting that Benedict cannot resign the office. No! Gänswein knows his history and canon law! Popes have resigned.

An *acceptance* of one's election to the papal office is indeed *irrevocable*. Benedict cannot, as if going back in time, revoke his acceptance of his election at the conclave in 2005. No! He may later resign the papal office as he did, but one cannot go back in time and undo or revoke that *original* acceptance. Benedict will always be a man who *accepted* the papacy upon his election. That does not mean he will always be 'irrevocably' pope.

It is a matter of fact that Benedict's acceptance of the office in April 2005 is irrevocable. There is nothing controversial in such a statement. This is simply a rhetorical point of emphasis. Gänswein is merely saying that the thought of abandoning the papal office, as if in some act of cowardice, or dereliction of duty, would be impossible for Benedict.

Consequently, instead of being an act of weakness, the archbishop portrays Benedict's resignation as an "extraordinary act of courage" which "renewed the office;" and with this "final effort he has strengthened it." Benedict strengthened the papacy by recognizing his lack of energy to fulfill the duties of his office, and accordingly, by stepping down from the throne of Peter to allow another to take his place.

Thus, in this vein, Gänswein says the role of "pope emeritus" has "renewed" the office. Benedict certainly appears to have had this in mind, setting a precedent for other enfeebled popes to follow. Thus, he set a precedent for style of dress (the wearing of a white cassock), a style of address ("pope emeritus" and "Your Holiness"), and even the example of not living in a secluded monastery.

Benedict is not like Pope Celestine V who resigned, hoping to become once again a hermit (but ended up locked away in prison). Rather, Benedict, in contrast, sets a new example as a former pope who will continue to pray for his "brothers and sisters," the Church, as his personal, spiritual mandate, mission, or ministry.

One need not agree with Gänswein's defense of Benedict on any of these points. We know the archbishop opposed the resignation of his friend, Pope Benedict XVI. We may not know Gänswein's true thoughts on the question beyond saying that in his speech at least, he tried to frame a *fait accompli* in a positive light, as something constructive for the Church.

Objection 5.6: Violation of law of non-contradiction

> If Pope Benedict's "resignation" was just like every previous Papal resignation, and "Pope Emeritus" is just a way of saying "resigned Pope", why is Pope Benedict XVI referred to by +Gänswein, with Pope Benedict's approval, as having created a "new institution" as "history's first Pope Emeritus?"
>
> How can Pope Benedict be simultaneously just exactly like all other resigned Popes, but at the same time "history's FIRST Pope Emeritus", "entirely different" from all previous Popes

that resigned, and that "to date there has never been a step taken like that of Benedict XVI"?

That is a stone-cold violation of the Law of Non-contradiction. Something can not BE and NOT BE at the same time. Pope Benedict cannot both be and not be the first "Pope Emeritus". Something cannot be both "entirely different" and "entirely the same" as something else. So, something MUST be wrong with the base premise, because the logical truth table here is yielding first-degree corollaries in violation the Second of the Three Laws of Thought.[252] [253]

Reply to Objection 5.6: The objector[254] has misstated the law of non-contradiction, or perhaps, we might say more charitably, she has stated it incompletely. The law of non-contradiction is *not* "something cannot be and not be at the same time." Rather, it is more properly put, "something cannot be and not be in the *same sense* at the *same time*." That is key to understanding the false contradictions found in the objection. The relevance of this we shall see shortly.

Having corrected the objector's error on this point, we can proceed to address the objection:

> How can Pope Benedict be simultaneously just exactly like all other resigned Popes, but at the same time "history's FIRST Pope Emeritus", "entirely different" from all previous Popes that resigned, and that "to date there has never been a step taken like that of Benedict XVI"?[255]

As noted above, Gänswein does explicitly say that Benedict "introduced into the Catholic Church the new institution of 'pope emeritus.'" What then about the objection?

As noted in the Reply to Objection 5.2, the title of *emeritus*, per Canon 185, "can be conferred upon the person who loses an office...by a resignation which has been accepted."[256] Granted, Canon 185 does not explicitly apply this to the context of the Roman Pontiff, as his is a resignation which is not accepted. However, as Benedict considered what title to use in his retirement, *emeritus* used an honorific for an "office lost by resignation" would make sense. Consequently, the honorific title *pope emeritus* refers to one who has lost the papal office due to resignation, i.e., meaning one is a *former* pope.

Thus, as to the title of *pope emeritus*, it is true to say Benedict is the first to use it, as the objector notes. So, in this sense, he is the first "pope emeritus." However, it is also true to say in another, *different sense* that Benedict was not the first *pope emeritus*. Recall Cardinal Brandmüller, who had publicly taken exception to Benedict's use of the title of "pope emeritus." Benedict responded to him as follows (italics added):

> In your recent interview with the FAZ [Frankfurter Allgemeine Zeitung] you say that I created, with the construction of the Pope Emeritus, a figure that does not exist in the entirety of Church history. Of course, you know very well that popes have retired, even if very rarely. *What were they afterwards? Pope Emeritus? Or what instead*?[257]

In context, Benedict is defending his use of pope emeritus. He takes issue with Brandmüller, who said *pope emeritus* did not exist in Church history. Benedict's implicit argument in his reply, whatever its merits, is that there have been other retired popes in history, like himself, and what were they, he asks, if not pope emeritus? That is to say, Benedict believed the previous retired popes were each a *pope emeritus* in fact, if not by title.

So, with respect to the principle of non-contradiction, Benedict is not the first *pope emeritus* even if he was the one who first introduced the title. That is, he only gave the name to the historical reality of a pope emeritus, i.e., a former, resigned pope. So, in one sense Benedict is the same as all other retired popes, but in another sense he is different in that he was the first to assume the honorific title.

Still, is there another, *different sense* wherein we might understand Benedict is the first *pope emeritus*? Well, it is clear he is the first to take the title, as noted above. However, beyond that, in the context of Gänswein's speech, which hearkens back to Benedict's last audience (see discussion in Chapter 3), Benedict is the first to speak of the bond of charity between him and the "sons and daughters" (i.e., the Church) he gained upon becoming pope, and that his decision to resign does not revoke this bond. His bond of charity persists, and because of it, Benedict believes himself to have a moral responsibility, a spiritual and "invisible"[258] mandate to continue in the service of prayer for the Church.

In the words of Gänswein, Benedict is to be a "power station" of prayer; which again hearkens back to the last audience where Benedict speaks of "remaining in the service of prayer." In this sense, Benedict is the first to put some thought into what a *pope emeritus* might constructively do for the Church and what a *pope emeritus* might be for the Church in retirement.

And, indeed, Benedict is the first to say so and do so. Here too, in one sense Benedict is the same as other retired popes but in this other sense, different. To underline this point, Gänswein points to the example of Pope Celestine V—who like Benedict is the only other pope to retire on his own, i.e., without doing so in response to some surrounding crisis, such as in the Great Schism. Speaking of Benedict, Gänswein notes in his speech:

> Since then, his role—allow me to repeat it once again—is entirely different from that, for example, of the holy Pope Celestine V, who after his resignation in 1294 would have liked to return to being a hermit, becoming instead a prisoner of his successor, Boniface VIII (to whom today in the Church we owe the establishment of jubilee years). To date, in fact, there has never been a step like that taken by Benedict XVI.[259]

Gänswein tells us his perspective as to why Benedict's role is unique in retirement. Whereas Celestine V wanted to resign in order to return to living as a hermit in seclusion, Benedict wanted to stay at the Vatican in the service of prayer for the whole Church. Again, in this sense, Benedict's decision is unique in terms of how he approaches his role as "pope emeritus"—and in this sense he is different from prior retired popes.

Consider how, in his interviews with Seewald, Benedict has spoken, certainly in his own case, of having a moral responsibility to resign the papacy when he no longer had the strength to fulfill its duties.

Finally, by his resignation Benedict clearly hoped to establish a precedent for future popes in yet another sense. He wanted to provide a positive example of how a former pope can continue to serve the Church through prayer rather than continuing on the papal throne in a weak and enfeebled state (think: John Paul II) when the Church might be better served by having a more energetic pope on the throne of Peter. Gänswein speaks of this move as an "extraordinary act of courage" which "renewed the office;" and with this "final effort he has strengthened it" [NB: This was addressed in more detail in the Reply to Objection 5.1]. Gänswein could only wonder if futures popes might follow Benedict's example in this regard.

In summary, there is no violation here of the law of non-contradiction: "something cannot be and not be in the *same sense* at the *same time*." Benedict can simultaneously be like all other retired popes, and yet the "first," and "entirely different" as well—if he is so in a *different sense*. Those different senses have been demonstrated in this reply.

Objection 5.7: Plain meaning of the words proves Benepapism

> Pope Benedict XVI himself made this perfectly clear in his "last audience" on 27 February, ARSH 2013, and it was reconfirmed WITH HIS APPROVAL on 20 May ARSH 2016 by his personal secretary (and incredibly suspicious character) Archbishop Georg Gänswein in a speech at the Pontifical Gregorian University in Rome laying out Pope Benedict's mindset vis-a-vis his failed partial-resignation. To deny the clarity of these words is FUNDAMENTALLY DISHONEST. As in, you have to LIE in order to argue that these words mean anything other than their plain meaning. In my experience, every person who has made this argument is FINANCIALLY DEPENDENT UPON THE INSTITUTIONAL CHURCH IDEOLOGY, be it for a salaried position, paid editorial writing gigs, a pension, or donations/blegging. To deny objective reality is pretty much the textbook definition of having no integrity.[260]

Reply to Objection 5.7: For the moment, let us set aside the suggestion Benedict gave his "approval" to Archbishop Gänswein's speech. This will be addressed in the Reply to Objection 5.8.

Setting aside also the *ad hominem*[261] aspects of the objection, the question is: have interpretations offered in rebuttal of the Benepapist case in this book been unfair to the "plain meaning" of either Benedict's last audience (see Chapter 3) or Gänswein's speech? I believe a brief review of the evidence demonstrates that it is the Benepapists who have misinterpreted the plain meaning of both Benedict and Gänswein.

Now, as to the question of "plain meaning," let us first consider Benedict's last audience. In the opening argument of Chapter 3, and in the replies to the objections therein, we saw that the Benepapists misinterpreted the meaning of the "always is also a forever." The Benepapists say this phrase speaks either of Benedict's belief that being elected pope leaves an indelible mark, like the sacrament of holy orders, or of Benedict intent to retain Petrine *munus*, and thus the papacy.

This is nonsense. Pope Benedict used both the "always" and the "forever" in the context of privacy. The "always" was used in the context of the loss of privacy upon one's election to the papacy. The "forever" was used in the context of "there can no longer be a return to the private sphere." Pope Benedict explicitly said his decision to resign did not revoke *this*. In context, and grammatically, the *this* refers to no longer being able to return to the private sphere.

What does Benedict mean when he speaks of "privacy?" Well, in his last audience, he told us. In defining his use of "always", Benedict explicitly said:

> Always—anyone who accepts the Petrine ministry no longer has any privacy. He belongs always and completely to everyone, to the whole Church. In a manner of speaking, the private dimension of his life is completely eliminated.[262]

By privacy, Benedict is speaking of belonging "always and completely to everyone, to the whole Church." Even though the private dimension of his life is destroyed, he goes on in the same paragraph to speak touchingly of *"one receives one's life precisely when one gives it away."* Benedict then says:

> [T]he Pope truly has brothers and sisters, sons and daughters, throughout the world, and that he feels secure in the embrace of your communion; because he no longer belongs to himself, he belongs to all and all belong to him.

Clearly, we see that Benedict is speaking of a bond of charity, a bond of love, between himself and his "brothers and sisters, sons and daughters." This is why he "no longer belongs to himself." We've seen this elsewhere in Benedict's writings, such as when as Archbishop Ratzinger he expressed similar sentiments in a homily about Pope Paul VI, saying "we can imagine how heavy the thought must be of *no longer belonging to ourselves*; *of no longer having a single private moment.*"

Consequently, it is clear that Benedict connects the loss of "privacy" to the responsibility of belonging to others, and not to oneself, i.e., a bond of charity, a bond of love. Thus, it is obvious what he meant when he said his resignation does not revoke this. Even though he has resigned, he will continue to love his "brothers and sisters, sons and daughters," the Church. This is the "plain meaning," and it should be clear to anyone who takes the time to read the full text rather than take snippets of it out of context.

Finally, with regard to "plain meaning," let us now consider Gänswein's speech. The Benepapist treatment of the speech is a shallow one, neglecting for example its context. Gänswein spoke at a presentation for a new book authored by Fr. Roberto Regoli on the pontificate of Benedict XVI. Gänswein, who is a close friend of Benedict, was bound to sing his praises in an almost panegyric fashion. Further, given the great disappointment there had been over the resignation, it should not be surprising that Gänswein made glowing remarks defending Benedict's decision to resign, and giving it meaning and a purpose.

In this chapter, we explored Gänswein's use of expressions such as "expanded ministry." However, Gänswein clearly is speaking of a "de facto" expanded ministry, not an officially expanded one. He calls it "quasi-shared." He is not speaking of an *actual* shared ministry. Indeed, when speaking of this "expanded ministry," Gänswein references Benedict's coat-of-arms bearing 3 John 1:8, which speaks of "fellow workers in the truth." Being a "fellow worker in the truth" does not mean having the *same* office, it does mean having the same goal. Gänswein is not speaking of Benedict actually still sharing the same *munus* or office as Francis. He is speaking in an extended or figurative sense. That this is the case can also be seen, as noted earlier in the chapter, when Gänswein speaks of Fr. Regoli and Peter Seewald as also participating in an "enlarged Petrine ministry." This is the "plain meaning."

Contrary to the assertions in the *ad hominem* infested objection, the Benepapists have not read the "plain meaning" out of Benedict's last audience or Gänswein's speech. The reality is the leading Benepapists have demonstrated they have misinterpreted the key texts upon which their theories rely. This is very evident with their treatment of the last audience and Gänswein's speech, as we have seen.

The simple truth is the Benepapists fail to seriously consider that a more innocent and natural reading of the texts, which takes each on its own merits, is, in fact, far more probable than their own. A natural reading—not viewed through the prism of personal agendas, or doubtful theories that Benedict held erroneous and or even heretical opinions about the papacy, or that he faked his resignation as part of some "master plan."

Unlike the Benepapist theory, the interpretation offered in this chapter is a natural and simpler one, which has the benefit of accounting for—and being consistent with—all the evidence.

Objection 5.8: BXVI edited and approved Gänswein's speech

> On February 27, 2013, Pope Benedict XVI clearly spoke about his erroneous, attempted partial resignation during his last general audience. Further, Benedict's meaning in the last audience "was reconfirmed with his approval"[263] of Gänswein's speech on May 20, 2016. Indeed, Gänswein's speech carries all the more weight because Benedict personally approved this

speech, and thus we know it is consistent with Benedict's thinking in his last speech.[264]

Reply to Objection 5.8: The objector[265] appears to have a source who says that Benedict personally approved Gänswein's speech.[266] The suggestion seems to be, because there is proof Benedict approved of Gänswein's speech beforehand, then one cannot deny that Gänswein's speech is a reflection of what Benedict actually thought.

Although the claim of having such a source is interesting, the reality is, even if true, it is irrelevant. That is, I do not wish to deny Gänswein's speech is reflective of what Benedict said in his last audience. Indeed, in this current chapter and in the replies to the objections, I have argued that Gänswein's does reflect the key themes found in Benedict's last audience. Therefore, given Benedict's last general audience does not support a case for Benepapism as argued in Chapter 3, neither does Gänswein's speech. Quite simply, Gänswein's speech, properly understood, does not support the Benepapist case.

Gänswein admits Benedict resigned, that he "left the papal throne," that his pontificate ended in 2013, that he no longer wears the Fisherman's ring, that there is only one pope, not two, that Francis is his "successor," etc. Further, we have also seen that supposed controversial expressions such as "expanded ministry," etc., can be interpreted in natural, and more innocent ways that are consistent with Benedict's thought in his last general audience, e.g., continuing in the "service of prayer" for the Church after his resignation.

The interpretations of the last audience and Gänswein's speech offered in this book are far more probable than those offered by the Benepapists. So, the question of whether Benedict directly approved of Gänswein's speech or not is irrelevant. As argued in Chapter 3, Benedict's last general audience is consistent with a valid resignation. So, whether Benedict approved Gänswein's speech or not, we have seen his speech is consistent with Benedict's last audience, and thus consistent with the case for a valid resignation.

Chapter 6: Summation

When beginning this book, the author set for himself the goal of making the case against the Benepapists, who hold the renunciation of Pope Benedict XVI to be invalid. This task was not undertaken lightly, as if it were some academic exercise without real world application.

Indeed, some Benepapists have decided they will act with or without the Catholic hierarchy. A group of Benepapists have launched a Declaration and Petition which declare their fidelity to Benedict as the still-reigning pope. They have declared they will not accept the results of the next conclave if it fails to meet certain conditions which they outline. To say such a declaration and action are imprudent would be a gross understatement. It is utter folly. If these Benepapists stay true to their stated intentions, they will end up as a new generation of sedevacantists. With this in mind, let us review the case against the Benepapists.

"The 'Always' Is Also a 'Forever'"

One of the key defects of the arguments offered by the arch-Benepapists is that their interpretations of key documents are frequently found to be suspect. That is not to say one should doubt the sincerity of their intent. However, there are multiple examples where leading Benepapists have either read their theories into the text, or where they seem incapable, even unwilling, to consider the possibility there might be other, less controversial, and indeed, more probable readings other than their own.

In Chapter 5, for example, we examined Archbishop Georg Gänswein's speech. Benepapists demand we must understand the archbishop to be speaking of a true, literal "expanded Petrine ministry." Aside from the fact the archbishop denies such a

SUMMATION

meaning,[267] the text of his speech does not speak of such a thing as a real institution. It is evident from the text that Gänswein was speaking in a figurative, extended sense. This can be seen, for example, when he spoke of men like Fr. Regoli and Peter Seewald, who have written about Pope Benedict XVI, as having entered *"into that enlarged Petrine ministry."*[268] Gänswein even said *"Regoli himself now also takes part in the munus Petri of which I spoke."*[269] Clearly, Gänswein has spoken in a figurative sense throughout the speech, but the Benepapists simply do not address this fact, or allow for a less controversial interpretation that is consistent with a valid resignation.

Then, there are the famous words from Benedict's last audience, *"the 'always' is also a 'forever.'"* This phrase has been pressed into the service of Benepapism (see discussion in *Chapter 3*). Perhaps no other single phrase in this entire controversy has been so egregiously misinterpreted and misrepresented.

The Benepapists have warped these words to make it seem Pope Benedict XVI was saying one of two things. Either, that he would always bear the indelible mark of the papacy "forever" in some way even after his resignation, or that he intended to retain the Petrine *munus* "forever"—and thus would remain the one and only pope until his death.

However, such interpretations do not stand up to scrutiny. When examining the last audience in full context, it becomes clear that Benedict used the "always" in reference to the "loss of privacy," and "belonging to others" and "others belonging to him" upon being elected pope. Benedict explicitly made this clear himself (italics added):

> Here, allow me to go back once again to 19 April 2005. The real gravity of the decision was also due to the fact that from that moment on I was engaged *always and forever* by the Lord. *Always—anyone who accepts the Petrine ministry no longer has any privacy. He belongs always and completely to everyone, to the whole Church.*[270]

This theme of a papal "loss of privacy" and of "belonging to others" was also used by Benedict XVI when, as Cardinal

Ratzinger in 1978, he gave a homily on Pope Paul VI soon after his death. It is clear Pope Benedict XVI, and earlier as Cardinal Ratzinger, was speaking of a mutual *bond of charity* between the pope and his sons and daughters, the Church. There can be no doubt about it. Given Benedict defines what he means earlier in the text, we can understand what he means when he says a bit further on:

> *The "always" is also a "for ever"—there can no longer be a return to the private sphere. My decision to resign the active exercise of the ministry does not revoke this.*

The "forever" has reference to there "no longer being a return to the private sphere." Benedict already told us of the "loss of privacy" on becoming pope by which he came to "belong" to his "sons and daughters" in the Church, and they to him. He is speaking of a mutual *bond of charity*. Nothing more.

When he says his resignation "does not revoke this," the *this* both grammatically and logically refers back to there "no longer being a return to the private sphere." He is saying his resignation does not revoke the mutual bond of charity with the "sons and daughters" he has gained upon becoming pope. Thus, as he explains further on, he will continue to pray for the Church when he is no longer pope. It is unfortunate that Benedict's beautiful reflection on his love for his "sons and daughters" has been so abused by the Benepapists, who have sought to stuff their theories into the text.

Benedict XVI: Theological Fool or Strategic Genius?

Benepapist theories are ultimately based on fantastical assumptions. These assumptions, as argued in this book, and seen in the example above, are read into key texts which then, not surprisingly, yield back confirmation of the same, original assumptions. Some arch-Benepapists claim Benedict held erroneous opinions about the nature of the papacy. Others suggest Pope Benedict XVI was something of a strategic genius, executing a master plan by which he willfully fooled the world into thinking

SUMMATION

he had resigned his papal office when he really had not. Let us briefly review the two main theories.

The first of these two theories holds that Benedict committed a "substantial error" whereby his renunciation was invalidated per Canon 188. It is alleged Benedict held erroneous views of the papacy. For example, it is suggested that he believed that he could *partially* resign the papacy, perhaps to create a papal "diarchy" of sort, or a two-member "synodal papacy." Another related theory is that Benedict had an erroneous view of the Petrine *munus*. Rather than properly thinking of the papal *munus* as a jurisdictional office that could be renounced, some Benepapists say Benedict erroneously believed it to be a sacramental *munus* that he would still retain in some way even if he resigned.

Unfortunately for the Benepapists, they have no proof that withstands close scrutiny. We already reviewed examples of their forced interpretations of Benedict's last audience and Gänswein's speech. In addition, as seen in Chapter 1, Benepapists offered as proof the *Miller Dissertation*, but this document offered no evidence of Ratzinger himself proposing any errors regarding the papacy. None. Similarly, a paper authored by Cardinal Ratzinger, *The Primacy of the Pope and the unity of the People of God*, was offered as evidence he held erroneous views of the papacy. However, the text clearly showed Benedict was commenting on the views of others, rather than proposing his agreement with them.

Another Benepapist cited portions of two of Ratzinger's books to attempt to prove Ratzinger held an erroneous view of the Petrine *munus*. However, as demonstrated in Chapter 1, Ratzinger's original text in *Principles of Catholic Theology* was inaccurately paraphrased. For example, it was claimed Ratzinger said he "disagreed with those who say the papacy is not a sacrament." However, Ratzinger said no such thing in the text, either explicitly or implicitly. Rather, Ratzinger was speaking in the context of providing the Orthodox Church's perspective that the West had an exaggerated view of the papacy, and thus *they* chastise the Church in the West by declaring the "papacy is not a sacrament." Benedict was not arguing it is a sacrament!

Further, the same Benepapist cited another work of Ratzinger, *Theological Highlights of Vatican II*, quoting him to say in effect "*The ministry of the bishop is not an externally assigned 'administrative power' but...is itself sacramentally-based.*" Yet, the full, immediate quote from the book is as follows, with omitted sentence added back in italics:

> The ministry of the bishop is not an externally assigned "administrative power," *but rather arises from the necessary plurality of the eucharistic communities (i.e., of the Churches in the Church) and, as representing these,* is itself sacramentally based. The ruling of the Church and its spiritual mystery are inseparable.[271]

Again, a review of the full context does not support the ultimate thesis that Benedict believed the papacy was a sacrament, or a higher level of holy orders. Furthermore, there is nothing here to suggest the pope cannot really and fully resign the papal *munus*. That is, there is nothing here to suggest the *munus* or office cannot be lost.

Rather, Ratzinger would more likely say that given the "ruling" power "*necessarily arises*" from a bishop "*representing*" a eucharistic community (i.e., a local Church); and given that "*in the eucharistic office, both the sacrament and the 'ruling power' interpenetrate one another*"; if a bishop should cease being over that eucharistic community as its head, he would lose his "ruling power" over that local Church (i.e., there would no longer be an interpenetration of the "ruling power"). Regardless, there is nothing here that demonstrates Benedict believed the papacy was a sacrament, as if it were the next level of holy orders. Indeed, Lumen Gentium 21 explicitly teaches episcopal consecration confers the fullness of the sacrament of Holy Orders.[272] There is no evidence Josef Ratzinger as a theologian embraced heresy by rejecting this teaching by holding the fullness of Orders is conferred upon papal election.

The argument that suggests Benedict wrongly believed he could maintain the Petrine *munus* after his resignation is a bit unique. Here, the Benepapist claims Benedict would not have

SUMMATION

resigned if he had known his view was in error, and that *this* was his "substantial error." However, this is mind reading, only pure speculation as to what Benedict believed and what he would or would not do.[273]

The reality is we know why Benedict resigned. He told us. He said he resigned due to weakness and lack of strength. Furthermore, in a Seewald interview before his resignation, Benedict stated that if he ever got to such a point of weakness, then he would have a moral obligation to resign.[274] Thus, given he resigned out of a moral obligation, what he believed as to whether he might or might not retain the Petrine *munus* is at best, then, a moot point. That is, under a moral obligation he had to resign regardless. Thus, even under this Benepapist theory, the resignation would necessarily be valid.

The premise of the "substantial error" thesis is a curious one. In their attempt to save the Church from one erroneous pope, the Benepapists would only give it back another erroneous pope. If Benedict's understanding of the *munus* was so warped, then it would seem there is the *reductio ad absurdum* that we could never be sure if he really resigned, even if he had used the word "*munus*" as demanded by some Benepapists. Moreover, we might wonder if Benedict's understanding of the papacy was so erroneous that we could never be sure he had properly resigned from it, should we then wonder too whether his acceptance of his election was valid, if he never properly understood what it was he had accepted?

The truth of the matter is, though, the arch-Benepapists have not produced evidence to demonstrate Benedict held erroneous views of the papacy as a theologian before his election. Yet, even setting that aside, they have failed to demonstrate he held such opinions *after* his election, or that any such alleged error impacted the validity of his resignation. The Benepapists do not have grounds to allege a "substantial error" on Benedict's part. If there is any "substantial error," it is the Benepapists who have committed it.

Having considered the "substantial error" branch of Benepapism, let us look at the so-called *Plan B* theory. Benepapists who accept the *Plan B* theory reject the notion

Benedict committed any "substantial error." Rather, they believe Benedict, essentially, sabotaged his own renunciation by willfully using the word *ministerium* instead of *munus* in his *Declaratio*. He did this for the purpose of retaining the papal *munus*, the papal office, for himself. Thus, per this theory, Benedict's resignation of the "exercise" of the papacy was canonically and juridically meaningless.

So, in essence, Pope Benedict XVI essentially fooled the Church and the world into thinking he had resigned the papacy, when in fact he retained it. The claim that he, at most, gave up the exercise of the papal office was addressed earlier in this chapter, and in Chapter 1, and will be touched on later in this chapter.

The underlying premise of the *Plan B* theory is that Pope Benedict XVI *willfully* resigned in such a manner that his renunciation would be null and void with respect to the papal office. These Benepapists claim the null resignation was part of some sort of master strategy to keep the papacy out of the hands of antichristic modernists.

Per this theory, Benedict may have fooled the modernists, but he would have also fooled the entire Catholic world—that is, except for those Catholics who claim to understand the cryptic language by which Benedict communicates he is still pope. This supposed cryptic language or code used by Benedict for this purpose is called by some the *Ratzinger Code*.[275]

In Chapter 4, we examined this ludicrous concept of a "Ratzinger Code," and an example of how it was used to muddle Benedict's clear words on February 28, 2013 when he proclaimed that "*I am no longer the Supreme Pontiff of the Catholic Church, or I will be until 8:00 this evening and then no longer.*" The attempt to create a false distinction between *Sommo Pontefice* and *Pontefice Sommo* was demonstrated to be specious nonsense through multiple examples of the latter, some of them from the *Acta Apostolicae Sedis*. The absurd application of the "Ratzinger Code" to this key text certainly proves the adage, *falsus in uno, falsus in omnibus*. This idea that there is a *Ratzinger Code* that only a select group of the true faithful have discerned, and by which they can decode Benedict's supposed hidden strategy and message is gnostic nonsense.

SUMMATION

Beyond the nonsense of the Ratzinger Code, it is inescapable that the *Plan B* theory would make Benedict into a liar and a fraud, for faking his resignation and misleading a billion Catholics, and indeed the whole world. Even worse, Benedict would have to be a true, amoral monster.

Consider the implications of the theory. Having willfully submitted a null and void resignation, Benedict would have known that the conclave of 2013 was invalid. Thus, he would have known most of the Catholic world would have accepted an anti-pope, a false pope, as a true pope. He would have known much of the Catholic world might potentially be led astray by an antichristic modernist pope.

Essentially, the *Plan B* theory asks one to believe the absurdity that Benedict essentially decided it was better to pretend not to be pope, than to actually be pope and do what a pope should do, i.e., to feed and protect the Lord's flock (cf. Jn 21:15-17). As stated previously in this book, a pope can do more good for the Lord's flock by *being* the shepherd and *doing* precisely what the Lord commanded, rather than pretending not to be that shepherd. Thus, it stretches credulity to the breaking point to ask anyone to accept that Benedict believed that giving up the power to exercise the papacy, or pretending to, is a better course of action than to actually exercise one's Petrine authority to save the Church. This, of course, is nonsense. Lest you think this assessment unnecessarily harsh, I am not alone in making it.

A civil war of a sort has broken out in recent months among some of the arch-Benepapists, between those advocating the "substantial error" theory and those advocating the Plan B/Ratzinger Code theory.[276] For example, one arch-Benepapist behind the "substantial error" theory described the *Plan B* and *Ratzinger Code* theory as "deluded"[277] and "categorical nonsense."[278] A leading arch-Benepapist supporting the *Plan B* theory called the "substantial error" theory "absurd."[279]

It is quite remarkable that the same set of facts has resulted in two opposing, irreconcilable theories wherein Benedict is either a theological fool or a master strategist. However, in truth, these opposing arguments are two halves of one, combined, invincible argument which lays bare the utter absurdity of the whole Benepapist enterprise.

A "Pope Emeritus" Wearing White?

Whether Benedict XVI handled the externals of his resignation wisely or not may be the subject for honest debate. Might it have been more prudent to return to being called Cardinal Ratzinger? Was it prudent to keep wearing white, and to continue living on Vatican grounds? Undoubtedly, seeing two men dressed in white within the Vatican, with one called pope and the other "pope emeritus," has been a cause for confusion for some Catholics. Perhaps in the future, should we have another pope emeritus, it might be best that he live out the remainder of his years in some remote monastery. There, access to him would be limited and even restricted, given the obvious potential for confusion and mischief.

However, the wisdom of Benedict XVI's choices aside, do these "externals" demonstrate that he thinks himself pope as the Benepapists say? Let us briefly consider some of them.

While the Benepapists make much of Benedict still wearing white, they neglect the fact he did change his attire from when he was pope. For example, Benedict now wears a simple cassock. Benedict no longer wears the *mozzetta*, or red shoes, as he did before his resignation. Both of these were signs of authority.

Furthermore, Benedict no longer wears the Fisherman's ring, which he received in the mass inaugurating his papacy. As to Benedict having given an apostolic blessing on a couple of occasions, this does not prove he still believes himself pope. Others can give apostolic blessings[280] and this authority can be delegated by a pope.[281]

The title of *pope emeritus* is new. However, in deciding upon *emeritus* as a post resignation honorific, Benedict certainly could look to Canon 185. This canon says that one who loses an office due to resignation can adopt the honorific of emeritus. Thus, the use of *emeritus* emphasizes the fact that the one bearing the title no longer holds the office. For example, in common conversation, one may speak of a "professor emeritus," who is one who is no longer a professor.[282] The use of pope *emeritus* is therefore an obvious admission by Benedict that he no longer holds the office of the papacy. That is why, in his correspondence with Cardinal Brandmüller, Benedict implicitly argued that previous resigned popes were *emeritus* in fact, if not in name.

If the Roman Pontiff Renounces His Office (*Munus*)....

Ultimately, of course, the dispute over whether Pope Benedict XVI validly resigned comes down to his *Declaratio* wherein he declares:

> For this reason, and well aware of the seriousness of this act, with full freedom I declare that I renounce the ministry (*ministerio*) of Bishop of Rome, Successor of Saint Peter, entrusted to me by the Cardinals on 19 April 2005, in such a way, that as from 28 February 2013, at 20:00 hours, the See of Rome, the See of Saint Peter, will be vacant and a Conclave to elect the new Supreme Pontiff will have to be convoked by those whose competence it is.[283]

Pope Benedict XVI declares clearly that he resigned the "*ministry of the bishop of Rome...in such a way*" that the "*See of Rome, the See of Saint Peter*" would be "vacant" and a Conclave would be needed to elect a "new Supreme Pontiff." Reading this, it is clear what Pope Benedict XVI intended. If the "See of Rome, the See of Saint Peter" is vacant, then obviously, there is no pope. Pope Benedict XVI would no longer be pope. Further, this truth is underlined by the fact he calls for a conclave to elect a *new Supreme Pontiff*; not an additional Supreme Pontiff to himself, but a new one.

Despite the obvious import of this declaration, objections have been raised as to its meaning, centered on Canon 332§2 which governs papal renunciations. The canon reads:

> If it should happen that the Roman Pontiff resigns his office [*munus*], it is required for validity that he makes the resignation freely and that it be duly manifested, but not that it be accepted by anyone.[284]

VALID? THE RESIGNATION OF POPE BENEDICT XVI

The Benepapists protest that Benedict, in the Latin, had renounced the *ministerio* and not the *munus*. The *munus* refers to the office, say the Benepapists, and the *ministerium* refers to the active *exercise* of it. Those who believe in the "substantial error" theory generally claim the word *munus* must be explicitly used because of Canon 332§2.

However, the Benepapists are mistaken on the necessity of the word *munus*. Contrary to their argument, Canon 332§2 clearly states there are only two specific requirements for a valid renunciation. The first is that the renunciation must be made freely, and the second that it be properly manifested. The use of *munus* is simply not said to be a requirement.

So, the truth is, there is no formula for papal renunciations in current canon law. For that matter, the history of the papal teaching and early canon law both address the question of papal resignations. The papal teaching declared a pope may resign the "*papacy,*" and subsequently the canon said that the "*Roman pontiff may resign freely.*"[285] Thus, by common sense, the explicit word *munus* is not required. Any word or words that sufficiently convey the meaning that the reigning pontiff resigns the *papacy* will suffice.

On the other hand, Benepapists of the *Plan B* variety generally do not assert the word *munus* must be used explicitly. They only claim a suitable synonym for *munus* must be used, which *ministerium*, for them, is not. They argue that *ministerium* does not suffice, as they restrict its meaning here to the *exercise* of the office, and not the *office* itself.

Yet, even if we accept, arguendo, that Benedict renounced the "active exercise" of the papacy through the use of *ministerium*, the Benepapist argument would still fail. As Fr. Rickert argued (see Chapter 1):

> If a pope renounces the administration of his office, he necessarily renounces the office itself, because the office *per se* (*vi muneris*)[286] entails the right to act. Thus, Pope Benedict's renunciation of his administration entails renunciation of the papal office. That is why he goes on to express the results, which

SUMMATION

he is clearly cognizant of: the Chair of St. Peter will be vacant, and a new pope must be elected.[287]

Even though Fr. Rickert's answer above is, in itself, a sufficient one, the truth is that *ministerium* is a synonym for *munus*. The Benepapists want a clear distinction in the meanings of *munus* and *ministerium*. However, in Chapter 1, we cited Fr. John Rickert, FSSP, Ph.D. who wrote the *"distinction attempted is not based on a correct interpretation of the words."*[288] Fr. Rickert pointed to *A Latin Dictionary* by Lewis and Short which explicitly lists *ministerium* and *munus* as synonyms.[289] Furthermore, if one consults *The Dictionary of Ecclesiastical Latin* by Leo F. Stelten one finds overlapping definitions of the two words.[290] For example, both can mean *duty* and *office*.

Furthermore, it may be observed, as also shown in Chapter 1, that *Lumen Gentium* 20 clearly states that *"among these ministries (ministerio)"* the *"chief place belongs to the office (munus) of those"* appointed to the episcopate. Therefore, the text states the office or *munus* of the bishop is a ministry or *ministerio,* for it is "among these ministries." Put another way, *Lumen Gentium* 20 states an *office (munus)* is a ministry *(ministerio)*. It is indisputable that the Church has used the terms synonymously.[291] Thus, because a *munus* is a ministry; if one resigns the Petrine *ministry*, one is, therefore, *necessarily* resigning the Petrine *munus*.

In addition, in place of the old coronation mass to inaugurate a papacy, the mass to mark Benedict XVI's assumption of the papacy was called, in Latin, *"Sollemne Initium Ministerii Summi Eccelesiae Pastoris,"*[292] or the "solemn commencement of the ministry of the supreme pastor of the church." During inauguration masses, the popes receive the pallium and the Fisherman's ring which signify the office. At the mass inaugurating his Petrine ministry, Pope John Paul I speaks of the "solemn beginning of the ministry" (*ministerii*) of the Supreme Pastor of the Church being placed upon his shoulders.[293] Here he uses a form of *ministerium*. Clearly, the context of the mass, in place of the older mass of coronation, and John Paul I's words in Latin demonstrate that the papacy is the object.

VALID? THE RESIGNATION OF POPE BENEDICT XVI

Soon after his election, Pope Benedict XVI in a homily during a mass in the Sistine Chapel repeatedly used *ministerium* in a reflection on his election.[294] Pope Benedict, in Latin, spoke of *"The Eucharist, the heart of Christian life and the source of the good news of the Church, is an essential, permanent and central part of the Petrine ministry (ministerii) entrusted to us."*[295]

Here Benedict speaks of the Petrine ministry "entrusted" to him. In his *Declaratio*, he uses similar language when he resigned: "I renounce the ministry (*ministerio*) of Bishop of Rome, Successor of Saint Peter, *entrusted to me* by the Cardinals."[296] Thus, Benedict is speaking of his election as Supreme Pontiff because that is what the cardinals entrusted him with, i.e., the papacy. Consequently, it should not be surprising that the use of *ministerium* by Pope Benedict XVI to mark the beginning of his papacy was also used when he renounced it.

Valid as these arguments are, there is an even more devastating one to the Benepapist case which was raised by Fr. Rickert (see Chapter 1). The title of Pope Benedict XVI's *Declaratio* that was entered into the *Acta Apostolicae Sedis,* as noted in Fr. Rickert's argument, reads:

> *Declaratio Summi Pontificis De Muneris Episcopi Romae, Successoris Sancti Petri Abdicatione.*[297]

The *Acta Apostolicae Sedis* is the official record of the Holy See. The Latin title for Benedict's renunciation document above may be translated as follows:

> *Declaration of the Supreme Pontiff on the abdication of the office (munus) of the Bishop Rome, Successor of Saint Peter.*

A few things should be evident from this title. First, the title says the Declaration regards the abdication of the *muneris*, which is the proper form of *munus* to use here.[298] Thus, it is evident that the object of the declaration is in fact the renunciation of the Petrine *munus*. Thus, for those Benepapists who erroneously insist the word *munus* must be used, they should note that it was used in the official record of the Holy See.

SUMMATION

Secondly, the title explicitly informs the reader how the text of the declaration below is to be understood. That is to say, Benedict's words "*I declare that I renounce the ministry (ministerio) of Bishop of Rome, Successor of Saint Peter*" must necessarily, and *definitively* be understood as being synonymous with the document's title. Again, that title may be translated as follows: *Declaration of Supreme Pontiff on the abdication of the office (munus) of the Bishop Rome, Successor of Saint Peter*.

There is no doubt that *ministerium* is a synonym for *munus*. However, the naysayers who proclaimed it could not be in the case of a papal resignation are proven wrong. The title explains the meaning of the text. There can be no real doubt. Pope Benedict XVI did, in fact, renounce the papacy.

That the Renunciation Be Freely Made...

With regard to whether Pope Benedict XVI resigned the papacy under duress, no evidence has been brought forward that demonstrates his renunciation was not freely made. While we do know the group of cardinals and bishops known as the St. Gallen mafia opposed Cardinal Ratzinger and his election, there is no firm, convincing, and definitive proof coercion played a role in his resignation.

We do know that Benedict had relayed to others his decision to resign at some point in the summer of 2012.[299] These individuals included Cardinal Bertone, and Benedict's personal secretary, Archbishop Georg Gänswein. None of these men have given any indication that Benedict's real reason for renouncing the papacy was other than what he announced publicly, i.e., weakness and lack of strength.

Despite speculations to the contrary, the evidence supports the case the resignation was offered freely. For one, most obviously, Pope Benedict XVI said it was freely made in his *Declaratio*. Benedict also said as much in his interviews with Peter Seewald. For example, in his discussion of the Vatileaks scandal, it is clear Benedict was cognizant of the fact that he could not validly resign under pressure.[300] That is why, according to Benedict, he deferred his resignation until the Vatileaks controversy had reached a resolution in October 2012 following the completion of the trial.[301] Thus, it is clear that Benedict did not act in the belief he was being forced out of his papal office.

Ultimately, the suggestion Benedict was forced out simply does not correspond with the observable facts. Over the last nine years, the former pope has received guests, been interviewed, and even co-authored a book. There have been no suggestions by any who have visited him, or talked with him, to my knowledge, that Benedict has given any indication he had been coerced to leave office, or that he was somehow imprisoned, or still living under a threat.

Consequently, given the evidence his resignation was free, and absent any demonstrable proof to the contrary, it is unreasonable to say his resignation must be rejected on this ground.

The claim Benedict was forced to resign is unfortunate, as it implicitly impugns the character of the pope. The claim makes this holy man who devoted most of his life to the Church into a coward.

That the Renunciation Be Duly Manifested...

We move on to now consider whether Benedict's renunciation was *duly manifested* as required by Canon 332§2. While Canon 332§2 does not specify a precise meaning of what makes a renunciation "duly manifested," there can be no real doubt that Pope Benedict XVI's renunciation met this requirement.

Benedict drafted a written declaration of his renunciation, dated February 10, 2013. Pope Benedict XVI read this declaration before a consistory of cardinals. This reading of the *Declaratio* was captured on video. What's more, and perhaps most decisively, as indicated earlier in this chapter, Benedict's *Declaratio* was published in the *Acta Apostolicae Sedis*, the official record of the Holy See.

If the above is not sufficient to be counted as "duly manifested," it is hard to imagine what might be lacking. Consequently, there are no reasonable grounds to doubt Benedict's renunciation was *duly manifested*.

SUMMATION
Not That It Be Accepted by Anyone

Canon 332§2 says of a papal renunciation that it is required that it be freely made and duly manifested, but *"not that it be accepted by anyone."*[302] Yet, the arch-Benepapists are, in an act of sheer hubris, violating the very canon to which they pretend to give lip service.

The canon explicitly says the renunciation is not required to be "accepted by anyone." However, by definitively rejecting the renunciation, the arch-Benepapists are attempting to usurp a role and authority that is explicitly not granted by the canon to them or to anyone else.

The arch-Benepapists have ignored the maxim, *supra papas omnes canones.*[303] It is the pope, not they, who are over the canons. They have declared the resignation invalid, even though papal acts must be presumed valid, reflecting the authority and will of the Supreme Legislator in the Church on earth, the pope.

Clearly, Benedict does not believe himself to be pope, as it is evident Benedict is not behaving as someone who still believes himself to be pope. Further, he has called any doubts about the validity of his resignation "absurd."[304] Still, even if one were to entertain the thought or hypothesis that there might be a question on the matter, any judgment on the question can only come from a future pope.

Concluding Remarks

To be clear, this book is not intended as a defense of the course of events in the Church after 8 p.m. on February 28, 2013. The author has no desire to offer any such defense. Indeed, as outlined in the Introduction, the author shares the concerns of many Catholics regarding the current crisis in the Church.

It is natural and perhaps inevitable that Catholics would wonder about the state of the Church in such times as ours, and would attempt to either fit a theory that both explains what has happened, or suggest a course of action to deal with the crisis. Indeed, various theories and or courses of action have been suggested, such as the Open Letter,[305] and a "formal correction."[306]

VALID? THE RESIGNATION OF POPE BENEDICT XVI

Without professing any opinion on how all this will end, there is one thing of which we can be certain. A resolution to this crisis will come in time—perhaps not in our time, but certainly in the Lord's time. As recalled in the Introduction of this book, the case of Pope Honorius was not ultimately decided until some forty years after his death by Pope St. Leo II.[307] Furthermore, such an example, and others like it, should be a healthy reminder for Catholics that the ultimate authority within the Church to judge such matters rests with the pope. Thus, what the Church needs is prayer, patience, and prudence.

While the search for a credible theory and solution may be understandable and even necessary, any ultimate theory must stand on its own legs. Wishing and wanting a particular theory to be true because it seemingly provides an easy out does not suffice to make it true. A bad theory is no substitute for a good one. Benepapism is a bad theory that only provides a facile solution; one which, as argued in this work, does not withstand close scrutiny.

The Benepapists promised proof of Benedict's erroneous views of the papacy. The evidence shows they have failed. Benepapist interpretations of key documents are demonstrably suspect. The Benepapists have ignored and excluded key documents, such as *Normas Nonnullas*, in their analysis, which torpedoes their arguments suggesting Benedict intended to establish some new form of a papacy in his resignation. Benepapists claim the word *munus* must be used. This was proven wrong. Canon law requires no formula. The *Liber Sextus* shows that other words might be used. Benepapists deny *munus* is a synonym of *ministerium*. They were proven wrong via various sources. Benepapists claim Benedict intended to resign only the "active ministry" of the papacy. However, even assuming, arguendo, this was the case, it was demonstrated that by giving up the "active ministry" one would still be resigning the entire papacy. The Benepapists claim Benedict willfully submitted a null and void resignation. The claim was demonstrated to be patently absurd, as it would make Benedict a liar, a fraud, and a monster. The Benepapists claim there is a *Ratzinger Code* by which the faithful few can understand

SUMMATION

that Benedict communicates to us that he is still pope. This claim is was demonstrated to be gnostic nonsense.

Thus, whatever the ultimate resolution to the current crisis in the Church may be, it will not be found in Benepapism. Benepapism should be rejected with extreme prejudice as it tends towards schism and sedevacantism, and will certainly result in one or both on its present course. That is where the arch-Benepapists are leading their followers. No Catholic should follow them.

Unlike the Benepapist arguments, the case for the validity of Pope Benedict XVI's resignation is consistent with all the evidence. It does not exclude key documents. It does not rely on forced interpretations. It does not restrict the meaning of words, which otherwise explode one's pet theory. It does not require one to believe Benedict was in error, or even heretical in his views regarding the nature of papacy. It does not make Benedict a liar, a fraud, or a monster.

On February 11, 2013, Pope Benedict XVI declared the following:

> I declare that I renounce the ministry of Bishop of Rome, Successor of Saint Peter, entrusted to me by the Cardinals on 19 April 2005, in such a way, that as from 28 February 2013, at 20:00 hours, the See of Rome, the See of Saint Peter, will be vacant and a Conclave to elect the new Supreme Pontiff will have to be convoked by those whose competence it is.

If the *See of Rome, the See of Peter* is vacant, then there is no pope. If in such an instance a conclave is necessary, then there is no pope. This is inescapable. Furthermore, *ministerium* is a suitable word to use when renouncing the papacy. This is certainly demonstrated by the title of the *Declaratio* in the *Acta Apostolicae Sedis*, the official record of the Holy See, which reads: *Declaration of the Supreme Pontiff on the abdication of the office (munus) of the Bishop Rome, Successor of Saint Peter.*

On February 22, 2013, Pope Benedict XVI issued the *motu proprio, Normas Nonnullas*, which amended some of the existing rules for papal conclaves. None of these amendments were consistent with any theory that Benedict intended to create a papal "diarchy," a "synodal papacy," or to separate the Petrine ministry from the See of Rome. These amendments were consistent with existing conclave rules. Thus, Benedict understood his immediate Successor would be the *Supreme Pontiff* (*Normas Nonnullas* 87), elected by the conclave necessitated by his resignation, who would *immediately* be the *Bishop of Rome*, and *true pope*; thereby receiving *full* and *supreme* power over the universal Church. Moreover, these considerations, plus the timing of the *Normas Nonnullas*, just days before the effective date of his resignation, constitute a proof Benedict knew he would be giving up the *entire* papacy, while retaining none of it.

On February 27, 2013, Pope Benedict XVI held his last general audience. In it, Benedict spoke of his *bond of charity* with the faithful, and how his resignation would *not revoke this*. Thus, Benedict said that even though he no longer bears the "*power of governance of the Church*," he would continue on in the "*service of prayer*" for the Church.

On February 28, 2013, shortly before the effective hour of his resignation stated in the *Declaratio*, Pope Benedict XVI publicly affirmed "*I will no longer be the Supreme Pontiff of the Catholic Church*" as of that hour.

Therefore, in light of the above, and the other evidence considered in this work, and in light of the insufficiency of the evidence presented to the contrary, not only is it more probable than not, but it is clearly the case that Pope Benedict XVI's renunciation of the papacy was valid.

Bibliography and Works Referenced

Acosta, Estefania, "Adversus Fallacies: A Reply in Defense of the Book 'Benedict XVI: Pope "Emeritus?"'", Katejon.com.br, May 13, 2021. https://katejon.com.br/wordpress/wp-content/uploads/2021/05/reply_complete-blqd.pdf

Acosta, Estefania, *Benedict XVI Pope "Emeritus"? "The 'always' is also a 'forever'",* Independently published, 2021.

Acosta, Estefania, "His Holiness Benedict XVI's Declaratio and the Myth of 'Substantial Error:' Part I", Patrick Coffin Media. (www.PatrickCoffin.media), https://www.patrickcoffin.media/his-holiness-benedict-xvis-declaratio-and-the-myth-of-substantial-error-part-i/

Acosta, Estefania, "His Holiness Benedict XVI's Declaratio and the Myth of 'Substantial Error:' Part II", Patrick Coffin Media. (www.PatrickCoffin.media), https://www.patrickcoffin.media/his-holiness-benedict-xvis-declaratio-and-the-myth-of-substantial-error-part-ii/

ATM Marketplace, "Bank of Italy shuts down Vatican ATMs over AML issues," ATM Marketplace, January 7, 2013. https://www.atmmarketplace.com/news/bank-of-italy-shuts-down-vatican-atms-over-aml-issues/

Arendzen, J. (1909). Gnosticism. In *The Catholic Encyclopedia.* New York: Robert Appleton Company. Retrieved July 8, 2022 from New Advent. http://www.newadvent.org/cathen/06592a.htm

Barnhardt, Ann, "Breaking: Pope Benedict's personal secretary, Archbishop Gänswein sobbing repeatedly when talking about the

VALID? THE RESIGNATION OF POPE BENEDICT XVI failed attempted resignation. NOTHING TO SEE HERE.", Barnhardt.biz, June 19, 2022. https://www.barnhardt.biz/2022/06/19/breaking-pope-benedicts-personal-secretary-archbishop-ganswein-sobbing-repeatedly-when-talking-about-the-failed-attempted-resignation-nothing-to-see-here/

Barnhardt, Ann, "If Pope Benedict is the first-ever 'Pope Emeritus', doesn't that mean that his ontological state is DIFFERENT from the Popes who actually resigned?", Barnhardt.biz, May 1, 2022. https://www.barnhardt.biz/2018/12/10/if-pope-benedict-is-the-first-ever-pope-emeritus-doesnt-that-mean-that-his-ontological-state-is-different-from-the-popes-who-actually-resigned/

Barnhardt, Ann, "NonVeni Crosspost: Jesus doesn't require any 'secret codes' for men to be saved. The Church is VISIBLE, including at her Earthly Head," Barnhardt.biz, May 23, 2022. https://www.barnhardt.biz/2022/05/23/nonveni-crosspost-jesus-doesnt-require-any-secret-codes-for-men-to-be-saved-the-church-is-visible-including-at-her-earthly-head/

Barnhardt, Ann, "The Papacy Is…," Barnhardt.biz, May 25, 2022. https://www.barnhardt.biz/2022/05/25/the-papacy-is/

Barnhardt, Ann, "REPOST BY REQUEST: The Mountain of Evidence that Pope Benedict never validly resigned is like Kilauea – it just keeps spewing truth magma," Barnhart.biz, April 11, 2021. https://www.barnhardt.biz/2021/04/11/eight-years-ago-today-in-a-packed-piazza-san-pietro-pope-benedict-made-it-clear-that-he-was-not-validly-resigning-the-papacy/

Barnhardt, Ann, "Speech edited and approved by Pope Benedict and delivered by his Personal Secretary Archbishop Georg Gänswein on May 20, ARSH 2016 – the full text. JUST READ IT", Barnhardt.biz, May 29, 2022. https://www.barnhardt.biz/2022/05/29/speech-edited-and-approved-by-pope-benedict-and-delivered-by-his-personal-secretary-archbishop-georg-ganswein-on-may-20-arsh-2016-the-full-text-just-read-it/

BIBLIOGRAPHY and WORKS REFERENCED

Barnhardt, Ann, "Thermonuclear Substantial Error...", Barnhardt.biz, January 13, 2019. https://www.barnhardt.biz/2019/01/13/thermonuclear-substantial-error-in-1978-joseph-ratzinger-posited-that-a-monarchical-papacy-was-intrinsically-arian-in-nature-and-the-papacy-should-reflect-the-trinity-a-p/

Barreiro, Msgr. Ignacio; Rev. Brian W. Harrison, O.S., M.A., S.T.D, Peter A. Kwasniewski, et al. *"The Apostolic Exhortation Amoris laetitia: a theological critique and Letter to Cardinal Sodano."* June 29, 2016. Originally published on the website of The Australian. Reprinted on the website CatholicCulture.org. https://www.catholicculture.org/culture/library/view.cfm?recnum=11324

Beal, John P., James A. Coriden, Thomas J. Green, eds. *New Commentary on the Code of Canon Law*, Commissioned by the Canon Law Society of America, New York NY/Mahwah NJ: Paulist Press, 2000.

Pope Benedict XVI, "Angelus, Saint Peter's Square, Sunday, 24 February 2013", Libreria Editrice Vaticana. February 24, 2013. https://www.vatican.va/content/benedict-xvi/en/angelus/2013/documents/hf_ben-xvi_ang_20130224.html

Pope Benedict XVI, "Declaratio", Libreria Editrice Vaticana. February 10, 2013. https://www.vatican.va/content/benedict-xvi/en/speeches/2013/february/documents/hf_ben-xvi_spe_20130211_declaratio.html

Pope Benedict XVI, "Declaratio Summi Pontificis: De Muneris Episcopi Romae, Successoris Sancti Petri Abdicatione," Acta Apostolicae Sedis, Vol. 105, Nº. 3, 2013, March 1, 2013. Libreria Editrice Vaticana. April 22, 2013.

Pope Benedict XVI, "General Audience (Wednesday, February 27, 2013)", Libreria Editrice Vaticana. February 27, 2013. https://www.vatican.va/content/benedict-xvi/en/audiences/2013/documents/hf_ben-xvi_aud_20130227.html

VALID? THE RESIGNATION OF POPE BENEDICT XVI

Pope Benedict XVI, "Greeting of His Holiness Benedict XVI to the Faithful of the Diocese of Albano (Thursday, February 28, 2013)", Libreria Editrice Vaticana. February 27, 2013. https://www.vatican.va/content/benedict-xvi/en/speeches/2013/february/documents/hf_ben-xvi_spe_20130228_fedeli-albano.html

Pope Benedict XVI, "Mass, Imposition of the Pallium, and conferral of the Fisherman's Ring for the Beginning of the Petrine Ministry of the Bishop of Rome, Homily of His Holiness Benedict XVI", Libreria Editrice Vaticana. Sunday, April 24, 2005. https://www.vatican.va/content/benedict-xvi/en/homilies/2005/documents/hf_ben-xvi_hom_20050424_inizio-pontificato.html

Pope Benedict XVI, "Normas Nonnullas", Libreria Editrice Vaticana. February 22, 2013. https://www.vatican.va/content/benedict-xvi/en/motu_proprio/documents/hf_ben-xvi_motu-proprio_20130222_normas-nonnullas.html

Pope Benedict XVI, "Pontificatus Exordia", Acta Apostolicae Sedis, ISSN 0001-5199, Vol. 97, Nº. 2 5, 2005, May 7, 2005, Libreria Editrice Vaticana. Homily given April 20, 2005.

Pope Benedict XVI, "Post-Synodal Apostolic Exhortation *Sacramentum Caritatis*", Libreria Editrice Vaticana. February 22, 2007. https://www.vatican.va/content/benedict-xvi/en/apost_exhortations/documents/hf_ben-xvi_exh_20070222_sacramentum-caritatis.html

Bugnolo, Alexis, "Catholics Worldwide warn the Cardinals that Benedict XVI is the pope," FromRome.info, November 22, 2021. https://www.fromrome.info/2021/11/22/catholics-worldwide-warn-the-cardinals-that-benedict-xvi-is-the-pope/

Bugnolo, Alexis (Brother), "MARK DOCHERTY RESPONDS TO CIONCI ET ALIA ON THE RATZINGER CODE & PLAN B", FromRome.Info, May 23, 2022.

BIBLIOGRAPHY and WORKS REFERENCED

https://www.fromrome.info/2022/05/23/mark-docherty-responds-to-cionci-et-alia-on-the-ratzinger-code-plan-b/

Buscemi, Georges; Robert Cassidy STL; Fr. Thomas Crean OP, et al, "Open Letter to the Bishops of the Catholic Church," Easter Week, 2019. Document found on DocumentCloud.org, contributed by Peter Baklinski of LifeSiteNews. https://www.documentcloud.org/documents/5983408-Open-Letter-to-the-Bishops-of-the-Catholic.html

CBC, "5 papal things Benedict gives up in retirement," CBC.CA, February 28, 2013, https://www.cbc.ca/news/world/5-papal-things-benedict-gives-up-in-retirement-1.1332261

Chapman, J. (1910). Pope Honorius I. In *The Catholic Encyclopedia*. New York: Robert Appleton Company. Retrieved July 6, 2022 from New Advent. http://www.newadvent.org/cathen/07452b.htm

Cionci, Andrea, "Andrea Cionci responds to MSGR. Athanasius Schneider's appeal to accept Bergoglio as pope," FromRome.info, June 15, 2022. https://www.fromrome.info/2022/06/15/andrea-cionci-responds-to-msgr-athanasius-schneiders-appeal-to-accept-bergoglio-as-pope/

Cionci, Andrea, "Benedict XVI and the absurd Substantial Error thesis: 'Pope Ratzinger has misconceptions'?", PatrickCoffinMedia, undated (June 2022). https://www.patrickcoffin.media/benedict-xvi-the-absurd-substantial-error-thesis/

Cionci, Andrea, "Cionci: The Possible Reconstruction of Benedict XVI's 'Plan B'", Published by Marco Tosatti, April 11, 2021. https://www.marcotosatti.com/2021/04/11/cionci-the-possible-reconstruction-of-benedict-xvis-plan-b/

Cionci, Andrea, *Codice Ratzinger*, Milano: Byoblu Edizione, 2022.

Cionci, Andrea, "'Codice Ratzinger': trovato il più clamoroso dei messaggi, in mondovisione da Castel Gandolfo", LiberoQuotidiano.it, December18, 2021.
https://www.liberoquotidiano.it/articolo_blog/blog/andrea-cionci/29829255/trovato-clamoroso-messaggio-in-codice-ratzinger-benedetto-sbaglio-apposta-il-titolo-pontificale-in-mondovisione-da-castel-ga.html)

Cionci, Andrea, "'Good Night!'. Ratzinger Code on the 'Roman' hour of Benedict XVI's impeded see: Francis is not the pope", Sfero Social Italiano (www.sfero.me), April 4, 2022.
https://sfero.me/article/good-night-ratzinger-code-on-the-roman-hour-of-benedict-xvi-s-impeded-see-francis-is-not-the-pope

Cionci, Andrea, "Ratzinger, dagli Usa tre obiezioni alla tesi del 'Piano B'. Rispondiamo punto per punto." LiberoQuotidiano.it, July 25, 2021.
https://www.liberoquotidiano.it/articolo_blog/blog/andrea-cionci/28098801/papa-ratzinger-tre-obiezioni-usa-teoria-piano-b-rispondiamo-punto-per-punto.html

CNA, "Is Francis the last Pope? A rare interview with Archbishop Gänswein", Catholic News Agency, June 26, 2016.
https://www.catholicnewsagency.com/news/34096/is-francis-the-last-pope-a-rare-interview-with-archbishop-ganswein

Coffin, Patrick, "#248: Is Benedict XVI Still the Pope?—Dr. Edmund Mazza," Produced by Patrick Coffin (www.PatrickCoffin.Media), The Patrick Coffin Show, September 14, 2021, 1:31:06.
https://www.patrickcoffin.media/is-benedict-xvi-still-the-pope/

Coriden, James A., Thomas J. Green, Donald E. Heintschel, eds. *The Code of Canon Law: A Text and Commentary*, Commissioned by the Canon Law Society of America, New York/Mahwah: Paulist Press, 1985.

Declaratiouniversa, "Declaratio," November 10, 2021.
https://declaratiouniversa.wixsite.com/declaratio

BIBLIOGRAPHY and WORKS REFERENCED

Docherty, Mark, "Count me in: Moral Certitude and the invalid abdication of Pope Benedict XVI, still reigning", NonVeniPacem.com, July 3, 2017.
https://nonvenipacem.com/2017/07/03/count-me-in-moral-certitude-and-the-invalid-abdication-of-pope-benedict-xvi-still-reigning/

Docherty, Mark, "Examining the Benedictine Option," NonVeniPacem.com, June 26, 2016.
https://nonvenipacem.com/2016/06/26/examining-the-benedictine-option/

Docherty, Mark, "FAQ: Did Pope Benedict reveal his intent to bifurcate the papacy in the actual Declaratio?", NonVeniPacem.com, July 22, 2017.
https://nonvenipacem.com/2017/07/22/faq-did-pope-benedict-reveal-his-intent-to-bifurcate-the-papacy-in-the-actual-declaratio/

Feser, Edward, Ph.D., "Benedict is not the pope: A reply to some critics", EdwardFeser.Blog, May 5, 2022.
https://edwardfeser.blogspot.com/2022/05/benedict-is-not-pope-reply-to-some.html

Feser, Edward, Ph.D., "Benevacantism is scandalous and pointless", Catholic World Report, April 14, 2022.
https://www.catholicworldreport.com/2022/04/14/benevacantism-is-scandalous-and-pointless/

Filteau, Jerry, "Pope Pius XII was prepared to resign as pope," National Catholic Reporter (www.ncronline.org), blogs, February 28, 2013. https://www.ncronline.org/blogs/ncr-today/pope-pius-xii-was-prepared-resign-pope

Pope Francis, "Post Synodal Apostolic Exhortation *Amoris Laetitia*," Libreria Editrice Vaticana. March 19, 2016.
https://www.vatican.va/content/dam/francesco/pdf/apost_exhortations/documents/papa-francesco_esortazione-ap_20160319_amoris-laetitia_en.pdf

Pope Francis, Al-Azhar Ahmad Al-Tayyeb (Grand Imam), "*A Document on Human Fraternity for World Peace and Living*

Together," Libreria Editrice Vaticana. February 4, 2019. https://www.vatican.va/content/francesco/en/travels/2019/outside/documents/papa-francesco_20190204_documento-fratellanza-umana.html

Gagliarducci, Andrea, "What Could Pope Francis' Message Be With His Choice of New Cardinals?", National Catholic Register, May 30, 2022. https://www.ncregister.com/cna/what-could-pope-francis-message-be-with-his-choice-of-new-cardinals

Gordon, Timothy J., "DEBATE: Is Benedict Still Pope?", Produced by Timothy J. Gordon (www.timothyjgordon.com), Rules for Retrogrades Podcast, February 11, 2022, 1:44:26. https://www.youtube.com/watch?v=G9t-2dCKcKM

Grant, Ryan, "Rise of the Benevacantists: Who Is Pope?", OnePeterFive, December 14, 2018. https://onepeterfive.com/benevacantists/

Haynes, Michael, "Bishop Schneider: Theory that Benedict XVI is pope and not Francis defies 'tradition of the Church'," LifeSiteNews, June 9, 2022. https://www.lifesitenews.com/news/bishop-schneider-theory-that-benedict-xvi-is-pope-and-not-francis-defies-tradition-of-the-church/

Hickson, Maike, "Bp. Schneider: Pope must formally correct statement that God wills false religions," LifeSiteNews, May 8, 2019. https://www.lifesitenews.com/news/bp.-schneider-pope-must-formally-correct-statement-that-god-wills-false-religions/

Hickson, Maike, "Six cardinals and bishops who condemned pagan 'Pachamama' rituals at Vatican," LifeSiteNews, blogs, October 30, 2019. https://www.lifesitenews.com/blogs/six-cardinals-and-bishops-who-condemned-pagan-pachamama-rituals-at-vatican/

Ivereigh, Austin, *The Great Reformer and the Making of a Radical Pope,* New York: Henry Holt and Company, 2014.

BIBLIOGRAPHY and WORKS REFERENCED

Pope John Paul I, "Holy Mass for the Inauguration of the Petrine Ministry of the Bishop of Rome, Homily of His Holiness John Paul I", Libreria Editrice Vaticana. September 3, 1978. https://www.vatican.va/content/john-paul-i/en/homilies/documents/hf_jp-i_hom_03091978.html

Pope John Paul II, "Post-Synodal Apostolic Exhortation *Familiaris Consortio*," Libreria Editrice Vaticana. November 22, 1981. https://www.vatican.va/content/john-paul-ii/en/apost_exhortations/documents/hf_jp-ii_exh_19811122_familiaris-consortio.html

Pope John Paul II, "Post-Synodal Apostolic Exhortation *Reconciliatio et Paenitentia*," Libreria Editrice Vaticana. December 2, 1984. https://www.vatican.va/content/john-paul-ii/en/apost_exhortations/documents/hf_jp-ii_exh_02121984_reconciliatio-et-paenitentia.html

Pope John Paul II, "Apostolic Constitution *Universi Dominici Gregis*," Libreria Editrice Vaticana. February 22, 1996. https://www.vatican.va/content/john-paul-ii/en/apost_constitutions/documents/hf_jp-ii_apc_22021996_universi-dominici-gregis.html

Pope John XXIII, "Ad christifideles in foro Sancti Petri coadunatos, quo urnae sollemniter delatae sunt, in quibus S. Pii Papae X et S. Ioannis Bosco sacrae asservantur exuviae", Acta Apostolicae Sedis. Vol. 51 (LI), (Series III, v. 1), No. 1, 1959, January 24, 1959, Libreria Editrice Vaticana. May 11, 1959. https://www.vatican.va/archive/aas/documents/AAS-51-1959-ocr.pdf

Pope John XXIII, "Ad Praelatos Auditores ceterosque Officiales, Advocatos et Procuratores Tribunalis Sacrae Romanae Rotae", Acta Apostolicae Sedis. Vol. 51 (LI), (Series III, v. 1), No. 1, 1959, January 24, 1959, Libreria Editrice Vaticana. https://www.vatican.va/archive/aas/documents/AAS-51-1959-ocr.pdf

Pope John XXIII, "Adhortatio ad Clerum, Qui E Tota Venetorum Regione Venetias Convenerat, in Basilica S. Marci Sacras Exuvias Sancti PII Papae X Veneraturus", Acta Apostolicae Sedis. Vol. 51 (LI), (Series III, v. 1), No. 1, 1959, January 24, 1959, Libreria Editrice Vaticana. https://www.vatican.va/archive/aas/documents/AAS-51-1959-ocr.pdf

Kirsch, J.P. (1910). Pope John XXII. In *The Catholic Encyclopedia.* New York: Robert Appleton Company. Retrieved July 6, 2022 from New Advent. http://www.newadvent.org/cathen/08431a.htm

Lewis, Charlton T., Charles Short, ed. *A Latin Dictionary*. Omaha, NE: Patristic Publishing, 2019 (in public domain).

Liber Sextus. UCLA Digital Library (https://digital.library.ucla.edu/catalog/ark:/21198/zz0014rx8d?cv=35)

Lumen Gentium, Dogmatic Constitution on the Church, Promulgated by Pope Paul VI, November 21, 1964. https://www.vatican.va/archive/hist_councils/ii_vatican_council/documents/vat-ii_const_19641121_lumen-gentium_en.html

Marshall, Taylor, Ph.D,, "Is Benedict XVI Still the Pope? Did Pope Benedict XVI Fully Resign the Papacy or Just a Part of It?", Produced by Dr. Taylor Marshall (https://www.youtube.com/c/DrTaylorMarshall), Dr Taylor Marshall Podcast, May 27, 2022, 1:41:07. https://www.youtube.com/watch?v=bABWi2CoVlc

Marshall, Taylor, Ph.D, "Is Pope Benedict XVI Still Pope (but Francis Bishop of Rome?) Mazza Thesis Revisited", Produced by Dr. Taylor Marshall (https://www.youtube.com/c/DrTaylorMarshall), Dr Taylor Marshall Podcast, June 10, 2022, 2:05:24. https://www.youtube.com/watch?v=iK1Zg1WyKI4

Mazza, Edmund J., Ph.D., "Guest Post: Dr. Edmund Mazza's Position Paper on the Invalidity of Pope Benedict's Resignation:

BIBLIOGRAPHY and WORKS REFERENCED

Pope Emeritus: Enigma: An Explanation at Last", Barnhardt.biz, May 27, 2020. https://www.barnhardt.biz/2020/05/27/guest-post-dr-edmund-mazzas-position-paper-on-the-invalidity-of-pope-benedicts-resignation/

Mazza, Edmund, Ph.D., "'Leave the Throne, Take the Ministry' The Sacred Powers of Pope Emeritus," www.EdmundMazza.com, April 21, 2021. https://www.edmundmazza.com/2021/04/21/leave-the-throne-take-the-ministry-the-sacred-powers-of-pope-emeritus/

McClean, Dorothy Cummings, "Vatican newspaper features 'Pachamama' bowl used at Amazon Synod's closing Mass", LifeSiteNews, November 7, 2019. https://www.lifesitenews.com/news/vatican-newspaper-features-pachamama-bowl-used-at-amazon-synods-closing-mass/

McCloon, David, "Cdl. Müller: Pope Francis resigning with Benedict still alive would be a 'big problem'", LifeSiteNews, June 22, 2022. https://www.lifesitenews.com/news/cdl-muller-pope-francis-resigning-with-benedict-still-alive-would-be-a-big-problem/

Montagna, Diane, "Did Benedict really resign? Gänswein, Burke and Brandmüller weigh in", LifeSiteNews, February 14, 2019. https://www.lifesitenews.com/news/did-benedict-really-resign-gaenswein-burke-and-brandmueller-weigh-in/

O'Connell, Gerard, *The Election of Pope Francis: An Inside Account of the Conclave that Changed History,* New York: Orbis Books, 2019.

O'Reilly, Steven. "Benedict is still NOT pope", https://romalocutaest.com/2017/09/14/benedict-is-still-not-pope/; "Pope Francis, the Open Letter, and the Pesky Preface", (see https://onepeterfive.com/pope-francis-the-open-letter-and-the-pesky-preface/; "The Errors of Mr. Walford's 'Pope Francis, The Family and Divorce'", https://romalocutaest.com/2018/10/08/the-errors-of-mr-walfords-pope-francis-the-family-and-divorce/; "Part II: The Development of Mr. Walford's Errors", https://romalocutaest.com/2018/10/19/part-ii-the-development-of-mr-walfords-errors/; "Part III: Mr. Walford and the Magisterium", https://romalocutaest.com/2018/11/13/part-iii-mr-walford-and-the-magisterium/; "The Conclave Chronicles" on Roma Locuta Est, https://romalocutaest.com/2020/09/23/the-conclave-chronicles/; "Why Blame Scalfari?", https://romalocutaest.com/2019/11/08/why-blame-scalfari/ "Benedict is Still Pope and Other Errors", January 15, 2019. https://romalocutaest.com/2019/01/15/benedict-is-still-not-pope-and-other-errors/; "Benedict's Plan 'B' from Outer Space," April 12, 2021. https://romalocutaest.com/2021/04/12/benedicts-plan-b-from-outer-space/; "Benedict's Plan B from Outer Space – the Sequel", August 3, 2021, https://romalocutaest.com/2021/08/03/benedicts-plan-b-from-outer-space-the-sequel/ ; "Benedict is really, really still not pope! Really!", September 22, 2018. https://romalocutaest.com/2018/09/22/benedict-is-really-really-still-not-pope-really/; "Summa Contra Dr. Mazza", November 2, 2020. https://romalocutaest.com/2020/11/02/the-summa-contra-dr-mazza/; "On the 8th Anniversary of the Resignation of Pope Benedict XVI," February 28, 2021. https://romalocutaest.com/2021/02/28/on-the-8th-anniversary-of-the-resignation-of-pope-benedict-xvi/; "Regarding Benedict's Last Audience", February 27, 2022. https://romalocutaest.com/2022/02/27/regarding-benedicts-last-audience/

Patricio, Ryan Sayre, "Pius XII Planned to Resign if Seized by Nazis", First Things , May 6, 2009. https://www.firstthings.com/blogs/firstthoughts/2009/05/pius-xii-planned-to-resign-if-seized-by-nazis

Pentin, Edward. "Cardinal Danneels Admits to Being Part of 'Mafia' Club Opposed to Benedict XVI", National Catholic Register, blog, September 23, 2015. https://www.ncregister.com/blog/cardinal-danneels-admits-to-being-part-of-mafia-club-opposed-to-benedict-xvi

BIBLIOGRAPHY and WORKS REFERENCED

Pentin, Edward, "Debate Intensifies Over Benedict XVI's Resignation and Role as Pope Emeritus," Edward Pentin, March 6, 2020. https://edwardpentin.co.uk/debate-intensifies-over-benedict-xvis-resignation-and-role-as-pope-emeritus/

Pentin, Edward. "Full Text and Explanatory Notes of Cardinals' Questions on 'Amoris Laetitia'", National Catholic Register, blog, November 14, 2016. https://www.ncregister.com/blog/full-text-and-explanatory-notes-of-cardinals-questions-on-amoris-laetitia

Pentin, Edward, "Benedict XVI Discusses His Resignation in Newly Published Letters", National Catholic Register, blog, September 19, 2018. https://www.ncregister.com/blog/benedict-xvi-discusses-his-resignation-in-newly-published-letters

Peters, Edward, JD, JCD, Ref. Sig. Ap., "Lighter fare: can bad Latin save a papacy?", CanonLawblog, October 1, 2014. https://canonlawblog.wordpress.com/2014/10/01/lighter-fare-can-bad-latin-save-a-papacy/)

Pope Pius X, "Communion Rerum", Italian translation of the Encyclical Communion Rerum. Acta Apostolicae Sedis, Vol. 1, Nº. 1, 1909, January 1, 1909, Libreria Editrice Vaticana. April 21, 1909. https://www.vatican.va/archive/aas/documents/AAS-01-1909-ocr.pdf

"Quando II Luglio MDCCCLVII La Santita Del Pontefice Sommo Papa Pio IX Letificava Di Sua Sacra Augusta Presenza La Citta di Modena," Le Confraternite Laicale a Perennare la Memoria di tal Giorno Volevano Pubblicato il Sequente Omaggio Poetico che Riverenti Ponevano a Piedi del Supremo Gerarca, found in the Italian History of the Risorgimento Period, the Collection of H. Nelson Gay, A.M., 1896, bought from the bequest of Archibald Gary Coolidge, A.B. 1887, 1931. https://play.google.com/books/reader?id=FPIQQCOqdhoC&pg=GBS.PP2&hl=en

Ratzinger, Josef Cardinal. Congregation for the Doctrine of the Faith. *"Letter to the Bishops of the Catholic Church Concerning the Reception of Holy Communion by the Divorced and Remarried Members of the Faithful,*" Libreria Editrice Vaticana, September 14, 1994. https://www.vatican.va/roman_curia/congregations/cfaith/documents/rc_con_cfaith_doc_14091994_rec-holy-comm-by-divorced_en.html

Ratzinger, Josef Cardinal, "The Primacy of the Pope and the Unity of the People of God," Communio International Catholic Review. https://www.communio-icr.com/files/ratzinger41-1.pdf

Ratzinger, Josef, *Principles of Catholic Theology: Building Stone for a Fundamental Theology.* San Francisco: Ignatius Press, 1987.

Ratzinger, Josef, *Theological Highlights of Vatican II*, New York/Mahwah NJ: Paulist Press, 1966.

Ratzinger, Josef Cardinal, "The Transfiguration," originally a homily given August 10, 1979. Reprinted in L'Osservatore Romano, Weekly Edition in English, 7-14 August 2013, page 3, published online on EWTN. https://www.ewtn.com/catholicism/library/transfiguration-1723

Rickert, Fr. John, FSSP, Ph.D., "Antipope Claims: Substantial Error — Guest Post by Fr John Rickert, FSSP," William M. Briggs, March 20, 2017. https://www.wmbriggs.com/post/21231/

Rickert, Fr. John, FSSP, Ph.D., "Countering The Claim That Francis Is An Antipope — Guest Post by Fr. John Rickert, FSSP", William M. Briggs, March 6, 2017. https://www.wmbriggs.com/post/21193/

Rickert, Fr. John, FSSP, Ph.D., "Follow The Munus! Why Benedict Is [Likely] Pope — Guest Post by Edmund J. Mazza; Rejoinder by Fr John Rickert", William M. Briggs, April 26, 2022. https://www.wmbriggs.com/post/39752/

Rickert, Fr. John, FSSP, Ph.D., "Munus, Ministerium & Pope Emeritus Benedict — Guest Post by Fr John Rickert", William

BIBLIOGRAPHY and WORKS REFERENCED

M. Briggs, April 20, 2022.
https://www.wmbriggs.com/post/39718/

Roberts, James, "Scalfari claims Pope does not believe Jesus 'the man' was divine", The Tablet, October 10, 2019.
https://www.thetablet.co.uk/news/12111/scalfari-claims-pope-does-not-believe-jesus-the-man-was-divine

Salzano, Bishop Tommaso Michele, "Brevi Riflessioni sul modo di Risolvere E Sull'Opportunita di Definire l'Infallibilita del Pontefice Sommo", Typography by Stanislao de Lella, Napoli. 1870. Found in the Fordham University Libraries, Digital Collection.
https://cdm17265.contentdm.oclc.org/digital/collection/italianPamp/id/33077

Schneider, Athanasius (Bishop), "EXCLUSIVE: Bishop Schneider wins clarification on 'diversity of religions' from Pope Francis, brands abuse summit a 'failure,'" Article and Interview by Diane Montagna, LifeSiteNews, March 7, 2019.
https://www.lifesitenews.com/news/bishop-schneider-extracts-clarification-on-diversity-of-religions-from-pope-francis-brands-abuse-summit-a-failure/

Seewald, Peter, *Benedict XVI: A Life. Volume 2: Professor and Prefect to Pope and Pope Emeritus 1966–The Present.* (English Translation, Kindle Edition). Great Britain: Bloomsbury Continuum, 2021.

Seewald, Peter, *Benedict XVI: Last Testament in his own words.* London: Bloomsbury Publishing Company Plc, 2016.

Seewald, Peter, *Light of the World*, San Francisco: Ignatius Press, 2010.

Skojec, Steve, "The Evidence Suggests The Francis-Scalfari Connection is No Accident", OnePeterFive, October 11, 2019.
https://onepeterfive.com/the-francis-scalfari-connection-is-no-accident/

Smits, Jeanne, "Pagan ceremony at the Vatican was just the beginning of the irreverent activity taking place at Synod", LifeSiteNews, October 11, 2019. https://www.lifesitenews.com/news/pagan-ceremony-at-the-vatican-was-just-the-beginning-of-the-irreverent-activity-taking-place-at-synod/

Stelten, Leo F., *Dictionary of Ecclesiastical Latin*, Peabody, Massachusetts: Hendrickson Publishers, 1995.

Viganò, Carlo Maria, "Testimony," Wall Street Journal Online, August, 22, 2018. https://online.wsj.com/media/Viganos-letter.pdf

Vogt, Andrea, "'Plot to kill pope' sparks Italian media storm", The Guardian, February 10, 2012. https://www.theguardian.com/world/2012/feb/10/plot-kill-pope-italian-media

Walford, Stephen, *The Pope, The Family, and Divorce: In Defense of Truth and Mercy*, Paulist Press, 2018.

William, Thomas D., Ph.D., "Top Theologian: In Abu Dhabi Statement, Pope 'Undermines' the Gospel", Breitbart, June 5, 2019. https://www.breitbart.com/faith/2019/06/05/top-theologian-in-abu-dhabi-statement-pope-undermines-the-gospel/

Wooden, Cindy, "Resignation letter prepared by Blessed Paul VI published", National Catholic Reporter (ncronline.org), blogs, May 16, 2018. https://www.ncronline.org/news/vatican/resignation-letter-prepared-blessed-paul-vi-published

www.correctiofilialis.org, "Correctio filialis de haeresibus propagates", July 16, 2017. http://www.correctiofilialis.org/wp-content/uploads/2017/08/Correctio-filialis_English_1.pdf

Zenit Staff, "Benedict XVI Says Doubts on Resignation Are 'Absurd'", Zenit (www.Zenit.org), February 26, 2014. https://zenit.org/2014/02/26/benedict-xvi-says-doubts-on-resignation-are-absurd/

End Notes

[1] Pope Benedict XVI, *Declaratio,* Libreria Editrice Vaticana. February 10, 2013. https://www.vatican.va/content/benedict-xvi/en/speeches/2013/february/documents/hf_ben-xvi_spe_20130211_declaratio.html

[2] Ibid.

[3] The first known use of the acronym BiP for "Benedict is (still) pope," at least to the author's knowledge, is his first use of it on the blog *Roma Locuta Est* in one of his articles. See: https://romalocutaest.com/2017/09/14/benedict-is-still-not-pope/

[4] The descriptiveness of BiP for "Benedict is (still) pope" is contingent on Benedict's longevity, long may he live. However, given this acronym will fail to be accurate once Benedict passes, the author opted on the use of the terms *Benepapism* and *Benepapist* for this book. The terms are not intended to be pejorative. They encompass the belief that Benedict remained pope after February 28, 2013. Other terms that have been in circulation for some time, such as "Benevacantism" or "Beneplenism," were rejected as being either inaccurate or failing to encompass the range of Benepapist theories.

[5] See note 351 in section 305. Pope Francis, "Post Synodal Apostolic Exhortation *Amoris Laetitia*," Libreria Editrice Vaticana, p. 237. March 19, 2016. https://www.vatican.va/content/dam/francesco/pdf/apost_exhortations/documents/papa-francesco_esortazione-ap_20160319_amoris-laetitia_en.pdf

[6] Pope John Paul II, "Post-Synodal Apostolic Exhortation *Familiaris Consortio*," Libreria Editrice Vaticana. November 22, 1981, p. 84. https://www.vatican.va/content/john-paul-ii/en/apost_exhortations/documents/hf_jp-ii_exh_19811122_familiaris-consortio.html

[7] Pope John Paul II, "Post-Synodal Apostolic Exhortation *Reconciliatio et Paenitentia*," Libreria Editrice Vaticana. December 2, 1984, p. 34. https://www.vatican.va/content/john-paul-

ii/en/apost_exhortations/documents/hf_jp-ii_exh_02121984_reconciliatio-et-paenitentia.html

[8] See Josef Cardinal Ratzinger, Congregation for the Doctrine of the Faith. *"Letter to the Bishops of the Catholic Church Concerning the Reception of Holy Communion by the Divorced and Remarried Members of the Faithful,"* Libreria Editrice Vaticana, September 14, 1994. https://www.vatican.va/roman_curia/congregations/cfaith/documents/rc_con_cfaith_doc_14091994_rec-holy-comm-by-divorced_en.html

[9] See Pope Benedict XVI. "Post-Synodal Apostolic Exhortation *Sacramentum Caritatis.*" Libreria Editrice Vaticana, p. 29. February 22, 2007. https://www.vatican.va/content/benedict-xvi/en/apost_exhortations/documents/hf_ben-xvi_exh_20070222_sacramentum-caritatis.html

[10] See Msgr. Ignacio Barreiro; Rev. Brian W. Harrison, O.S., M.A., S.T.D, Peter A. Kwasniewski, et al, *"The Apostolic Exhortation Amoris laetitia: a theological critique and Letter to Cardinal Sodano."* June 29, 2016. Originally published on the website of The Australian. Reprinted on the website CatholicCulture.org, see: https://www.catholicculture.org/culture/library/view.cfm?recnum=11324

[11] The four *"Dubia"* cardinals include Cardinal Carlo Caffara and Cardinal Joachim Meisner, who have since passed away. The surviving *Dubia* cardinals include Cardinal Raymond Burke and Cardinal Walter Brandmüller.

[12] Edward Pentin provides both the *Dubia* and the explanatory note provided by the four cardinals. See Edward Pentin, "Full Text and Explanatory Notes of Cardinals' Questions on 'Amoris Laetitia'," National Catholic Register, blog, November 14, 2016. https://www.ncregister.com/blog/full-text-and-explanatory-notes-of-cardinals-questions-on-amoris-laetitia

[13] See "Correctio filialis de haeresibus propagates," www.correctiofilialis.org, July 16, 2017, retrieved April 18, 2020, 5:38 p.m. http://www.correctiofilialis.org/wp-content/uploads/2017/08/Correctio-filialis_English_1.pdf

[14] See Georges Buscemi, Robert Cassidy STL, Fr. Thomas Crean OP, et al, "Open Letter to the Bishops of the Catholic Church," Easter

ENDNOTES

Week, 2019. Document found on DocumentCloud.org, contributed by Peter Baklinski of LifeSiteNews, retrieved April 18, 2022, 5:45 p.m. https://www.documentcloud.org/documents/5983408-Open-Letter-to-the-Bishops-of-the-Catholic.html

[15] Among these writers is Stephen Walford, who has written a book for which Pope Francis provided the preface. See Stephen Walford, *The Pope, The Family, and Divorce: In Defense of Truth and Mercy*, Paulist Press, 2018. I have commented on the Pope's preface in an article titled "Pope Francis, the Open Letter, and the Pesky Preface" (see https://onepeterfive.com/pope-francis-the-open-letter-and-the-pesky-preface/), and have provided a three-part rebuttal of Mr. Walford's book, see "The Errors of Mr. Walford's 'Pope Francis, The Family and Divorce'" (https://romalocutaest.com/2018/10/08/the-errors-of-mr-walfords-pope-francis-the-family-and-divorce/); "Part II: The Development of Mr. Walford's Errors" (https://romalocutaest.com/2018/10/19/part-ii-the-development-of-mr-walfords-errors/); and "Part III: Mr. Walford and the Magisterium" (https://romalocutaest.com/2018/11/13/part-iii-mr-walford-and-the-magisterium/).

[16] See Edward Pentin, "Cardinal Danneels Admits to Being Part of 'Mafia' Club Opposed to Benedict XVI," National Catholic Register, blog, September 23, 2015. https://www.ncregister.com/blog/cardinal-danneels-admits-to-being-part-of-mafia-club-opposed-to-benedict-xvi

[17] See Gerard O'Connell, *"The Election of Pope Francis: An Inside Account of the Conclave that Changed History,"* New York: Orbis Books, 2019, pp. 20-22. In his book, O'Connell says there was "no time for canvassing," and there was not even a "semblance of a campaign." O'Connell recounts how the first edition of Austin Ivereigh's book, *The Great Reformer and the Making of a Radical Pope* had "suggested otherwise." Ivereigh, closely associated with Cardinal Murphy-O'Connor, corrected himself in a later edition of his book after the Vatican press secretary said four cardinals denied events transpired as reported in the book. O'Connell quotes Ivereigh's original version from the first edition, as well as the subsequent change Ivereigh made in the later edition:

[Existing]
They had learned their lessons from 2005. They first secured Bergoglio's assent. Asked if he was willing, he said that he believed that at this time of the crisis for the Church no cardinal could refuse if asked.

[New]
In keeping with the conclave rules, they did not ask Bergoglio if he would be willing to be a candidate. But they believed this time that the crisis in the Church would make it hard for him to refuse if elected.

[18] See Carlo Maria Viganò, "Testimony," August, 22, 2018, Wall Street Journal Online, p. 6; https://online.wsj.com/media/Viganos-letter.pdf, and also see the referenced video: (https://www.youtube.com/watch?v=b3iaBLqt8vg&t=41s)

[19] See linked articles in "The Conclave Chronicles" on *Roma Locuta Est*. https://romalocutaest.com/2020/09/23/the-conclave-chronicles/

[20] See Pope Francis and Grand Imam Al-Azhar Ahmad Al-Tayyeb, "*A Document on Human Fraternity for World Peace and Living Together*," Libreria Editrice Vaticana. February 4, 2019. https://www.vatican.va/content/francesco/en/travels/2019/outside/documents/papa-francesco_20190204_documento-fratellanza-umana.html

[21] Fr. Thomas Weinandy called the Abu Dhabi text "most egregious." See Thomas D. William Ph.D., "Top Theologian: In Abu Dhabi Statement, Pope 'Undermines' the Gospel," Breitbart, June 5, 2019. https://www.breitbart.com/faith/2019/06/05/top-theologian-in-abu-dhabi-statement-pope-undermines-the-gospel/

[22] See Bishop Athanasius Schneider, "EXCLUSIVE: Bishop Schneider wins clarification on 'diversity of religions' from Pope Francis, brands abuse summit a 'failure,'" Article and Interview by Diane Montagna, LifeSiteNews, March 7, 2019. https://www.lifesitenews.com/news/bishop-schneider-extracts-clarification-on-diversity-of-religions-from-pope-francis-brands-abuse-summit-a-failure/

[23] Bishop Athanasius Schnieder comments on this. See Maike Hickson, "Bp. Schneider: Pope must formally correct statement that God wills

ENDNOTES

false religions," LifeSiteNews, May 8, 2019.
https://www.lifesitenews.com/news/bp.-schneider-pope-must-formally-correct-statement-that-god-wills-false-religions/

[24] For commentary on and a catalog with links of Scalfari's interactions with Pope Francis, see Steve Skojec, "The Evidence Suggests The Francis-Scalfari Connection is No Accident," OnePeterFive, October 11, 2019.
https://onepeterfive.com/the-francis-scalfari-connection-is-no-accident/

[25] Roberts, James, "Scalfari claims Pope does not believe Jesus 'the man' was divine," The Tablet, October 10, 2019.
https://www.thetablet.co.uk/news/12111/scalfari-claims-pope-does-not-believe-jesus-the-man-was-divine

[26] See discussion of this point on *Roma Locuta Est*, in an article entitled "Why Blame Scalfari?"
https://romalocutaest.com/2019/11/08/why-blame-scalfari/

[27] For reporting on this event, see Jeanne Smits, "Pagan ceremony at the Vatican was just the beginning of the irreverent activity taking place at Synod," LifeSiteNews, October 11, 2019.
https://www.lifesitenews.com/news/pagan-ceremony-at-the-vatican-was-just-the-beginning-of-the-irreverent-activity-taking-place-at-synod/ Videos of the event may be found on Youtube.

[28] For example, see Maike Hickson, "Six cardinals and bishops who condemned pagan 'Pachamama' rituals at Vatican," LifeSiteNews, blogs, October 30, 2019.
https://www.lifesitenews.com/blogs/six-cardinals-and-bishops-who-condemned-pagan-pachamama-rituals-at-vatican/

[29] For reporting on this event see Dorothy Cummings McClean, "Vatican newspaper features 'Pachamama' bowl used at Amazon Synod's closing Mass," LifeSiteNews, November 7, 2019.
https://www.lifesitenews.com/news/vatican-newspaper-features-pachamama-bowl-used-at-amazon-synods-closing-mass/

[30] A future Pope and council might benefit from such a detailed listing especially.

[31] Ms. Barnhardt's articles may be found on her blog site:
https://www.barnhardt.biz/

[32] Mr. Docherty's articles may be found on his blog site:
https://nonvenipacem.com/

[33] Coriden, James A., Thomas J. Green, Donald E. Heintschel, eds. *The Code of Canon Law: A Text and Commentary*, Commissioned by the Canon Law Society of America, New York/Mahwah: Paulist Press, 1985, p. 109.

[34] Brother Alexis Bugnolo has said (italics added): "Mark Docherty is a close associate of Ann Barnhardt. So as he opens his article you will find no mention of the Franciscan Friar whom she hates with a diabolic passion. Nevertheless, I include myself in that list, and perhaps have the best personal history to respond to Mark, since I wrote an entire Scholastic Question demonstration the substantial error, but also was first to propose the Plan B thesis, which asserts that Pope Benedict XVI did with full knowledge and consent, renounce the ministerium rather than the munus to save the Church from Ecclesiastical Freemasonry." See Brother Alexis Bugnolo, "MARK DOCHERTY RESPONDS TO CIONCI ET ALIA ON THE RATZINGER CODE & PLAN B," FromRome.Info, May 23, 2022. Retrieved September 11, 2022, 7:39 p.m. https://www.fromrome.info/2022/05/23/mark-docherty-responds-to-cionci-et-alia-on-the-ratzinger-code-plan-b/

[35] Andrea Cionci, *Codice Ratzinger*, Milano: Byoblu Edizione, 2022.

[36] At this point of the Francis pontificate, nine years into it, a comprehensive list of his words and acts which raise concerns and confusion among the Catholic faithful would be quite long.

[37] The earliest blogs published about Benepapism include those operated by the aforementioned Ann Barnhardt, Mark Docherty, and Brother Bugnolo.

[38] For Edward Pentin's commentary on the continued controversy, see Edward Pentin, "Debate Intensifies Over Benedict XVI's Resignation and Role as Pope Emeritus," Edward Pentin, March 6, 2020. https://edwardpentin.co.uk/debate-intensifies-over-benedict-xvis-resignation-and-role-as-pope-emeritus/

[39] For example, the blogs of various Italian vaticanisti, such as Marco Tosatti and Sandro Magister, have republished articles with a Benepapist angle, certainly showing there is some traction for the theory.

[40] The English release of Socci's book led to controversy among some when it was titled "The Secret of Benedict XVI: Is he still pope?".

For whatever reason, the English publisher softened the definitive Italian "why he is still pope" to a question: "Is he still pope?" This led to some raised eyebrows among the more conspiratorial-minded Benepapists at the time.

[41] For example, Dr. Edmund Mazza has appeared on separate programs hosted by Taylor Marshall, Patrick Coffin, and John-Henry Westin.

[42] The author describes this Benepapist division in the following articles, "A Benepapist Civil War?", May 22, 2022, https://romalocutaest.com/2022/05/22/a-benepapist-civil-war/; and "Benedict XVI: strategic genius or theological fool?," May 29, 2002, https://romalocutaest.com/2022/05/29/benedict-xvi-strategic-genius-or-theological-fool/

[43] Cionci calls Barnhardt's "substantial error" theory "absurd." See (Cionci, Andrea, "Benedict XVI and the absurd Substantial Error thesis: 'Pope Ratzinger has misconceptions'?", PatrickCoffinMedia, undated (June 2022). https://www.patrickcoffin.media/benedict-xvi-the-absurd-substantial-error-thesis/ While Barnhardt indirectly calls Cionci's *Plan B* theory "nonsense." See Ann Barnhardt, "Breaking: Pope Benedict's personal secretary, Archbishop Ganswein sobbing repeatedly when talking about the failed attempted resignation. NOTHING TO SEE HERE.", Barnhardt.biz, June 19, 2022. https://www.barnhardt.biz/2022/06/19/breaking-pope-benedicts-personal-secretary-archbishop-ganswein-sobbing-repeatedly-when-talking-about-the-failed-attempted-resignation-nothing-to-see-here/

[44] See my article on this very point: https://romalocutaest.com/2022/05/29/benedict-xvi-strategic-genius-or-theological-fool/

[45] See this Declaration here (retrieved April 18, 2022 at 7:22 p.m.): https://declaratiouniversa.wixsite.com/declaratio

[46] Ibid.

[47] Ibid.

[48] A list of signatories may be found here (retrieved April 18, 2022 at 7:39 a.m.): https://52a99a74-6392-456d-bed5-847351b08fbf.filesusr.com/ugd/ff0010_420104a4a8384ef2b44e24da371db389.pdf?index=true

⁴⁹ Chapman, J. (1910). Pope Honorius I. In *The Catholic Encyclopedia*. New York: Robert Appleton Company. Retrieved July 6, 2022 from New Advent: http://www.newadvent.org/cathen/07452b.htm

⁵⁰ Kirsch, J.P. (1910). Pope John XXII. In *The Catholic Encyclopedia.* New York: Robert Appleton Company. Retrieved July 6, 2022 from New Advent: http://www.newadvent.org/cathen/08431a.htm

⁵¹ For example, Ryan Grant has written one article on the subject (see https://onepeterfive.com/benevacantists/),

Fr. John Rickert, FSSP, Ph.D. has written four articles (see
https://www.wmbriggs.com/post/39718/;
https://www.wmbriggs.com/post/21231/;
https://www.wmbriggs.com/post/21193/; and
https://www.wmbriggs.com/post/39752/), and

Dr. Edward Feser, Ph.D., has written at least two (see https://edwardfeser.blogspot.com/2022/05/benedict-is-not-pope-reply-to-some.html; and
https://www.catholicworldreport.com/2022/04/14/benevacantism-is-scandalous-and-pointless/).

On our own blog, *Roma Locuta Est*, there are two summary articles which have compiled the links to multiple other articles written by the author:
(see https://romalocutaest.com/2020/02/11/summa-contra-the-bip-theory-why-benedict-xvi-is-not-the-pope/, and
https://romalocutaest.com/2022/03/21/the-case-against-those-who-claim-benedict-is-still-pope/).

⁵² The substantial-error theory.

⁵³ The Benepapists who believe in "Plan B."

⁵⁴ Pope Benedict XVI, *Declaratio.*

⁵⁵ Canon 332§2 reads as follows: "If it should happen that the Roman Pontiff resigns his office (*munus*), it is required for validity that he makes the resignation freely and that it be duly manifested, but not that it be accepted by anyone." (Coriden, James A., et al, eds. *The Code of Canon Law: Text and Commentary,* p. 270)

⁵⁶ See Pope Benedict XVI, "Declaratio Summi Pontificis: De Muneris Episcopi Romae, Successoris Sancti Petri Abdicatione," Acta Apostolicae Sedis, Vol. 105, N°. 3, 2013, March 1, 2013. Libreria

ENDNOTES

Editrice Vaticana. Declaratio given April 22, 2013, pp. 239-240. Credit to Fr. John Rickert FSSP, Ph.D. for making this very point in his rebuttal of Dr. Mazza. See Fr. John Rickert, FSSP, Ph.D., "Follow The Munus! Why Benedict Is [Likely] Pope — Guest Post by Edmund J. Mazza; Rejoinder by Fr John Rickert," William M. Briggs (www.WMBriggs.com), April 26, 2022. https://www.wmbriggs.com/post/39752/

[57] Credit to Fr. John Rickert FSSP, PH.D. for making this very point in his rebuttal of Dr. Mazza. See Fr. John Rickert, FSSP, PH.D., "Follow The Munus! Why Benedict Is [Likely] Pope — Guest Post by Edmund J. Mazza; Rejoinder by Fr John Rickert," William M. Briggs (www.WMBriggs.com), April 26, 2022, https://www.wmbriggs.com/post/39752/

[58] See "Benedict XVI Says Doubts on Resignation Are "Absurd"," Zenit, February 26, 2014, retrieved April 19, 2022 at 12:43 p.m. https://zenit.org/2014/02/26/benedict-xvi-says-doubts-on-resignation-are-absurd/ Pope Emeritus Benedict XVI was quoted as saying: "There is absolutely no doubt regarding the validity of my resignation from the Petrine ministry. The only condition for the validity of my resignation is the complete freedom of my decision. Speculations regarding its validity are simply absurd." Benedict's camp has not denied the validity of the quote, so there are no grounds to reject its veracity.

[59] See Peter Seewald, *Benedict XVI: A Life. Volume 2.* (English translation. Great Britain: Bloomsbury Continuum, 2021), p. 660. Seewald recounts that Pope Benedict XVI met cardinals on the morning of February 28, 2013, before his resignation became effective. Seewald notes that Benedict at that time told these cardinals, "And among you in the College of Cardinals is a future pope to whom today I promise my unconditional respect and my unconditional obedience."

[60] *Universi Dominici Gregis* 87 as amended by Pope Benedict XVI, "Motu Proprio *Normas Nonnullas*," Libreria Editrice Vaticana, February, 22, 2013. https://www.vatican.va/content/benedict-xvi/en/motu_proprio/documents/hf_ben-xvi_motu-proprio_20130222_normas-nonnullas.html

[61] *Universi Dominici Gregis* 88 (see Pope John Paul II, "Apostolic Constitution *Universi Dominici Gregis*," Libreria Editrice Vaticana.

February 22, 1996.) https://www.vatican.va/content/john-paul-ii/en/apost_constitutions/documents/hf_jp-ii_apc_22021996_universi-dominici-gregis.html

⁶² See Peter Seewald, *Benedict: A Life. Volume 2*, p 669. Seewald quotes Benedict from his interview as saying, "This legal-spiritual formula avoids any idea of there being two popes at the same time: a bishopric can only have one incumbent." Note: As is clearer in the discussion in the interview, Benedict is justifying his use of the title "pope emeritus," and at this point he is affirming there are not two popes, only one and that is Francis, and that there is only one incumbent of a bishopric, that is Francis and not Benedict.

⁶³ See discussion in: https://romalocutaest.com/2017/09/25/a-filial-correction-of-those-who-believe-benedict-is-still-pope/

⁶⁴ See Diane Montagna, "Did Benedict really resign? Gänswein, Burke and Brandmüller weigh in," LifeSiteNews, February 14, 2019. https://www.lifesitenews.com/news/did-benedict-really-resign-gaenswein-burke-and-brandmueller-weigh-in/ . In this article, both Cardinal Burke and Cardinal Brandmüller affirm the validity of Benedict's resignation.

⁶⁵ Cardinal Müller has affirmed Benedict is no longer pope. See David McCloon, "Cdl. Müller: Pope Francis resigning with Benedict still alive would be a 'big problem'," LifeSiteNews, June 22, 2022. https://www.lifesitenews.com/news/cdl-muller-pope-francis-resigning-with-benedict-still-alive-would-be-a-big-problem/

⁶⁶ Bishop Athanasius Schneider recently spoke out on the issue by video. See Michael Haynes, "Bishop Schneider: Theory that Benedict XVI is pope and not Francis defies 'tradition of the Church'," LifeSiteNews, June 9, 2022. https://www.lifesitenews.com/news/bishop-schneider-theory-that-benedict-xvi-is-pope-and-not-francis-defies-tradition-of-the-church/

⁶⁷ A papal resignation does not need to be "accepted by anyone." See note 55.

⁶⁸ See https://www.atmmarketplace.com/news/bank-of-italy-shuts-down-vatican-atms-over-aml-issues/

⁶⁹ For reporting on such rumors, see Andrea Vogt, "'Plot to kill pope' sparks Italian media storm," The Guardian, February 10, 2012.

https://www.theguardian.com/world/2012/feb/10/plot-kill-pope-italian-media

[70] Peter Seewald, *Benedict XVI: Last Testament in his own words* (London: Bloomsbury Publishing Company Plc, 2016), p. 23.

[71] Coriden, James A., et al, eds. *The Code of Canon Law: A Text and Commentary*, p. 437.

[72] Liber Sextus (I, VII, I), UCLA Digital Library, pp. 197-198, retrieved June 7, 2022, 4:57 p.m.
https://digital.library.ucla.edu/catalog/ark:/21198/zz0014rx8d?cv=35

[73] See Fr. John Rickert, FSSP, Ph.D., "Follow The Munus! Why Benedict Is [Likely] Pope — Guest Post by Edmund J. Mazza; Rejoinder by Fr John Rickert".
https://www.wmbriggs.com/post/39752/.
Permission to use and cite article granted by W.M. Briggs, and Fr. John Rickert, FSSP.

[74] Ibid.

[75] "Abdicatio, onis, f. abdico, I. a renouncing, disowning…". See Charlton T. Lewis, Charles Short, ed., Abdicatio. *A Latin Dictionary*. Omaha, NE: Patristic Publishing, 2019 (in public domain) p. 50.

[76] See Estefania Acosta, "Adversus Fallacies: A Reply in Defense of the Book 'Benedict XVI: Pope "Emeritus?"'", Katejon.com.br, May 13, 2021.
https://katejon.com.br/wordpress/wp-content/uploads/2021/05/reply_complete-blqd.pdf

[77] Ibid. Acosta provides these and other similar examples.

[78] I would like to thank Ryan Grant who brought the following citation and commentary to my attention. See: John P. Beal, John P., James A. Coriden, Thomas J. Green, eds., *New Commentary on the Code of Canon Law*, Commissioned by the Canon Law Society of America, New York NY/Mahwah NJ: Paulist Press, 2000, p. 437. On p. 438, the *editors of New Commentary on Code of Canon Law state that:* "The new law correctly provides for the resignation of a pope even if in a limited measure (c. 332, §2). Such a resignation must be freely submitted and duly manifested. However, its acceptance is not a requirement. The general provisions on resignation of an office are contained in canons 187-189. These legal regulations are only guidelines since, due to his supreme power, the pope can always pass

new laws, and stands above already valid laws *(Papa supra omnes canones)."*
[79] Ibid...p. 438.
[80] Ibid.
[81] See Brother Alexis Bugnolo, "Catholics Worldwide warn the Cardinals that Benedict XVI is the pope," FromRome.info, November 22, 2021.
https://www.fromrome.info/2021/11/22/catholics-worldwide-warn-the-cardinals-that-benedict-xvi-is-the-pope/
[82] Grant, Ryan, "Rise of the Benevacantists: Who Is Pope?", OnePeterFive, December 14, 2018.
https://onepeterfive.com/benevacantists/
[83] Ryan Grant is the first to my knowledge to make this case in this controversy.
[84] Ryan Grant, "Rise of the Benevacantists: Who is Pope?". https://onepeterfive.com/benevacantists/
[85] Fr. John Rickert, FSSP, Ph.D., "Munus, Ministerium & Pope Emeritus Benedict — Guest Post by Fr John Rickert," William M. Briggs, April 20, 2022.
https://www.wmbriggs.com/post/39718/
Permission to use and cite article granted by W.M. Briggs and Fr. John Rickert, FSSP.
[86] Ibid. "1. "Moenera militia," Lucr. 1,29), eris, n. root mu-; cf.: moenia, munis, munia, etc., *a service, office, post, employment, function, duty* (class.: syn.: officium, ministerium, honos). Etc." See Charlton T. Lewis, Charles Short, ed., Munus. *A Latin Dictionary.*
[87] See Leo F. Stelten, *Dictionary of Ecclesiastical Latin*, (Peabody, Massachusetts: Hendrickson Publishers, 1995). Per *Dictionary of Ecclesiastical Latin*: munus (-eris: n. ; gift, bounty, present, offering; duty, office, employment, responsibility, service; bribe), p. 166; ministerium (-ii: n; ministry, service, office, duty), p. 162.
[88] See Dianne Montagna, "Did Benedict really resign? Gänswein, Burke and Brandmüller weigh in".
https://www.lifesitenews.com/news/did-benedict-really-resign-gaenswein-burke-and-brandmueller-weigh-in/
[89] Ibid.
[90] Ibid.
[91] Ibid.

[92] Lumen Gentium, 20. The Latin from which the English is a translation is as follows: "Missio illa divina, a Christo Apostolis concredita, ad finem saeculi erit duratura, cum Evangelium, ab eis tradendum, sit in omne tempus pro Ecclesia totius vitae principium. Quapropter Apostoli, in hac societate hierarchice ordinata, de instituendis successoribus curam egerunt. Non solum enim varios adiutores in ministerio habuerunt, sed ut missio ipsis concredita post eorum mortem continuaretur, cooperatoribus suis immediatis, quasi per modum testamenti, demandaverunt munus perficiendi et confirmandi opus ab ipsis inceptum, commendantes illis ut attenderent universo gregi, in quo Spiritus Sanctus eos posuit pascere Ecclesiam Dei. Constituerunt itaque huius modi viros ac deinceps ordinationem dederunt, ut cum decessissent, ministerium eorum alii viri probati exciperent. Inter varia illa ministeria quae inde a primis temporibus in Ecclesia exercentur, teste traditione, praecipuum locum tenet munus illorum qui, in episcopatum constituti, per successionem ab initio decurrentem, apostolici seminis traduces habent."

[93] My thanks to Fr. John Rickert, FSSP, who, via private correspondence, brought to my attention both *Lumen Gentium* 20 and its relevance to the question of *ministerium* being a synonym of *munus*, i.e., that the *munus* of the episcopate is "among the ministries."

[94] Pope John Paul I, "Holy Mass for the Inauguration of the Petrine Ministry of the Bishop of Rome, Homily of His Holiness John Paul I," Libreria Editrice Vaticana, September 3, 1978.
https://www.vatican.va/content/john-paul-i/en/homilies/documents/hf_jp-i_hom_03091978.html

[95] "In hac sacra celebratione, qua solemne fit initium ministerii Summi Ecclesiae Pastoris, humeris Nostris impositi, mentem imprimis adorantes orantesque convertimus ad Deum, infinitum et aeternum, qui consilio suo, humanis argumentis inexplicabili, et benignissima dignatione sua ad Cathedram beati Petri Nos evexit. Sponte quidem in haec verba Sancti Pauli Apostoli erumpimus: « O altitudo divitiarum et sapientiae et scientiae Dei: quam incomprehensibilia sunt iudicia eius et investigabiles viae eius." See Pope John Paul I, "Holy Mass for the Inauguration of the Petrine Ministry of the Bishop of Rome, Homily of His Holiness John Paul I."

[96] Pope Benedict XVI, "Pontificatus Exordia," Acta Apostolicae Sedis, ISSN 0001-5199, Vol. 97, N°. 2 5, 2005, May 7, 2005, Libreria Editrice Vaticana. Homily given April 20, 2005, pp. 694-699.

[97] Ibid, p. 696. "Eucharistia, vitae christianae cor ac Ecclesiae evangelizantis fons, necessario permanentem mediamque partem constituit et fontem Petrini ministerii, Nobis commissi." For English translation an Internet translation site was used. (https://www.translate.com/latin-english)

[98] Pope Benedict XVI, *Declaratio.*

[99] Acta Apostolicae Sedis, ISSN 0001-5199, Vol. 97, N°. 2 5, 2005, pp. 706-712.

[100] See Fr. John Rickert, FSSP, Ph.D., "Munus, Ministerium & Pope Emeritus Benedict — Guest Post by Fr John Rickert". https://www.wmbriggs.com/post/39718/. Permission to use and cite article granted by W.M. Briggs, and Fr. John Rickert, FSSP.

[101] Ibid.

[102] See Acosta, Estefania, "Benedict XVI Pope 'Emeritus'? "The 'always' is also a 'forever'," (Independently Published, 2021), p. 55.

[103] Here, Fr. Rickert emphasizes that the word "muneris" is in fact a form of the same word, "munus." See Leo F. Stelten, *Dictionary of Ecclesiastical Latin*, (Peabody, Massachusetts: Hendrickson Publishers, 1995), and its entry on *munus.*

[104] Fr. John Rickert, FSSP, Ph.D., "Munus, Ministerium & Pope Emeritus Benedict — Guest Post by Fr John Rickert". https://www.wmbriggs.com/post/39718/ Permission to use and cite article granted by W.M. Briggs, and Fr. John Rickert, FSSP.

[105] Canon 188: "A resignation submitted out of grave fear, which has been unjustly inflicted, or because of fraud, substantial error or simony is invalid by the law itself." See James A. Coriden, et al, ed, *The Code of Canon Law: A Text and Commentary*, p. 109.

[106] Ibid.

[107] Ann Barnhardt, "The Papacy Is…," Barnhardt.biz, May 25, 2022, retrieved June 7, 2022 at 9:32pm. https://www.barnhardt.biz/2022/05/25/the-papacy-is/

[108] Ibid.

ENDNOTES

[109] Ann Barnhardt, "Thermonuclear Substantial Error...", Barnhardt.biz, January 13, 2019. https://www.barnhardt.biz/2019/01/13/thermonuclear-substantial-error-in-1978-joseph-ratzinger-posited-that-a-monarchical-papacy-was-intrinsically-arian-in-nature-and-the-papacy-should-reflect-the-trinity-a-p/

[110] Ibid.

[111] Cardinal Josef Ratzinger, "The Primacy of the Pope and the Unity of the People of God," Communio International Catholic Review, https://www.communio-icr.com/files/ratzinger41-1.pdf

[112] Ibid, pp. 114 and 115.

[113] Ibid, p. 115

[114] Ibid, p. 115

[115] Ibid, see footnote 9 on p. 115.

[116] See O'Reilly, "Benedict is Still Pope and Other Errors," *Roma Locuta Est*, January 15, 2019. https://romalocutaest.com/2019/01/15/benedict-is-still-not-pope-and-other-errors/

[117] James A. Coriden, et al, eds. *The Code of Canon Law: A Text and Commentary*, p. 109.

[118] See Diane Montagna, "Did Benedict really resign? Gänswein, Burke and Brandmüller weigh in". https://www.lifesitenews.com/news/did-benedict-really-resign-gaenswein-burke-and-brandmueller-weigh-in/)

[119] The objection is the author's summary reconstruction of the thesis advanced by Dr. Edmund Mazza on the Patrick Coffin Show. See Patrick Coffin, "#248: Is Benedict XVI Still the Pope?—Dr. Edmund Mazza," Produced by Patrick Coffin (www.PatrickCoffin.Media), The Patrick Coffin Show, September 14, 2021, 1:31:06. https://www.patrickcoffin.media/is-benedict-xvi-still-the-pope/

[120] *Lumen Gentium* 21.

[121] See Dr. Mazza on Patrick Coffin's show. See Patrick Coffin, "#248: Is Benedict XVI Still the Pope?—Dr. Edmund Mazza". Time stamp 30:01 to 30:55, retrieved 4/21/2022. Unofficial transcript by O'Reilly.

[122] Ibid. Time stamp 31:42 to 31:59. Unofficial transcript by O'Reilly.

¹²³ Josef Ratzinger, *Principles of Catholic Theology: Building Stone for a Fundamental Theology* (San Francisco: Ignatius Press, 1987), pp. 194-195.
¹²⁴ Ibid.
¹²⁵ Dr. Mazza on Patrick Coffin's show. See Patrick Coffin, "#248: Is Benedict XVI Still the Pope?—Dr. Edmund Mazza". Time Stamp 32:01 to 32:43. Unofficial transcript by O'Reilly.
¹²⁶ Josef Ratzinger, *Theological Highlights of Vatican II* (New York/Mahwah NJ: Paulist Press, 1966), pp. 189-190.
¹²⁷ Ibid.
¹²⁸ The author's summary reconstruction of the thesis advanced by Dr. Edmund Mazza on Patrick Coffin's podcast as part of the overall thesis presented on the Patrick Coffin Show. See Patrick Coffin, "#248: Is Benedict XVI Still the Pope?—Dr. Edmund Mazza". https://www.patrickcoffin.media/is-benedict-xvi-still-the-pope/
¹²⁹ Ibid. Time stamp 38:55 to 39:16. Unofficial transcript by O'Reilly.
¹³⁰ Ibid. Time stamp 59:39 to 59:46. Unofficial transcript by O'Reilly.
¹³¹ See Diane Montagna, "Did Benedict really resign? Gänswein, Burke and Brandmüller weigh in". https://www.lifesitenews.com/news/did-benedict-really-resign-gaenswein-burke-and-brandmueller-weigh-in/
¹³² See Timothy J. Gordon, "DEBATE: Is Benedict Still Pope?," Produced by Timothy J. Gordon (www.timothyjgordon.com), Rules for Retrogrades Podcast, February 11, 2022, 1:44:26. https://www.youtube.com/watch?v=G9t-2dCKcKM
¹³³ Patrick Coffin, "#248: Is Benedict XVI Still the Pope?—Dr. Edmund Mazza". Time stamp 38:55 to 39:16. Unofficial transcript by O'Reilly.
¹³⁴ Peter Seewald, *Light of the World* (San Francisco: Ignatius Press, 2010), p. 39.
¹³⁵ Peter Seewald, *Benedict XVI: Last Testament in his own words*, p. 66.
¹³⁶ Andrea Cionci, "Cionci: The Possible Reconstruction of Benedict XVI's 'Plan B'," published by Marco Tosatti, April 11, 2021. Retrieved on April 22, 2022 at 6:37 p.m. https://www.marcotosatti.com/2021/04/11/cionci-the-possible-reconstruction-of-benedict-xvis-plan-b/

ENDNOTES

[137] Ibid. Overall, the author's construction of this objection is based on or inspired by the article written by Andrea Cionci, as it appeared on Marco Tosatti's site.

[138] Fr. John Rickert, FSSP, Ph.D., "Munus, Ministerium & Pope Emeritus Benedict — Guest Post by Fr John Rickert". https://www.wmbriggs.com/post/39718/. Permission to use and cite article granted by W.M. Briggs, and Fr. John Rickert, FSSP.

[139] Andrea Cionci, "Cionci: The Possible Reconstruction of Benedict XVI's "Plan B"".

[140] Ibid. Mr. Cionci informs his reader that Pope Benedict XVI *"might have willingly prearranged an entirely invalid resignation."* Various articles by Mr. Cionci of a similar theme have appeared on a website operated by Br. Bugnolo, (www.FromRome.info).

[141] See O'Reilly, "Benedict's Plan "B" from Outer Space," April 12, 2021. https://romalocutaest.com/2021/04/12/benedicts-plan-b-from-outer-space/

[142] See O'Reilly, "Benedict's Plan B from Outer Space – the Sequel," August 3, 2021. https://romalocutaest.com/2021/08/03/benedicts-plan-b-from-outer-space-the-sequel/

[143] See Chapter 4 for discussion of the "Ratzinger Code."

[144] See Ann Barnhardt, "NonVeni Crosspost: Jesus doesn't require any "secret codes" for men to be saved. The Church is VISIBLE, including at her Earthly Head," Barnhardt.Biz, May 23, 2022, retrieved July 7, 2022. https://www.barnhardt.biz/2022/05/23/nonveni-crosspost-jesus-doesnt-require-any-secret-codes-for-men-to-be-saved-the-church-is-visible-including-at-her-earthly-head/ Ms. Barnhardt writes: "In the same vein, trying to delude oneself into thinking that Pope Benedict is playing some monstrous game of 15-D underwater chess crossed with Pink Slip Chicken at the proverbial quarry, is not only wrong, but assumes a moral monstrosity on the part of Pope Benedict that would be right up there with Judas Iscariot."

[145] See Ann Barnhardt, "Breaking: Pope Benedict's personal secretary, Archbishop Ganswein sobbing repeatedly when talking about the failed attempted resignation. NOTHING TO SEE HERE". https://www.barnhardt.biz/2022/06/19/breaking-pope-benedicts-

personal-secretary-archbishop-ganswein-sobbing-repeatedly-when-talking-about-the-failed-attempted-resignation-nothing-to-see-here/ Ms. Barnhardt writes in part: "Let us disabuse ourselves of ANY notion of any categorical nonsense like a 'Ratzinger Code'. Anyone pushing such a fiction – and FICTION truly is the word – is a profiteer, looking to make money off of this abject train wreck of a situation."

[146] See Andrea Cionci, "Ratzinger, dagli Usa tre obiezioni alla tesi del 'Piano B'. Rispondiamo punto per punto." LiberoQuotidiano.it, July 25, 2021. Retrieved April 22, 2022 at 7:30 p.m. https://www.liberoquotidiano.it/articolo_blog/blog/andrea-cionci/28098801/papa-ratzinger-tre-obiezioni-usa-teoria-piano-b-rispondiamo-punto-per-punto.html

[147] Gagliarducci, Andrea, "What Could Pope Francis' Message Be With His Choice of New Cardinals?", National Catholic Register, May 30, 2022. Retrieved July 7, 2022. https://www.ncregister.com/cna/what-could-pope-francis-message-be-with-his-choice-of-new-cardinals

In his article, Gagliarducci observes that as of the consistory in August 2022, about 65% of the Cardinals who are vote-eligible for a conclave will have been appointed by Pope Francis. This makes a Francis-like successor all the more probable. Given such a situation, the Plan B theory seems all the more nonsensical.

[148] See Andrea Cionci, "Ratzinger, dagli Usa tre obiezioni alla tesi del 'Piano B'". https://www.liberoquotidiano.it/articolo_blog/blog/andrea-cionci/28098801/papa-ratzinger-tre-obiezioni-usa-teoria-piano-b-rispondiamo-punto-per-punto.html

[149] Acosta, Estefania, *Benedict XVI Pope 'Emeritus'? The 'always' is also a 'forever'"* (Independently Published, 2021), p. 72.

[150] Ibid. The preceding two quotes from source, see note 149, form the core of author's (O'Reilly's) construction of this objection.

[151] See Dr. Edward Peters, "Lighter fare: can bad Latin save a papacy?", CanonLawblog, October 1, 2014, retrieved July 8, 2022, 11:02 a.m. https://canonlawblog.wordpress.com/2014/10/01/lighter-fare-can-bad-latin-save-a-papacy/

[152] Ibid.

[153] Ibid.

ENDNOTES

[154] Andrea Cionci, "Andrea Cionci responds to MSGR. Athanasius Schneider's appeal to accept Bergoglio as pope," FromRome.info, June 15, 2022, retrieved June 18, 2022, 1:53 p.m.
https://www.fromrome.info/2022/06/15/andrea-cionci-responds-to-msgr-athanasius-schneiders-appeal-to-accept-bergoglio-as-pope/

[155] Ryan Sayre Patricio, "Pius XII Planned to Resign if Seized by Nazis," First Things, May 6, 2009, retrieved June 18, 2022, 2:05 p.m.
https://www.firstthings.com/blogs/firstthoughts/2009/05/pius-xii-planned-to-resign-if-seized-by-nazis;
and see also, Jerry Filteau, "Pope Pius XII was prepared to resign as pope," National Catholic Reporter, blogs, February 28, 2013, retrieved June 18, 2022, 2:11 p.m.
https://www.ncronline.org/blogs/ncr-today/pope-pius-xii-was-prepared-resign-pope

[156] Cindy Wooden, "Resignation letter prepared by Blessed Paul VI published," National Catholic Reporter, blogs, May 16, 2018, June 18, 2022, 2:17 p.m. https://www.ncronline.org/news/vatican/resignation-letter-prepared-blessed-paul-vi-published

[157] James A. Coriden, et al, eds. *The Code of Canon Law: A Text and Commentary*, p. 110.

[158] The citation and use of Canon 189.4 in the reply to this objection was directly suggested to the author by an article written by Fr. John Rickert, FSSP who made the point regarding Canon 189§4 that *"He (Benedict) even had a window of opportunity to revoke this resignation."* See Fr. John Rickert FSSP, Ph.D., "Antipope Claims: Substantial Error — Guest Post by Fr John Rickert, FSSP," William M. Briggs, March 20, 2017. https://www.wmbriggs.com/post/21231/ Permission to use and cite article granted by W.M. Briggs and Fr. John Rickert, FSSP.

[159] *Universi Dominici Gregis* 87 was modified by Pope Benedict XVI in his motu proprio *Normas Nonnullas*, February 22, 2013.

[160] *Universi Dominici Gregis* 88.

[161] We will see this point underlined in Chapter 5. On February 2013, shortly before 8 p.m.—the effective date and time his renunciation became effective, Pope Benedict XVI told a group of pilgrims he would no longer be Supreme Pontiff as of 8 p.m.

[162] Dr. Mazza appeared on Dr. Taylor Marshall's podcast on two

occasions in 2029 wherein he advanced his bifurcation theory. See Dr. Taylor Marshall, "Is Benedict XVI Still the Pope? Did Pope Benedict XVI Fully Resign the Papacy or Just a Part of It?", Produced by Dr. Taylor Marshall (https://www.youtube.com/c/DrTaylorMarshall), Dr Taylor Marshall Podcast, May 27, 2020, 1:41:07. https://www.youtube.com/watch?v=bABWi2CoVlc For the second appearance, see Dr. Taylor Marshall, "Is Pope Benedict XVI Still Pope (but Francis Bishop of Rome?) Mazza Thesis Revisited", Produced by Dr. Taylor Marshall (https://www.youtube.com/c/DrTaylorMarshall), Dr Taylor Marshall Podcast, June 10, 2020, 2:05:24. https://www.youtube.com/watch?v=iK1Zg1WyKI4

[163] Canon 331: "The bishop of the Roman Church, in whom continues the office given by the Lord uniquely to Peter, the first of the Apostles, and to be transmitted to his successors, is the head of the college of bishops, the Vicar of Christ, and the pastor of the universal Church on earth. By virtue of his office he possesses supreme, full, immediate, and universal ordinary power in the Church, which he is always able to exercise freely." See John P. Beal, et al, eds. *New Commentary on the Code of Canon Law*.

[164] Dr. Mazza at one time did argue this thesis. It appears he has backed away from it in favor of the thesis he advanced on Patrick Coffin's Show. Regardless, it is impossible to separate the Petrine succession from the See of Rome. While theological arguments can demonstrate this point, e.g., based on Pastor Aeturnus, it suffices here to point out that the *Normas Nonnullas* specifically states that the one elected in the conclave is Bishop of Rome and Supreme Pontiff with full power over the universal Church. Thus, setting aside whether it is even possible to do as Dr. Mazza suggested, we need merely answer that *Normas Nonnullas* makes no provision for it, and thus it is evident this was not the intention of Pope Benedict XVI. Consequently, the Benepapist thesis on this ground alone fails.

[165] See the cover of Estefania Acosta's book, *Benedict XVI: Pope "Emeritus"? "The 'always' is also a 'forever'"*.

[166] Those Benepapists who accept the "substantial-error" theory.

[167] Those Benepapists who believe Pope Benedict XVI submitted a resignation that was "deficient" in the sense he did not really resign the papacy at all. These Benepapists are those who essentially accept some version of the Plan B theory.

ENDNOTES

[168] Pope Benedict XVI, excerpt from the General Audience, February 27, 2013.

[169] Ibid.

[170] Cardinal Josef Ratzinger, "The Transfiguration," originally a homily given August 10, 1979, Reprinted in L'Osservatore Romano, Weekly Edition in English, 7-14 August 2013, page 3, published online on EWTN (www.ewtn.com).
https://www.ewtn.com/catholicism/library/transfiguration-1723

[171] Pope Benedict XVI, "Mass, Imposition of the Pallium, and conferral of the Fisherman's Ring for the Beginning of the Petrine Ministry of the Bishop of Rome, Homily of His Holiness Benedict XVI," Libreria Editrice Vaticana. Sunday, April 24, 2005.
https://www.vatican.va/content/benedict-xvi/en/homilies/2005/documents/hf_ben-xvi_hom_20050424_inizio-pontificato.html

[172] Pope Benedict XVI, excerpt from the General Audience, February 27, 2013.

[173] Peter Seewald, *Benedict XVI: Last Testament in his own words*, p.73 (Kindle version).

[174] Peter Seewald, *Benedict XVI: A Life. Volume 2: Professor and Prefect to Pope and Pope Emeritus 1966–The Present*, p. 669.

[175] Pope Benedict XVI, last General Audience, February 27, 2013.

[176] Author's construction of this objection, inclusive of a direct quote, is based on article found on the site NonVeniPacem. See Mark Docherty, "FAQ: Did Pope Benedict reveal his intent to bifurcate the papacy in the actual *Declaratio*?", July 22, 2017. Retrieved July 8, 2022, 1:28 p.m. https://nonvenipacem.com/2017/07/22/faq-did-pope-benedict-reveal-his-intent-to-bifurcate-the-papacy-in-the-actual-declaratio/

[177] Pope Benedict XVI, last General Audience, February 27, 2013.

[178] Ibid.

[179] Close paraphrase, near verbatim, of statement found in Mark Docherty, "FAQ: Did Pope Benedict reveal his intent to bifurcate the papacy in the actual Declaratio?".
https://nonvenipacem.com/2017/07/22/faq-did-pope-benedict-reveal-his-intent-to-bifurcate-the-papacy-in-the-actual-declaratio/

[180] Mark Docherty, "FAQ: Did Pope Benedict reveal his intent to bifurcate the papacy in the actual Declaratio?"

¹⁸¹ Estefania Acosta, "Adversus Fallacies: A Reply in Defense of the Book 'Benedict XVI: Pope "Emeritus?"'".
https://katejon.com.br/wordpress/wp-content/uploads/2021/05/reply_complete-blqd.pdf
¹⁸² Ibid.
¹⁸³ Ibid.
¹⁸⁴ This objection was constructed by the author based on his reading and understanding of Dr. Mazza's theory. Compare to Dr. Edmund Mazza, "'Leave the Throne, Take the Ministry' The Sacred Powers of Pope Emeritus", www.EdmundMazza.com, April 21, 2021.
https://www.edmundmazza.com/2021/04/21/leave-the-throne-take-the-ministry-the-sacred-powers-of-pope-emeritus/
Note, for example, at one point in his article Dr. Mazza quotes from Benedict's last general audience, inserting his bracketed comments: *"My decision to resign the active exercise of the ministry does not revoke this…I am not abandoning the cross, but remaining in a new way at the side of the crucified Lord. I no longer bear the power of office for the governance* [potestas iurisdictionis] *of the Church, but in the service of prayer I remain, so to speak, in the enclosure of Saint Peter* [potestas ordinis]."
¹⁸⁵ Here Fr. John Rickert, FSSP emphasizes the word *muneris* is in fact a form of the same word, *munus*. See Leo F. Stelten, *Dictionary of Ecclesiastical Latin*, (Peabody, Massachusetts: Hendrickson Publishers, 1995), and its entry on *munus*.
¹⁸⁶ Fr. John Rickert, FSSP, Ph.D., "Munus, Ministerium & Pope Emeritus Benedict — Guest Post by Fr John Rickert".
https://www.wmbriggs.com/post/39718/
¹⁸⁷ Ibid.
¹⁸⁸ Code of Canon Law, Canon 331.
https://www.vatican.va/archive/cod-iuris-canonici/eng/documents/cic_lib2-cann330-367_en.html
¹⁸⁹ Pope Benedict XVI, "Greeting of His Holiness Benedict XVI to the Faithful of the Diocese of Albano (Thursday, February 28, 2013)", Libreria Editrice Vaticana. February 27, 2013.
https://www.vatican.va/content/benedict-xvi/en/speeches/2013/february/documents/hf_ben-xvi_spe_20130228_fedeli-albano.html

[190] Pope Benedict XVI, *Declaratio*.
[191] *Universi Dominici Gregis* (UDG) 88.
[192] See *Normas Nonnullas* which amended *Universi Dominici Gregis* 87.
[193] See Acosta, Estefania, *Benedict XVI Pope "Emeritus"? "The 'always' is also a 'forever'"* (Independently Published, 2021), p. 58.
[194] Ibid. There is no need to go into a discussion of Ms. Acosta's discussion of "parallelism."
[195] Ibid, p. 70.
[196] Curiously, one can find an article by Mark Docherty on his site (www.NonVeniPacem.com) back on June 26, 2016, in which he cited Benedict's words "*I am no longer Supreme Pontiff of the Catholic Church.*" However, he offered them as a proof *against* Ms. Ann Barnhardt's argument that Benedict is (still) pope. (See Mark Docherty, "Examining the Benedictine Option", June 26, 2016. https://nonvenipacem.com/2016/06/26/examining-the-benedictine-option/) Unfortunately, Mr. Docherty reversed his opposition to Ms. Barnhardt's thesis a little over a year later, declaring then his moral certitude had done a reverse-180, and he now believed Benedict's abdication was invalid (See Mark Docherty, "Count me in: Moral Certitude and the invalid abdication of Pope Benedict XVI, still reigning," July 3, 2017. https://nonvenipacem.com/2017/07/03/count-me-in-moral-certitude-and-the-invalid-abdication-of-pope-benedict-xvi-still-reigning/ Note: This reversal of moral certainty was apparently based on Ms. Barnhardt's *spurious* interpretations of Benedict's last audience and Gänswein's speech. The most interesting thing is that Mr. Docherty *never* publicly explained why Barnhardt's questionable interpretation of the last audience trumped the clear and obvious meaning of Benedict's words "*I am no longer the Supreme Pontiff of the Catholic Church.*" Unfortunately, to my knowledge, neither Ms. Barnhardt nor *Mr. Docherty the Benepapist* have answered the question posed by *Mr. Docherty the anti-Benepapist's*, essentially, "If you're a Benepapist, how do you explain Pope Benedict XVI's statement '*I am no longer the Supreme Pontiff of the Catholic Church*'?" Unfortunately, on this point, Mr. Docherty had less faith in his own better judgment than in Ms. Barnhardt's.
[197] See earlier discussion of unsuccessful attempts by Ms. Barnhardt

and Dr. Mazza to tie Josef Ratzinger, either as theologian or pope, to a "substantial error" related to the papacy and relevant to the Benepapist controversy.

[198] The term "Ratzinger Code" originated with Andrea Cionci, for example, see Andrea Cionci, "'Codice Ratzinger': trovato il più clamoroso dei messaggi, in mondovisione da Castel Gandolfo," LiberoQuotidiano.it, December18, 2021. https://www.liberoquotidiano.it/articolo_blog/blog/andrea-cionci/29829255/trovato-clamoroso-messaggio-in-codice-ratzinger-benedetto-sbaglio-apposta-il-titolo-pontificale-in-mondovisione-da-castel-ga.html)

[199] For statement in quotes, See Andrea Cionci; "Ratzinger Code": found the most sensational of messages, worldwide from Castel Gandolfo, December 18, 2021. Also see Andrea Cionci, https://sfero.me/article/ratzinger-code-the-sensational-messages-from December 18, 2021.
NOTE: Author (O'Reilly) based his construction of the overall objection on his reading and understanding of Mr. Cionci's "Ratzinger Code" thesis as applied to Benedict's statement to the pilgrims from Albano.

[200] Andrea Cionci, "Cionci: The Possible Reconstruction of Benedict XVI's 'Plan B'," Published by Marco Tosatti, April 11, 2021. Retrieved on April 22, 2022 at 6:37 p.m. https://www.marcotosatti.com/2021/04/11/cionci-the-possible-reconstruction-of-benedict-xvis-plan-b/

[201] Andrea Cionci, *Codice Ratzinger*.

[202] Estefania Acosta, *Benedict XVI Pope "Emeritus"? "The 'always' is also a 'forever,'"* p. 73.

[203] Andrea Cionci, "'Good Night!'. Ratzinger Code on the 'Roman' hour of Benedict XVI's impeded see: Francis is not the pope," Sfero Social Italiano, April 4, 2022. https://sfero.me/article/good-night-ratzinger-code-on-the-roman-hour-of-benedict-xvi-s-impeded-see-francis-is-not-the-pope

[204] Ibid.

[205] See J. Arendzen, (1909). Gnosticism. In *The Catholic Encyclopedia*. http://www.newadvent.org/cathen/06592a.htm

ENDNOTES

[206] Pope Benedict XVI. "Greeting of His Holiness Benedict XVI to the Faithful of the Diocese of Albano (Thursday, February 28, 2013)." https://www.vatican.va/content/benedict-xvi/en/speeches/2013/february/documents/hf_ben-xvi_spe_20130228_fedeli-albano.html

[207] Andrea Cionci, "'Codice Ratzinger': trovato il più clamoroso dei messaggi, in mondovisione da Castel Gandolfo," https://www.liberoquotidiano.it/articolo_blog/blog/andrea-cionci/29829255/trovato-clamoroso-messaggio-in-codice-ratzinger-benedetto-sbaglio-apposta-il-titolo-pontificale-in-mondovisione-da-castel-ga.html)

[208] Cionci is the author.

[209] Sapere.It, Pontefice. De Agostini Editore S.p.A, retrieved July 8, 2022, 7:02 p.m. https://www.sapere.it/enciclopedia/pont%C3%A9fice.html

[210] Translation by the author. Note: "Pontiff Supreme" is a strict *word-by-word* translation, but "Supreme Pontiff" is a proper translation.

[211] "*Quando II Luglio MDCCCLVII La Santita Del Pontefice Sommo Papa Pio IX Letificava Di Sua Sacra Augusta Presenza La Citta di Modena*," Le Confraternite Laicale a Perennare la Memoria di tal Giorno Volevano Pubblicato il Sequente Omaggio Poetico che Riverenti Ponevano a Piedi del Supremo Gerarca, found in the Italian History of the Risorgimento Period, the Collection of H. Nelson Gay, A.M., 1896, bought from the bequest of Archibald Gary Coolidge, A.B. 1887, 1931. https://play.google.com/books/reader?id=FPIQQCOqdhoC&pg=GBS.PP2&hl=en

[212] Bishop Tommaso Michele Salzano, *Brevi Riflessioni sul modo di Risolvere E Sull'Opportunita di Definire l'Infallibilita del Pontefice Sommo*, typography by Stanislao de Lella, Napoli. 1870. Found in the Fordham University Libraries, digital collection. https://cdm17265.contentdm.oclc.org/digital/collection/italianPamp/id/33077)

[213] Pope Pius X, *Communion Rerum*, Italian translation of the Encyclical Communion Rerum. *Acta Apostolicae Sedis*, Vol. 1, N°. 1, 1909, January 1, 1909, Libreria Editrice Vaticana. Encyclical *Communion Rerum*, April 21, 1909, pp.333-388.

https://www.vatican.va/archive/aas/documents/AAS-01-1909-ocr.pdf

[214] Pope John XXIII, "Ad christifideles in foro Sancti Petri coadunatos, quo urnae sollemniter delatae sunt, in quibus S. Pii Papae X et S. Ioannis Bosco sacrae asservantur exuviae," Acta Apostolicae Sedis. Vol. 51 (LI), (Series III, v. 1), No. 1, 1959, January 24, 1959, Libreria Editrice Vaticana, May 11, 1959, pp. 367-371.

https://www.vatican.va/archive/aas/documents/AAS-51-1959-ocr.pdf

[215] Pope John XXIII, "Adhortatio ad Clerum, Qui E Tota Venetorum Regione Venetias Convenerat, in Basilica S. Marci Sacras Exuvias Sancti PII Papae X Veneraturus," Acta Apostolicae Sedis. Vol. 51 (LI), (Series III, v. 1), No. 1, 1959, January 24, 1959, Libreria Editrice Vaticana, pp. 375-381.

https://www.vatican.va/archive/aas/documents/AAS-51-1959-ocr.pdf

[216] Pope John XXIII, "Ad Praelatos Auditores ceterosque Officiales, Advocatos et Procuratores Tribunalis Sacrae Romanae Rotae," Acta Apostolicae Sedis. Vol. 51 (LI), (Series III, v. 1), No. 1, 1959, January 24, 1959, Libreria Editrice Vaticana, October 19, 1959, p. 822.

https://www.vatican.va/archive/aas/documents/AAS-51-1959-ocr.pdf

[217] Excerpts from "Complete English Text: Archbishop Georg Gänswein's 'Expanded Petrine Office' Speech" by Diane Montagna, May 30, 2016. © Aleteia.org. Used with permission, no other use of this material is authorized.

[218] Discussed by O'Reilly here: "Benedict is really, really still not pope! Really!", September 22, 2018.

https://romalocutaest.com/2018/09/22/benedict-is-really-really-still-not-pope-really/

[219] Peter Seewald, *Benedict XVI: A Life. Volume 2: Professor and Prefect to Pope and Pope Emeritus 1966–The Present*, p. 669.

[220] Dr. Edmund J. Mazza, "Guest Post: Dr. Edmund Mazza's Position Paper on the Invalidity of Pope Benedict's Resignation: Pope Emeritus: Enigma: An Explanation at Last," Barnhardt.biz, May 27, 2020, retrieved July 8, 2022, 7:13 p.m.

https://www.barnhardt.biz/2020/05/27/guest-post-dr-edmund-mazzas-position-paper-on-the-invalidity-of-pope-benedicts-resignation/;

[221] Excerpts from "Complete English Text: Archbishop Georg Gänswein's 'Expanded Petrine Office' Speech" by Diane Montagna. May 30, 2016. © Aleteia.org. Used with permission, no other use of this material is authorized.

ENDNOTES

222 Ibid. © Aleteia.org. Used with permission, no other use of this material is authorized.

223 Taylor Marshall, Ph.D, "Is Benedict XVI Still the Pope? Did Pope Benedict XVI Fully Resign the Papacy or Just a Part of It?" https://www.youtube.com/watch?v=bABWi2CoVlc

224 Dr. Edmund J. Mazza, Ph.D, "Guest Post: Dr. Edmund Mazza's Position Paper on the Invalidity of Pope Benedict's Resignation: Pope Emeritus: Enigma: An Explanation at Last". https://www.barnhardt.biz/2020/05/27/guest-post-dr-edmund-mazzas-position-paper-on-the-invalidity-of-pope-benedicts-resignation/

225 Actually, to give due credit, the Benepapist website www.NonVeniPacem.com operated by Mark Docherty was the first, to my knowledge, to call attention to Gänswein's reference to Duns Scotus (see https://nonvenipacem.com/2018/12/09/was-the-immaculate-conception-a-proxy-for-the-expanded-petrine-ministryarchbishop-ganswein-thinks-so/). Due credit for being the first aside, Mr. Docherty's analysis regarding the import of the words at issue is wrong, as outlined in Chapter 5 and the replies to the objections.

226 The *Kobayashi Maru* is a reference found in the television and movie series *Star Trek*, probably something only a Trekkie gets. Essentially, and briefly, it refers to a no-win situation that was notably overcome by only one man, the story's hero, Captain Kirk. If you really must, you can read more here: https://en.wikipedia.org/wiki/Kobayashi_Maru

227 Dr. Mazza's theory is untenable, as proven in the discussion about *Normas Nonnullas* in Chapter 2. See O'Reilly's articles at *Roma Locuta Est* which rebut the theory proposed by Dr. Mazza on Dr. Taylor Marshall's podcast: see "Summa Contra Dr. Mazza," November 2, 2020. https://romalocutaest.com/2020/11/02/the-summa-contra-dr-mazza/

228 Dr. Mazza appears to have abandoned the theory he once advanced on Dr. Taylor Marshall's program, i.e., regarding the separation of the Petrine succession from the See of Rome. See Patrick Coffin, "#248: Is Benedict XVI Still the Pope?—Dr. Edmund Mazza."

229 Excerpts from "Complete English Text: Archbishop Georg Gänswein's 'Expanded Petrine Office' Speech" by Diane Montagna.

May 30, 2016. © Aleteia.org. Used with permission, no other use of this material is authorized.

[230] James Coriden, et al, eds., *The Code of Canon Law: A Text and Commentary*, p. 109.

[231] Edward Pentin, "Benedict XVI Discusses His Resignation in Newly Published Letters," National Catholic Register, blog, September 19, 2018. https://www.ncregister.com/blog/benedict-xvi-discusses-his-resignation-in-newly-published-letters

Author's discussion of issue on his blog, *Roma Locuta Est*, is here: "Benedict is really, really still not pope! Really!" https://romalocutaest.com/2018/09/22/benedict-is-really-really-still-not-pope-really/

[232] CBC, "5 papal things Benedict gives up in retirement," CBC.CA, February 28, 2013. https://www.cbc.ca/news/world/5-papal-things-benedict-gives-up-in-retirement-1.1332261

[233] Pope Benedict XVI, "Mass, Imposition of the Pallium, and conferral of the Fisherman's Ring for the Beginning of the Petrine Ministry of the Bishop of Rome, Homily of His Holiness Benedict XVI". https://www.vatican.va/content/benedict-xvi/en/homilies/2005/documents/hf_ben-xvi_hom_20050424_inizio-pontificato.html

[234] The author raised the example of a "professor emeritus" in his debate with Dr. Mazza on February 11, 2022. See Timothy J. Gordon, "DEBATE: Is Benedict Still Pope?", time stamp 45:40 to 46:05. https://www.youtube.com/watch?v=G9t-2dCKcKM

[235] Dr. Edward Feser makes the same point about the use of the title "pope emeritus." See Dr. Edward Feser, "Benedict is not the pope: A reply to some critics," EdwardFeser.Blog, May 5, 2022. https://edwardfeser.blogspot.com/2022/05/benedict-is-not-pope-reply-to-some.html

[236] James Coriden, et al, eds., *The Code of Canon Law: A Text and Commentary*, p. 109.

[237] Peter Seewald, *Benedict XVI: A Life. Volume 2: Professor and Prefect to Pope and Pope Emeritus 1966–The Present*, p. 669.

[238] Holweck, F. (1907). Apostolic Blessing. In *The Catholic Encyclopedia.* New York: Robert Appleton Company. Retrieved August 7, 2022 from New Advent:

http://www.newadvent.org/cathen/02602a.htm

[239] In this discussion of apostolic blessings, my thanks again go to Fr. John Rickert, FSSP. In private correspondence with him, it was he who specifically pointed my attention to several canons that were relevant to the debate over Benedict and apostolic blessings. These Canons include 1166, 1167, and 1168.

[240] John P. Beal, et al, eds., *New Commentary on the Code of Canon Law*, p. 1402.

[241] Ibid.

[242] In private correspondence with Fr. John Rickert, FSSP regarding the reply on apostolic blessings in this section, Fr. Rickert made this precise point.

[243] See Ann Barnhardt, "REPOST BY REQUEST: The Mountain of Evidence that Pope Benedict never validly resigned is like Kilauea – it just keeps spewing truth magma," Barnhart.biz, April 11, 2021, retrieved July 8, 2022, 10:45 p.m. https://www.barnhardt.biz/2021/04/11/eight-years-ago-today-in-a-packed-piazza-san-pietro-pope-benedict-made-it-clear-that-he-was-not-validly-resigning-the-papacy/

[244] See Diane Montagna, "Did Benedict really resign? Gänswein, Burke and Brandmüller weigh in", https://www.lifesitenews.com/news/did-benedict-really-resign-gaenswein-burke-and-brandmueller-weigh-in/

[245] Peter Seewald, *Benedict XVI: A Life. Volume 2: Professor and Prefect to Pope and Pope Emeritus 1966–The Present*, p. 668.

[246] Pope Benedict XVI, last General Audience, February 27 2013. See discussion in Chapter 3.

[247] See CNA, "Is Francis the last Pope? A rare interview with Archbishop Gänswein," Catholic News Agency, June 26, 2016. https://www.catholicnewsagency.com/news/34096/is-francis-the-last-pope-a-rare-interview-with-archbishop-ganswein; Diane Montagna, "Did Benedict really resign? Gänswein, Burke and Brandmüller weigh in," https://www.lifesitenews.com/news/did-benedict-really-resign-gaenswein-burke-and-brandmueller-weigh-in/: In her article, Ms. Montagna reports that Gänswein complained: "*I saw from among the reactions that I was imputed to have said a number of things that I did not say. Of course, Pope Francis is the legitimate and legitimately elected pope.*"

[248] CNA, "Is Francis the last Pope? A rare interview with Archbishop Gänswein". https://www.catholicnewsagency.com/news/34096/is-francis-the-last-pope-a-rare-interview-with-archbishop-ganswein

[249] See Diane Montagna, "Did Benedict really resign? Gänswein, Burke and Brandmüller weigh in". https://www.lifesitenews.com/news/did-benedict-really-resign-gaenswein-burke-and-brandmueller-weigh-in/

[250] Ibid.

[251] Ibid.

[252] Objection may be found in a blog post by Ann Barnhardt, "If Pope Benedict is the first-ever "Pope Emeritus", doesn't that mean that his ontological state is DIFFERENT from the Popes who actually resigned?", www.Barnhardt.biz, May 1, 2022, https://www.barnhardt.biz/2018/12/10/if-pope-benedict-is-the-first-ever-pope-emeritus-doesnt-that-mean-that-his-ontological-state-is-different-from-the-popes-who-actually-resigned/

[253] See Wikipedia article on the Three Traditional Laws: https://en.m.wikipedia.org/wiki/Law_of_thought#The_three_traditional_laws

[254] Ann Barnhardt.

[255] Ann Barnhardt, "If Pope Benedict is the first-ever "Pope Emeritus", doesn't that mean that his ontological state is DIFFERENT from the Popes who actually resigned?"

[256] James Coriden, et al, eds., *The Code of Canon Law: A Text and Commentary*, p. 109.

[257] Edward Pentin, "Benedict XVI Discusses His Resignation in Newly Published Letters." National Catholic Register, blog, September 19, 2018. https://www.ncregister.com/blog/benedict-xvi-discusses-his-resignation-in-newly-published-letters

[258] Peter Seewald, *Benedict XVI: A Life. Volume 2: Professor and Prefect to Pope and Pope Emeritus 1966–The Present*, p. 669. During his interview, Seewald asked about Benedict's use of the honorific title "emeritus." Benedict replied: *"In this formula both things are implied: no actual legal authority any longer, but a relationship which remains even if it is invisible."* Furthermore, Benedict told Seewald explicitly this *"legal-spiritual formula avoids any idea of there being two popes at the same time: a bishopric can only have one incumbent. But the*

ENDNOTES

formula also expresses a spiritual link, which cannot ever be taken away."

[259] Excerpts from "Complete English Text: Archbishop Georg Gänswein's 'Expanded Petrine Office' Speech" by Diane Montagna. May 30, 2016. © Aleteia.org. Used with permission, no other use of this material is authorized.

[260] The objection is excerpted from a blog post by Ann Barnhardt, "REPOST BY REQUEST: The Mountain of Evidence that Pope Benedict never validly resigned is like Kilauea – it just keeps spewing truth magma". https://www.barnhardt.biz/2021/04/11/eight-years-ago-today-in-a-packed-piazza-san-pietro-pope-benedict-made-it-clear-that-he-was-not-validly-resigning-the-papacy/

[261] I think it fair to characterize the objection as having an ad hominem component. Although the objection does not explicitstate the target or targets of its attention, I replied to the objection and its accusations on two previous occasions. See O'Reilly, "On the 8th Anniversary of the Resignation of Pope Benedict XVI," February 28, 2021. https://romalocutaest.com/2021/02/28/on-the-8th-anniversary-of-the-resignation-of-pope-benedict-xvi/; and see "Regarding Benedict's Last Audience," February 27, 2022. https://romalocutaest.com/2022/02/27/regarding-benedicts-last-audience/

For additional examples of ad hominem attacks used by other leading Benepapists, see O'Reilly, "Hey, leading Benepapists, "if you're 'ad hominem-ing'; you're not winning," July 13, 2022. https://romalocutaest.com/2022/07/13/hey-leading-benepapists-if-youre-ad-hominem-ing-youre-not-winning/

[262] Pope Benedict XVI, last General Audience, February 27, 2013.

[263] See Ann Barnhardt, "REPOST BY REQUEST: The Mountain of Evidence that Pope Benedict never validly resigned is like Kilauea – it just keeps spewing truth magma". https://www.barnhardt.biz/2021/04/11/eight-years-ago-today-in-a-packed-piazza-san-pietro-pope-benedict-made-it-clear-that-he-was-not-validly-resigning-the-papacy/

[264] The wording of this objection is based on the author's reading and understanding of Ann Barnhardt's statement that Benedict approved Gänswein's speech. Compare to Ann Barnhardt, "REPOST BY

REQUEST: The Mountain of Evidence that Pope Benedict never validly resigned is like Kilauea – it just keeps spewing truth magma", https://www.barnhardt.biz/2021/04/11/eight-years-ago-today-in-a-packed-piazza-san-pietro-pope-benedict-made-it-clear-that-he-was-not-validly-resigning-the-papacy/

[265] Ann Barnhardt.

[266] First it was said that Benedict approved the speech before it was given (for example, see https://www.barnhardt.biz/2021/04/11/eight-years-ago-today-in-a-packed-piazza-san-pietro-pope-benedict-made-it-clear-that-he-was-not-validly-resigning-the-papacy/). A more recent article adds that Benedict "edited and approved" the speech. See Barnhardt, Ann, "Speech edited and approved by Pope Benedict and delivered by his Personal Secretary Archbishop Georg Gänswein on May 20, ARSH 2016 – the full text. JUST READ IT," Barnhardt.biz, May 29, 2022. https://www.barnhardt.biz/2022/05/29/speech-edited-and-approved-by-pope-benedict-and-delivered-by-his-personal-secretary-archbishop-georg-ganswein-on-may-20-arsh-2016-the-full-text-just-read-it/

[267] See Diane Montagna, "Did Benedict really resign? Gänswein, Burke and Brandmüller weigh in". https://www.lifesitenews.com/news/did-benedict-really-resign-gaenswein-burke-and-brandmueller-weigh-in/

[268] Excerpts from "Complete English Text: Archbishop Georg Gänswein's 'Expanded Petrine Office' Speech" by Diane Montagna. May 30, 2016. © Aleteia.org. Used with permission, no other use of this material is authorized.

[269] Ibid.

[270] Pope Benedict XVI, last General Audience, February 27, 2013.

[271] Josef Ratzinger, *Theological Highlights of Vatican II* pp. 189-190.

[272] *Lumen Gentium* 21.

[273] Benedict's "substantial error"—per a theory advanced by Dr. Mazza—is that Benedict would not have resigned the papacy had he known that his understanding of the *munus* or the "sacramental papacy" was in error, a*nd that he would not retain anything of the munus at all after his resignation.* Dr. Edmund Mazza certainly appears to have admitted his theory of "substantial error" relies on his subjective interpretation of Benedict's intent, i.e., what *Dr. Mazza* "honestly believes" Benedict would or would not have done. For

example, in an interview on the Patrick Coffin Show, Dr. Mazza says at one point: *"Had he known that the truth of the matter is there is no such thing as a sacramental papacy and that when you renounce the office that's it, you're not papal in any way shape or form any more, I honestly believe based on everything he said over the last sixty years, he would not have resigned.* (O'Reilly, unofficial transcript). See Patrick Coffin, "#248: Is Benedict XVI Still the Pope?—Dr. Edmund Mazza". https://www.patrickcoffin.media/is-benedict-xvi-still-the-pope/

[274] Peter Seewald, *Light of the World*, p. 39.

[275] Andrea Cionci, "'Codice Ratzinger': trovato il più clamoroso dei messaggi, in mondovisione da Castel Gandolfo". https://www.liberoquotidiano.it/articolo_blog/blog/andrea-cionci/29829255/trovato-clamoroso-messaggio-in-codice-ratzinger-benedetto-sbaglio-apposta-il-titolo-pontificale-in-mondovisione-da-castel-ga.html)

[276] The author describes this Benepapist civil war in the following articles, "A Benepapist Civil War?", May 22, 2022. https://romalocutaest.com/2022/05/22/a-benepapist-civil-war/; and "Benedict XVI: strategic genius or theological fool?", May 29, 2002. https://romalocutaest.com/2022/05/29/benedict-xvi-strategic-genius-or-theological-fool/

[277] See Ann Barnhardt, "NonVeni Crosspost: Jesus doesn't require any 'secret codes' for men to be saved. The Church is VISIBLE, including at her Earthly Head". https://www.barnhardt.biz/2022/05/23/nonveni-crosspost-jesus-doesnt-require-any-secret-codes-for-men-to-be-saved-the-church-is-visible-including-at-her-earthly-head/ Ms. Barnhardt writes: *"In the same vein, trying to delude oneself into thinking that Pope Benedict is playing some monstrous game of 15-D underwater chess crossed with Pink Slip Chicken at the proverbial quarry, is not only wrong, but assumes a moral monstrosity on the part of Pope Benedict that would be right up there with Judas Iscariot."*

[278] See Ann Barnhardt, "Breaking: Pope Benedict's personal secretary, Archbishop Ganswein sobbing repeatedly when talking about the failed attempted resignation. NOTHING TO SEE HERE".

https://www.barnhardt.biz/2022/06/19/breaking-pope-benedicts-personal-secretary-archbishop-ganswein-sobbing-repeatedly-when-talking-about-the-failed-attempted-resignation-nothing-to-see-here/
Ms. Barnhardt writes in part: "*Let us disabuse ourselves of ANY notion of any categorical nonsense like a "Ratzinger Code". Anyone pushing such a fiction – and FICTION truly is the word – is a profiteer, looking to make money off of this abject train wreck of a situation.*"

[279] See Cionci, Andrea, "Benedict XVI and the absurd Substantial Error thesis: "Pope Ratzinger has misconceptions"?". https://www.patrickcoffin.media/benedict-xvi-the-absurd-substantial-error-thesis/

[280] Holweck, F. (1907). Apostolic Blessing. In *The Catholic Encyclopedia.* http://www.newadvent.org/cathen/02602a.htm

[281] Consequently, Benedict, while still pope, may have granted to himself the authority to continue to give private apostolic blessings as Pope Emeritus. It is also possible that Francis granted permission to Benedict as Pope Emeritus. The point is, there are a number of alternative explanations which do not require the leap in logic taken by the Benepapists.

[282] The author used this example in his previously cited debate with Dr. Mazza on February 11, 2022, on the Tim Gordon *Rules for Retrogrades* podcast. Separately, Dr. Edward Feser makes the same point in his own article: See Dr. Edward Feser, "Benedict is not the pope: A reply to some critics". https://edwardfeser.blogspot.com/2022/05/benedict-is-not-pope-reply-to-some.html

[283] Pope Benedict XVI, *Declaratio*.

[284] James A. Coriden, et al, eds. *The Code of Canon Law: A Text and Commentary*, p. 437.

[285] Liber Sextus (I, VII, I), UCLA Digital Library, pp. 197-198, retrieved June 7, 2022, 4:57 p.m. https://digital.library.ucla.edu/catalog/ark:/21198/zz0014rx8d?cv=35

[286] Here, Fr. Rickert emphasizes the word "muneris" is in fact a form of the same word, "munus." From personal correspondence with the author.

[287] Fr. John Rickert, FSSP, Ph.D., "Munus, Ministerium & Pope Emeritus Benedict — Guest Post by Fr John Rickert".

ENDNOTES

https://www.wmbriggs.com/post/39718/. Permission to use and cite this article was granted by W.M. Briggs, and Fr. John Rickert, FSSP.

[288] Ibid.

[289] Ibid. Also see: "1. "Moenera militia," Lucr. 1,29), eris, n. root mu-; cf.: moenia, munis, munia, etc., *a service, office, post, employment, function, duty* (class.: syn.: officium, ministerium, honos). Etc. See Charlton T. Lewis, Charles Short, ed., Munus. *A Latin Dictionary.*

[290] See Leo F. Stelten, *Dictionary of Ecclesiastical Latin.* Per *Dictionary of Ecclesiastical Latin,* munus (-eris: n. ; gift, bounty, present, offering; duty, office, employment, responsibility, service; bribe), p. 166; ministerium (-ii: n; ministry, service, office, duty), p. 162.

[291] See note 93.

[292] Acta Apostolicae Sedis, ISSN 0001-5199, Vol. 97, N°. 2 5, 2005, pp. 706-712.

[293] "In hac sacra celebratione, qua solemne fit initium ministerii Summi Ecclesiae Pastoris, humeris Nostris impositi, mentem imprimis adorantes orantesque convertimus ad Deum, infinitum et aeternum, qui consilio suo, humanis argumentis inexplicabili, et benignissima dignatione sua ad Cathedram beati Petri Nos evexit. Sponte quidem in haec verba Sancti Pauli Apostoli erumpimus: « O altitudo divitiarum et sapientiae et scientiae Dei: quam incomprehensibilia sunt iudicia eius et investigabiles viae eius." See Pope John Paul I, "Holy Mass for the Inauguration of the Petrine Ministry of the Bishop of Rome, Homily of His Holiness John Paul I". https://www.vatican.va/content/john-paul-i/en/homilies/documents/hf_jp-i_hom_03091978.html

[294] Pope Benedict XVI, "Pontificatus Exordia," Acta Apostolicae Sedis, ISSN 0001-5199, Vol. 97, N°. 2 5, 2005, May 7, 2005, Libreria Editrice Vaticana. Homily given April 20, 2005, pp. 694-699.

[295] Ibid, 696. "Eucharistia, vitae christianae cor ac Ecclesiae evangelizantis fons, necessario permanentem mediamque partem constituit et fontem Petrini ministerii, Nobis commissi." For English translation an online site was used (https://www.translate.com/latin-english).

[296] Pope Benedict XVI, *Declaratio.*

[297] See Fr. John Rickert, FSSP, Ph.D., "Munus, Ministerium & Pope Emeritus Benedict — Guest Post by Fr John Rickert".

https://www.wmbriggs.com/post/39718/ Permission to use and cite article granted by W.M. Briggs, and Fr. John Rickert.

[298] Per personal communication with Fr. Rickert on this subject.

[299] See "Martini: Benedict XVI's resignation and the 2005 Conclave," La Stampa, Vatican Insider (www.VaticanInsider.com), July 18, 2015, modified July 9, 2019, retrieved August 7, 2022, at 2:40 p.m. https://www.lastampa.it/vatican-insider/en/2015/07/18/news/martini-benedict-xvi-s-resignation-and-the-2005-conclave-1.35243041

[300] Benedict was quoted as saying: "Of course you are not permitted to yield to demands. Therefore I emphasized in my speech that I was acting freely. One is not allowed to go away if one is running away. One is not allowed to submit to coercion. One can only turn away when no one has demanded it. And no one demanded it of me during my time as pope. No one." See Peter Seewald, *Benedict XVI: Last Testament in his own words*, p. 26.

[301] Benedict was quoted as saying: "On the contrary, the Vatileaks controversy was completely resolved. I said while it was still happening – I believe it was to you – that one is not permitted to step back when things are going wrong, but only when things are at peace. I could resign because calm had returned to this situation. It was not a case of retreating under pressure or a feeling that things couldn't be coped with." See Peter Seewald, *Benedict XVI: Last Testament in his own words*, p. 23.

[302] James A. Coriden, et al, eds. *The Code of Canon Law: A Text and Commentary*, p. 437.

[303] John P. Beal, et al, eds., *New Commentary on the Code of Canon Law*, p. 437. On p. 438, the *editors of New Commentary on Code of Canon Law state that:* "The new law correctly provides for the resignation of a pope even if in a limited measure (c. 332, §2). Such a resignation must be freely submitted and duly manifested. However, its acceptance is not a requirement. The general provisions on resignation of an office are contained in canons 187-189. These legal regulations are only guidelines since, due to his supreme power, the pope can always pass new laws, and stands above already valid laws *(Papa supra omnes canones).*"

[304] See "Benedict XVI Says Doubts on Resignation Are 'Absurd'," https://zenit.org/2014/02/26/benedict-xvi-says-doubts-on-resignation-are-absurd/ Pope Emeritus Benedict XVI was quoted: "There is absolutely no doubt regarding the validity of my resignation from the Petrine ministry. The only condition for the validity of my resignation is the complete freedom of my decision. Speculations regarding its validity are simply absurd." Benedict's camp has not denied the validity of the quote, so there are no grounds to reject its veracity.

[305] The Open Letter to the Bishops of the Catholic Church, in which the signatories wrote to the bishops "...*first, to accuse Pope Francis of the canonical delict of heresy, and second, to request that you take the* While the authors of the Open Letter submitted their concerns to a higher authority, the Benepapists have taken their solution in their own hands. For information on the Open Letter, see Georges Buscemi; Robert Cassidy STL; Fr. Thomas Crean OP, et al, "Open Letter to the Bishops of the Catholic Church". https://www.documentcloud.org/documents/5983408-Open-Letter-to-the-Bishops-of-the-Catholic.html

[306] For example, see Edward Pentin, "Cardinal Burke Outlines Formal Correction of Pope Francis' Teaching," National Catholic Register, blog, August 17, 2017. https://www.ncregister.com/blog/cardinal-burke-outlines-formal-correction-of-pope-francis-teaching

[307] Pope Leo II in his letter of confirmation to the 6th Ecumenical Council wrote: "We anathematize the inventors of the new error, that is, Theodore, Sergius, ...and also Honorius, who did not attempt to sanctify this Apostolic Church with the teaching of Apostolic tradition, but by profane treachery permitted its purity to be polluted." See Chapman, J. (1910). Pope Honorius I. In *The Catholic Encyclopedia.* New York: Robert Appleton Company. Retrieved August 7, 2022 from New Advent: http://www.newadvent.org/cathen/07452b.htm

VALID? THE RESIGNATION OF POPE BENEDICT XVI

www.ingramcontent.com/pod-product-compliance
Lightning Source LLC
Chambersburg PA
CBHW071237070526
44583CB00017B/2225